Food Security in South Asia

About the Editor

Mr. Pradeep Chaturvedi has been involved with the food security and sustainable development issues for over two decades. His association with the World Food Day programme since 1981 at national, regional and global level has given an insight into different aspects of food and nutrition situation. Mr. Chaturvedi has effectively motivated a number of professional institutions with scientific and engineering background to support the cause of global food security. He has been able to identify the gaps that can be covered by inputs from professional and experienced scientists and engineers.

The Food Security movement has created awareness in different professional groups, Non-government organisations and citizens groups about the need for their involvement.

Mr. Chaturvedi is a Mechanical Engineers and has been associated with the Rural Wood Energy Development Programme for Asia and Pacific of the FAO, based at Bangkok for over a decade. His understanding of energy issues of importance to South and South East Asia region has been widely appreciated.

Mr. Chaturvedi was awarded the World Food Day Medal by the Director General of FAO in 1992. He is Chairman of the UNESCO sponsored, World Renewable Energy Network, Vice-Chairman of the World Environment Foundation; and President of the Bio Energy Society of India.

Mr. Chaturvedi has authored six books and edited 25 books on Energy, Food Security and Sustainable Development.

Food Security in South Asia

Edited by
Pradeep Chaturvedi

Published for
Indian Association for the Advancement of Science, New Delhi

by

CONCEPT PUBLISHING COMPANY, NEW DELHI 110059

ISBN-81-7022-972-3

First Published 2002

Published and Printed by
Ashok Kumar Mittal
Concept Publishing Company
A/15-16, Commercial Block, Mohan Garden,
NEW DELHI-110059 (India)

Phones : 5351460, 5351794
Fax : 0091-11-5357103
E-mail : **publishing@conceptpub.com**

अजित सिंह
Ajit Singh

सत्यमेव जयते

कृषि मंत्री
भारत सरकार
कृषि भवन
नई दिल्ली-110 001
Minister of Agriculture
Government of India
Krishi Bhawan
New Delhi-110 001

FOREWORD

There is no other issue apart from that of pure drinking water, which is of such vital concern for the well being of humanity like the availability of good and nutritious food to those that are in need. When we speak of a nation's food security it has to be kept in mind that self sufficiency and even as surplus state at the national level does not, by itself, solve the problem. Every one should have easy access to the food and it should be wholesome and nutritious if the objective is to be achieved. It is, therefore, most important that production programmes of the country should be fully oriented towards this objective of food security.

For motivating the producer farmers towards higher levels of production, it is essential that he should have a stake in that programme whose results are vital interest to him. From this point of view the reforms that are being attempted in land tenure system should be receiving our continuous attention. A vast area of the country still remains un-irrigated and dependent on the natural showers which often turn out to be inadequate, erratic or whimsical. Technology generation for rain-fed areas has made a good deal of progress but the implementation and dissemination of that knowledge has to be more wide spread and at a faster pace.

I am glad to notice that the Indian Association for the Advancement of Science is publishing a book entitled " Food Security in South Asia " based on the discussions at all levels—local, regional, national and international. Such a publication of this nature without much time lag is but a timely step and it is indeed most heartening that the Non-Government Organisations are extending their warm and willing support to the government and to international bodies in their efforts for ensuring food security to all.

I wish this endeavour a grand success.

(AJIT SINGH)

CONTENTS

PART – II : Food Security Issues in India

Overview Papers

INTRODUCTION

Food Security is a central issue to social and economic development in India and other developing countries. FAO has focused global attention on Food Security at the World Food Summit, at Rome, in November 1996. Subsequently, the review of the progress on pledges made by 185 countries were considered necessary five years later, in 2001, when it became clear that the original World Food Summit goal would not be met without additional efforts. The world leaders will soon gather in Rome, in June 2002, at the World Food Summit: *five years later*. In the light of the likely negative economic impact of recent global events, and worsening plight of the hungry, a major commitment is required to press forward with renewed effort to reduce poverty and hunger.

FAO's State of Food Insecurity Report 2001 showed a disturbing slowdown in the 1990s in the reduction of the world's undernourished population to approximately 6 million people a year, against the implicit target rate of about 20 million per year. Hunger incidence is not being reduced quickly enough to be able to cut by half the number of hungry people by the year 2015.

The Report suggests, 'At this juncture, a distinction may be made between (long-run or) growth-mediated food security and (short-run or) support-led or entitlement-mediated food security. Growth-mediated food security has to do with human capabilities to meet food and other basic needs. Broad-based economic growth enhances the attainment of such capabilities. Support-led food security recognizes social concerns other than growth and reflects society's aversion to starvation and other less terminal forms of nutritional deprivation.

The distinction highlights potential trade-offs between the short – and long-run benefits (and costs) of public sector intervention to enhance food security'.

India lies in the Asia Pacific zone of FAO's global demarcation. It will therefore, be relevant to consider the situation in this region.

Food insecurity in Asia-Pacific developing economies is essentially a poverty problem, reflecting in large part a failure of food entitlements due to low returns to assets owned by the poor.

Thus, the bulk of the food insecure are also largely the rural poor. The prevalence of undernourishment correlates well with poverty incidence. National incomes (measured by GNP per capita) are lowest in countries where undernourishment is pervasive. In this regard, it is thus of great concern that countries with over 20 percent undernourishment showed only a negligible improvement of per capita incomes during the last decade. While some progress has been made in reducing the incidence of hunger, Asia Pacific countries still account for 64 percent of the 780 million hungry people in the developing world. They face a deficit in basic daily dietary energy ranging 100 to 400 kilocalories. With 522 million or 44 percent of the world's poor in 1998, South Asia correspondingly had the largest incidence of undernourishment (294 million) or more than 39 percent of the world's hungry people.

India has 26 percent of its population below poverty line, and about 18 percent suffering from malnutrition. In numbers: India has 50 percent of South Asia's poor and 60 percent of under-nourished. A review of food security at this stage is important and relevant for India.

The Indian Association for the Advancement of Science is actively involved in preparatory phase of the 'World Food Summit: *five years later*' at Asia Pacific Regional level as well as at the national level.

The Book is a collection of papers presented at Asia Pacific Regional and National Consultations, and reflects the present situation and steps taken alongwith initiatives required in India and the Asia Pacific region.

First part of the Book is NGOs/CSOs Perceptions in South Asia

Food Security can be ensured only by active involvement of NGOs and the Civil Society Organisations. Dr. R.B.Singh, Assistant Director General, FAO, provided help and support for prominent NGOs/CSOs from Asia-Pacific Region to meet in Bangkok during August 26-27, 2001 to consider various options of attaining food security. Selected Papers from India, Bangladesh, Nepal and Srilanka, presented in this Consultation, have been included to reflect the situation in South Asia Region. Welcome Address and the Inaugural Address outline various issues at global and Asia-Pacific region. The Declaration from the NGOs/CSOs Consultation has been annexed to present the collective view of NGOs/CSOs.

The second part of the Book is a reflection of situation in India.

In India, following three National Workshops were organized by IAAS in collaboration with FAO, during 2001:

i) Workshop on Post Harvest Management
ii) Workshop on Engineers and Food Security
iii) Workshop on Fight Hunger to Reduce Poverty

These Workshops attracted contributions from policy-makers; scientists and NGOs and covered whole gamut of post-harvest management. Selected papers have been included in the volume.

The Indian Association for the Advancement of Science had also undertaken a survey on Food and Nutrition in India – 2001 at six different geographical locations to reflect the situation. The data were benchmarked against the results of the study conducted by the Association in 1992. A brief summary of the same is also presented.

The Book thus, presents the Status and Issues involved in Food Security in Asia and Pacific Region, especially in South Asia and India.

I hope the readers will find it an informative reference volume.

Release of the Book on the eve of FAO's 26th Regional Conference for Asia-Pacific at Kathmandu gives another opportunity to highlight important regional food security issues to governments, NGOs and CSOs.

Some of the inputs from this Book may become important information for discussion and decision making at WSF:fyl.

The book reflects the work undertaken by the IAAS in collaboration with FAO Delhi office and FAO – RAP, Bangkok.

May 11, 2002

Pradeep Chaturvedi
Secretary General
Indian Association for the
Advancement of Science

ACKNOWLEDGEMENTS

We wish to greatfully acknowledge the contribution of foreword by Hon'ble Shri Ajit Singh, Minister for Agriculture, Government of India.

My grateful thanks to Dr.R.B.Singh, Assistant Director General, FAO, Regional Office for Asia and the Pacific for his encouragement and support for publication and release of the Book. Support of Mr. T.K.Mudbhary, Nutrition Policy Officer, FAO, Regional Officer for Asia and the Pacific is also acknowledged.

The Association would like to acknowledge encouragement and support of Mr. Peer Hijmans, FAO Representative in India and Bhutan for his support. Mr.Gopil Ghosh, National Professional Officer, and Mr.G.Petros, Nutrition Programme Officer of FAO Delhi office.

The Association also acknowledges support from regional focal points of NGOs/CSOs consultations viz Asian NGO Coalition for Agrarian Reform and Rural Development, (ANGOC), Institute for Motivating Self Employment (IMSE), Pesticide Action Network – Asia Pacific (PAN-AP). Special thanks to Mr.Biplab Halim, India; Mr. Zasfar Ahmed, Bangladesh; Mr.Cyril R. Ekanayake, Srilanka; Mr. Roel R.Ravanera, Philippines for giving consent to include their papers in this book.

We would also like to acknowledge contribution of authors of all the papers included in this Book.

Our thanks to the Institution of Engineers (India), Delhi State Centre and the Rotary Club of Delhi South Metropolitan for organizing World Food Day activities in 2001.

We also acknowledge the initiative of Shri Ashok Mittal, Managing Director, Concept Publishing Company to undertake design, layout and publication of the Book.

Pradeep Chaturvedi
Secretary General
Indian Association for the
Advancement of Science

PART - I

Food Security Issues in South Asia

1

Food Security Issues in Asia and Pacific

Welcome Address

R.B. Singh
Assistant Director-General and Regional Representative
FAO Regional Office for Asia and the Pacific

It is a privilege for FAO to be invited to address this regional consultation of non-governmental and civil society organizations from the Asia and Pacific region. On behalf of the FAO Director-General, Jacques Diouf, the Regional Office for Asia and the Pacific and on my own behalf, I wish to congratulate the three main organizers of the consultation – the Asian NGO Coalition for Agrarian Reform and Rural Development (ANGOC), the Institute of Motivating Self-Employment (IMSE) and the Pesticide Action Network Asia-Pacific (PAN-AP) – as well as the 120 delegates for this initiative to assess regional progress towards achieving the goal of the November 1996 World Food Summit to reduce the number of hungry people in the world by half by the year 2015.

Realizing that our shared ideal of 'food for all' cannot be achieved by governments alone, FAO continues to value highly the active involvement of civil society in tackling the hurdles to eradicating hunger from the world. I recall that in 1996 a pre-Summit NGO Consultation for the Asia-Pacific region was held at the FAO regional office in Bangkok. The resulting Bangkok Declaration was an important input to the NGOs collective advocacy at the World Food Summit.

I believe many of the civil society representatives present today were participants at the 1996 NGO meeting. Your involvement in national, regional and global networking on food security has been a hallmark of the World Food Summit follow-up. The accumulated expertise available in this consultation will no doubt generate an important input for the deliberations at the forthcoming parallel NGO forum in Rome and the NGO declaration to be presented at the World Food Summit: five years later (WFS: fyl).

I also wish to recall the outcome of the NGOs/CSOs regional consultation held in Yokohama last year in August, in parallel with FAO's 25th Regional Conference for Asia and the Pacific. The Yokohama meeting made concrete suggestions on ways in which civil society can work more effectively with FAO in the fight against hunger.

Allow me also to stress the significance of the attendance today of the Honourable Secretary of the Department of Agriculture, Philippines who took part in the Yokohama consultation as a leading NGO representative. The presence of NGO representatives in senior government positions is another tribute to a most significant political development of the last years of the 20th century: the power of civil society advocacy for a more equitable world order.

Food is essential to life. It is the most basic of basic needs. As an ancient Hindu scripture said: "All actions stem from food...Food depends on food." Unless there is enough food today for all - men and women, young and old – the prospects for food security tomorrow are greatly diminished.

Recognizing this, government leaders from 185 countries present at the World Food Summit pledged their political will and common and national commitment "to achieving food security for all and to an on-going effort to eradicate hunger in all countries, with an immediate view to reducing the number of undernourished people to half their present level no later than 2015."

Information to date assembled and analysed by FAO indicates that there has been some progress toward that goal. However, the current annual reduction by eight million in the number of undernourished people in the world is far below the rate of 20 million per year needed to reach the 2015 target set by the WFS. If we continue at such a slow pace, it is obvious that the World Food Summit goals will not be met. The business-as-usual scenario will see the target met not earlier than 2030, 15 years too late.

In the Asia-Pacific region, unprecedented progress was achieved during the last 3 to 4 decades. The percentage of undernourished people in Asian developing countries had fallen from 21 per cent in 1990-92 to 17 per cent in 1996-98. However, the region still has 524 million hungry people today, accounting for two-thirds of the undernourished population in the developing world. To reach the WFS target, the region ought to annually reduce the number of undernourished by 14 million (out of 20 million at global level).

The sad part of this reality is that this is happening even in parts of the world where there is plenty of food to meet everyone's needs. In my own country India, where the warehouses of the national food agency are brimming with 60 million tones of grains, food security is a core issue for about 200 million people – one-fourth of the world's undernourished population. The paradox of the coexistence of mountains of grains and millions of hungry is a shame for humanity.

The battle against food insecurity is therefore, far from over. It is obvious that while adequate production of food is an essential condition, it is not sufficient to ensure comprehensive food security. Access to food, especially on the part of vulnerable people, is thus now a major concern.

We must act for the poor, the hungry and the deprived of the world, and for the children of the poor and the marginalized of today, who will be hungry a decade from now, if we do not act now. Hunger manifests itself in physical and intellectual dwarfism. Society has no right to abbreviate the lives of such unfortunate children who came to this world as equals.

The hungry child can't wait. It is today that his bones and sinews are being formed. "You can't tell him tomorrow", a farmer novelist has said, "His name is today."

The 1990s saw a 15 per cent fall in overseas development assistance, while the portfolio of multilateral development lenders like the World Bank and regional development banks has shrunk by 40 per cent since the WFS. FAO member countries too have not stepped up contributions, leading to a 14 per cent decline in the organization's budget in real terms. In addition, FAO's field programmes have been cut back by nearly a fifth in these years even as emergency assistance rose more than four times.

Part of the problem is the conspicuous lack of focus on food security issues within the global poverty reduction debate. Lack of minimum nutrition undermines the productive capacities of the poor pushing them deeper into poverty. Battling hunger is a crucial first step in the war against poverty given that 70 per cent of the world's poor live in rural areas.

It is against this backdrop that FAO is organizing the WFS: fyl global forum within the framework of the biennial FAO Conference in November this year to take stock of the situation and to facilitate mobilization of the necessary political will to ensure that the required decisions are taken by leaders who are in a position to influence policy for all sectors of the economy and all segments of society. World leaders will be requested to outline the measures they envisage to achieve the goals, which they had set in adopting the documents of the World Food Summit. In addition, they will be asked to take the decisions necessary to accelerate the rate of implementation of these measures aimed at halving the number of the world's hungry by 2015.

The new millennium has opened as an era of global economic interdependence, which holds out the promise of global prosperity. But globalization can be a double-edged sword and the evident pitfalls have given rise to parallel global civil society assertiveness of the rights of those marginalized by the new international economic order. The violent protests, which began on the streets of Seattle two years ago and culminated last month in the Italian city of Genoa, have pitchforked concerns of poverty and hunger onto the global stage as never before.

A level playing field must not remain an illusion in a region like ours. The Asia-Pacific region has the distinction of having 75 per cent of the world's farming households. About 80 per cent of these are small-scale farmers, and the majority of them are resource poor.

In order to provide a level playing field for small farmers, explicit provisions in the form of a livelihood security box should be made in the WTO agreement. Alongside, mechanisms should be in place to increase the profitability and protect the viability and sustainability of small farms.

In recognition, the G-8 Genoa summit endorsed the need to make hunger reduction a central objective of poverty reduction, stressing the need to target the most food insecure regions in sub-Saharan Africa and South Asia. It also emphasized FAO's own concern that food security depends on availability of food that is nutritionally adequate and safe, especially food that is produced by the new cutting edge farm technologies.

Distinguished Delegates

The results of this consultation will further enhance the dialogue with governments and other stakeholders and feed into the deliberations of the WFS: fyl. It should therefore clearly spell out civil society views on major food security issues and make concrete recommendations for policy reforms and priority actions expected from the governments and FAO. We are ready to support the outcome of your consultation, making sure that your voice is heard by those in power and the general public.

The *WFS : fyl* is a unique opportunity for the world to give higher political priority to food security and safety for all humankind. It will be a chance for the richer nations to demonstrate their commitment with generous funding to the new FAO Trust Fund to support food security projects in the poorest countries. I look forward to seeing your consultation address this latest initiative by FAO's Director-General.

Finally, I should like to acknowledge the generous funding from the Government of Japan under the project Information, Awareness and Support in Japan for FAO Sustainable Agricultural and Rural Development Activities for the regional NGOs/CSOs consultation.

Allow me to wish each one of you full success in our collective pursuit of the goals of food for all. I also wish you all an enjoyable stay in Bangkok.

2

Hunger and Poverty : Issues and Challenges for the FAO, Government, and Civil Society

Leonardo Q. Montemayor
Secretary
Department of Agriculture, Philippines

This is an opportunity to reunite with the representatives of the world's most prominent NGOs and CSOs. It has been five years since we joined the World Food Summit in Rome to reaffirm our commitment to the cause of global food security.

That same year we met as NGOs and CSOs in this equally ancient and beautiful city of Bangkok to share experiences and start a more active collaboration with the FAO in policy and information sharing.

Time flies fast indeed. Here I am now talking before you as part of my country's newly installed government. I assure you that this does not in any way loosen my links with civil society, which helped put me there in the first place. But it only goes to show how much our lives and the world can change in five years.

This assessment of how far we have gone in implementing our World Food Summit commitments as NGOs, and how we can further dialogue with government and other stakeholders, is most welcome and commendable. I particularly thank the ANGOC, the IMSE of India (CSOs), the PAN-AP of Malaysia, and of course the FAO Asia Pacific for organizing this consultation.

With that, let me delve into the topic that you have asked me to discuss today: hunger and poverty.

Link between Hunger and Poverty

Since we issued the WFS declaration five years ago, the number of hungry people in the developing world has remained the same. Today, close to 800 million people in the developing world are considered chronically undernourished (FAO, 1999). Optimistic forecasts see this number declining to some 700 million ten years from now, but this offers scant relief to the one out of every 8 persons in the world's poorest countries who will remain chronically hungry.

The global food balance may look adequate in the aggregate and may in fact lead to a progressively improving food situation in the industrial and developing world through 2010. Yet the same projection comes with an important qualifier: it will hold true only for those with an "effective demand for food", which means those with ample resources to produce food on their own or the income to buy it from outside sources.

FAO has long acknowledged this vital link between hunger and poverty when it said: "Food security is becoming less a problem of global food supplies, overall stability, and global stock levels as such, but more a problem of inadequate access to food supplies for vulnerable groups resulting from, *inter alia,* lack of purchasing power."

The Asia-Pacific region has some of the highest density populations in the world. It is also home to a large number of the world's poor. Considering the relationship between poverty and hunger, it is no wonder that 525 million, or two-thirds of the developing world's chronically hungry, are found in the region. Hence, the Asia-Pacific deserves particular attention in our efforts to achieve global food security.

Poverty has effectively reduced people's food intake and increased the number affected by deficiencies in iron, vitamin A, and iodine. The 3-As of food security – Availability, Accessibility, Affordability – have to be addressed as a whole - from the production areas up to the level of the individual consumers.

At the end of the World Food Summit five years ago, we approved a Plan of Action vowing to cut the number of undernourished people to half the 1996 level not later than 2015. This means reducing the ranks of the hungry by an average of 13 million every year until 2015.

At the current rate of progress, there is no way this target can be met.

No less than the UN, the World Bank, the IMF, and the OECD confirmed this through a joint report "2000 : A Better World for All." The report tells us what we already know: the poor are still with us, and their number, far from being cut by half, is rising.

Developing country experience in globalization tells us much more. We have seen cheap, heavily supported developed country exports flood developing country markets, to the prejudice of small, resource-poor farmers. With the sheer imbalance in the playing field of international trade and despite the WTO's unified multilateral rules and disciplines, small farmer agriculture in developing countries is finding it more and more difficult to survive, much more to compete. These have negatively affected incomes, income distribution, and therefore food security.

As stated earlier, poverty and food insecurity are closely intertwined phenomena. Lack of sufficient and reliable income is at the heart of food insecurity, hunger and malnutrition. Hence, unless poverty is significantly reduced, the goal of halving the number of undernourished in the world will remain a distant dream.

Wanted : Political Will

We have ushered in the new millennium with a growing consensus that the major goal of development is the elimination of poverty.

The Summits of the 1990s, including the WFS, sharpened our people's awareness of major global problems and secured high level commitments for joint responses by countries and international agencies.

However, these problem-specific summits overcrowded the development agenda and shifted government attention from one major theme to another, affecting priority setting and diffusing efforts.

There was also a marked change in perspective regarding the role of government. All around the world, governments began to withdraw from activities, which were felt to be better handled by the private sector. Concentrating on their role as providers of public goods, many governments have cut down on public services and tightened fiscal discipline.

Thus, official development assistance decreased during the 1990s from 0.33 per cent to 0.25 per cent of the GNP of the OECD countries. Despite their pledges at the Summit, few countries embarked on large-scale programmes for improving food security. Nor were they encouraged to do so by their development partners who, despite having discredited the "trickle down" assumptions, continued to emphasize policies and investments which supported economic growth as the main goal of development in their country assistance strategies.

The over-riding concern of a number of developed countries for economic growth, efficiency and undistorted trade, combined with the pressures on their citizens to increase consumption, are increasingly at odds with the concerns for the environment, social equity and the welfare of poor people elsewhere in the world.

Commitment among donors to help address humanitarian and development issues has been further eroded by the disillusionment over the alleged ineffectiveness of aid and inability of recipients to "absorb" it, concerns over corruption, a diminishing geopolitical rationale for assistance and, in some cases, the need to apply austerity policies domestically.

In response to pressing global issues such as food security, we have seen the rise of transnational civil society advocacy movements, which bring together coalitions of interest groups to influence the conduct of global affairs. This perhaps is one of the most significant political developments in the last few years of the 20th century.

These movements, which include all of us here, bypass normal institutional mechanisms. They have successfully demonstrated their influence by tapping the power of mass media and information technology to build global constituencies for causes they support, including human rights, enivornment, and food safety.

As our gathering today proves, our movements have global reach – proving that there is out there, and in here, a critical mass of people who want to see the world managed more equitably and sustainably.

That this voice is being heard is evident in the speed and extent of response of world leaders, the UN, the Bretton Woods institutions, transnational corporations, and private philanthropists.

Among the notable successes of such movements has been the acceleration and deepening of debt relief for Highly Indebted Poor Countries. The 1999 G-8 Cologne Summit has, for example, accelerated debt relief through practical measures by developing countries to address poverty. The recent G-8 in Genoa also focused on reducing world poverty. Poverty alleviation is again at the centre of the world's development agenda.

Although hunger is the most direct manifestation of poverty, there is still a conspicuous lack of focus within poverty reduction strategies on food security issues. Concern over hunger tends to be confined largely to emergency situations. Both developed and developing countries have not allocated the resources required to achieve the eradication of hunger in its entirety.

Then there is the need for fundamental reform in world trade in food and agriculture. So long as there exist imbalances, primarily between developing and developed countries in their structure of protection and support to agriculture, the world trading system cannot adequately cope up with growing poverty and food insecurity in the developing world.

There is imminent danger that debates on poverty reduction strategies will continue in the world's corridors of power, delaying commitment to even the most obvious of actions, while almost 800 million people, many of them children, are deprived of the opportunity to live a full life. There is also a real risk that the very success of the agricultural revolution of the 20th century and the current general adequacy of world food supplies may encourage widespread indifference towards the need for urgent solutions to chronic hunger.

Political will is therefore needed to meet the goals we ourselves have set through the 1996 Rome Declaration.

Meeting the WFS Goals: Focus on the Philippines

A few years back, as a representative of small farmers, I advocated the "empowerment of the poor" as a strategy for alleviating poverty and thereby ensuring food security. Today, as Secretary of Agriculture in my home country, we are mainstreaming this very idea into our agricultural development plan.

Poverty in the Philippines is a rural phenomenon. Even urban poverty has its rural origins. Thus, the main thrust of our poverty alleviation programme has to be agricultural modernization founded on social equity, coupled with a thoroughgoing agrarian reform program.

Unfortunately, for so many years now, our agricultural sector has not been performing well. From 1990 to 1998, it grew by an average of only 1.5 per cent a year, much lower than Thailand, Indonesia, Vietnam and China. .

This can be attributed to the sector's failure to secure sources of productivity growth and income diversification.

We in the new government of President Macapagal-Arroyo are addressing this situation through our Agricultural and Fisheries Modernization Programme.

We have adopted the framework of Strategic Agricultural and Fisheries Development Zones to preserve and develop agricultural areas in a holistic manner.

To boost agricultural productivity, we have prioritized the expansion of needed rural infrastructure such as farm to-market roads : and small communal irrigation systems, which are both efficient and environmentally sustainable.

At the same time, we are adopting appropriate technologies such as organic farming, IPM, effective post-harvest facilities, and sustainable agriculture.

We have launched innovative non-collateralized credit schemes for farmers and other small borrowers, which tap non-traditional lending conduits like people's organizations.

We have resolved to fully implement the safety nets necessary so that the most vulnerable are sheltered from the adjustment shocks brought about by globalization.

The Macapagal-Arroyo government is also forging stronger partnerships with local governments, farmers/fisherfolk associations and cooperatives, NGOs, and business groups in order to harness the resources and creativity of all sectors of society.

Last May, President Macapagal-Arroyo met with the rural-based NGOs and CSOs as well as with agriculture-related government workers and other stakeholders at an "Agricultural Stakeholders' Summit." The Summit enabled agriculture-oriented groups with diverse political and economic agenda to present their views and recommendations on various rural development issues and policies, including those we are taking up in this consultation.

By encouraging the wide-ranging participation of civil society, we are strengthening our nation's political will to fully harness our agricultural potentials and to address hunger and poverty problems in the Philippines.

I'm sure the global community of NGOs and civil society organizations will not run out of such "political will." But we should infect our international funding institutions and donor countries with the virus of our determination. Development assistance must focus on reducing poverty to achieve the International Development Goal of cutting poverty by half by 2015.

In this context, I welcome the growing consensus to raise ODA allocation towards the 0.7 per cent GDP goal and give priority to assisting poor countries.

On the international trade front, the Philippines has been one of the strongest advocates of special and differential treatment (SND) for developing countries at the WTO. The Philippines feels strongly that fundamental reform in the agricultural policies of the developed countries will drive WTO's next and crucial reform process in agricultural trade. Such reform will be crucial in defining the future positive role of the international trading system in addressing global as well as individual national food security. We invite our partners in civil society in the region to support our proposals for a fair trading environment in the WTO.

Harnessing Resources

Accelerating the fight against hunger depends not only on political will, but also on sufficient and available resources.

The FAO estimates that developing countries will have to invest a total of US$ 180.4 billion a year in their agriculture sector for the period upto 2015. A continuation of the current annual investment rates until 2015 will be inadequate to achieve the WFS target.

Unfortunately, developing countries seem to continue investing at the same rate which resulted in the insufficient progress observed since the early1990s.

We therefore must come up with innovative ways of increasing investments in our agriculture sectors.

The largest share of investment in primary production is undertaken at the farm level. A conducive climate for private investment at this level is therefore needed.

Public investment, on the other hand, plays an important role in providing essential public goods, i.e., knowledge generation, information and education, and infrastructure, without which private initiative cannot flourish.

Recipient countries and donor institutions have to allocate resources to these areas, according to the requisites of attaining food security and alleviating poverty.

Issues and Challenges

What are the issues and challenges that the FAO, the governments, and civil society must address? First is the impact of and the response to globalization and trade liberalization on agriculture and the food security situation in developing countries. Relatedly, what adjustments, if any, should be made in land reform programmes so that smallholder beneficiaries can withstand the pressures of greater competition arising from freer trade?

Second is giving local communities greater control over their resources. Government must recognize the expertise and resources of NGOs and CSOs, particularly in local communities. Especially where government services are inadequate, these groups should be tapped in providing the alternative service delivery required.

Third is improving governance in both government and NGOs/CSOs.

Effective governance should be a primary means of reducing poverty and attaining food security. At the core of efforts towards these ends is the synergy of key actors in governance : government, civil society and the private sector.

Governance is not the exclusive domain of the public sector. It requires the distinct contribution of entrepreneurs and producers in creating wealth and employment, and of civil society as a whole in promoting moral values and accountability.

Fourth is involving all stakeholders in initiatives aimed at improving the prospects of peace. Without peace; development cannot proceed.

Fifth is strengthening collaboration among public and private institutions.

Well functioning institutions, economic openness, and a bias for social justice will remain the prerequisites for sustainable economic growth and sustainable improvements in the quality of life. NGOs must be encouraged to link up with government and international institutions.

As part of government, I have become more appreciative of government's awesome responsibilities, in which the NGOs and CSOs must share to speed up poverty alleviation and rural development.

Our NGOs and CSOs must explore project cost-sharing with national and local governments through such schemes as "counterpart funding." Networking with appropriate agencies of the government should also be enhanced.

Government-civil society cooperation has been proven most viable and productive in matters related to the environment and resource sustainability, such as IPM and community-based resource management schemes. Knowing that environmental degradation is tightly linked to poverty, we in the Philippines expect more collaboration in these areas.

Along this line, I will recommend inviting an NGO representative to be a member of the official Philippine delegation to the World Food Summit Five Years Later.

At the international level, partnership among stakeholders, particularly between the FAO and POs/NGOs should be enhanced. We have to strengthen our system for regular exchanges on current and emerging concerns such as modern biotechnology and improved governance.

Conclusion

We in the Philippines remain committed to working closely with the FAO and the international NGO community. We welcome your continuing support, even as we do our share in reducing hunger and poverty in Asia and the other parts of the world.

Today, the challenges of food security, poverty alleviation, and sustainable agricultural development remain as daunting as they were five years ago, when we signed the Rome Declaration.

But we can overcome them, if we maintain our unity, our cooperation, and above all, our political will.

3

Right to Food : The People's Perspective

Biplab Halim
President
Institute of Motivating Self-Employment

Introduction

Respected and dear friends, first of all I take this opportunity to extend my heartfelt thanks to ANGOC and FAO for giving me the opportunity to share my views and experiences in this August gathering. Since time is short, very briefly I would say a few words on my perception about the human rights to adequate food – in theory and practice.

A Few Words about Right to Food

It is known to all of us that the contemporary International human rights system was born on December 10th in 1948 when the United Nations General Assembly adopted the Universal Declaration on Human Rights popularly known as UDHR. In the Article 25 of the UDHR it was clearly stated that "everyone has the right to a standard of living, adequate for the health and well being of himself and of his family, including food, clothing, housing ...." etc. which are essential for all human beings to lead a dignified life.

Thereafter, noticing the growing awareness of the people about the human rights particularly about their violations, on

December 16, 1966 United Nations General Assembly adopted a resolution which finally came into force on January 3, 1976 as an International law, called International Covenant on Economic, Social and Cultural Rights. By 1995 this covenant was ratified by roughly 133 States in all over the world. As per Article 11 of this International Covenant, the States Parties to the present Covenant recognize the right of everyone to an adequate standard of living including adequate food. Article 11 also says that the States Parties will also take appropriate steps to ensure the realization of the right recognizing to this effect the essential importance of international cooperation based on free consent.

However, in spite of the acceptance of right to food in the Universal Declaration of 1948 and subsequently in the International Covenant on Economic, Social and Cultural Rights (ICESCR), the economic, social and cultural rights in general and right to food in particular were not given adequate attention at the national and International levels for several decades.

The 1987 "Report on the Right to Adequate Food as a Human Right" was the first study of the UN human rights system on economic right.

The Rome Declaration

Anyway, it is encouraging to note that the situation is gradually changing now; and there is no doubt that the various NGOs/CSOs have played an important role for developing a better understanding of the inter-dependence, indivisibility and universality of all human rights.

The increasing demand from the NGOs and various social movements all over the world for full implementation of the right to food from their respective authorities, finally prompted the heads of States and governments gathered at the World Food Summit in Rome in November in 1996 to recognize the intolerable situation that more than 800 million people throughout the world, and particularly in developing countries, do not have enough food to meet their basic nutritional needs. The Rome `Declaration on World Food Security' adopted by them reaffirmed "the right to everyone to have access to safe and nutritious food consistent with the right to adequate food and the fundamental right of everyone to be free from hunger." Thus it was recognized that the promotion and implementation of the right to adequate food must be a central objective of all States and other relevant actors in order to end hunger and malnutrition.

NGO Forum on Food Security

More than 1200 organizations from some 80 countries, from all regions of the World participated in the parallel NGO Forum at the World Food Summit in 1996 in Rome. The statement made by the NGO Forum at the WFS known as `Profit For Few or Food For All' mentioned that "the globalization of the world economy, along with the lack of accountability of transnational corporations and spreading patterns of over consumption have increased world poverty." This statement highlights that the multi stakeholders of the civil society have great responsibilities in supporting the realization of the right to food. However, the participants of the NGO parallel also emphasized the special role of States in guaranteeing it by saying `The shame of global hunger and malnutrition compels action by all. At the same time, we insist that governments have the primary and ultimate responsibility to ensure national and global food security."

Code of Conduct on the Human Right to Adequate Food

While the right to adequate food is now theoretically firmly established as a fundamental human right, NGOs/CSOs gathered in Rome in 1996 on the occasion of World Food Summit strongly felt the need of elaboration of the same further to facilitate its implementation. The Rome Declaration and the Plan of Action adopted by the World Food Summit offered a milestone opportunity for this endeavour. In commitment 7, objective 7.4 of the Plan of Action "invites the UN High Commissioner for Human Rights in consultation with relevant treaty bodies, and in collaboration with relevant specialized agencies and programmes of the UN system and appropriate inter-governmental mechanisms, to better define the rights related to food in Article 11 of the covenant on Economic Social and Cultural Rights and to propose ways to implement and realize these rights as a means of achieving the commitments and objectives of the World Food Summit, taking into account the possibility of formulating voluntary guidelines for food security for all."

To facilitate the process of translating the Plan of Action into a reality, the NGOs and social movements evolved the idea of a Code of Conduct on the right to adequate food because they visualized two of the major functions of such a code as quite important. Firstly a Code of Conduct would reduce existing weaknesses in the human rights instruments that recognize the right to adequate food, such as lack of precise descriptions of the legal concepts contained in the right to adequate food and the corresponding State obligations mentioned in the ICESCR. Secondly there are legal lacunae as to what impact so called inter-governmental policies imposed by the World Bank, IMF, GATT/WTO and private actors like TNCs would have on the right to adequate food and which could also be addressed, in a first step, by formulating a Code of Conduct on the right to adequate food. Some NGOs at the NGO Forum in Rome were given the responsibility to formulate a Code of Conduct and accordingly the Food First Information and Action Network popularly known as FIAN with assistance from to other international NGOs have drafted the Code of Conduct on the Human Right to Adequate Food which has been available since 1997. The International Core Planning Group of the NGOs/CSOs has decided to place the proposed Code of Conduct on to the agendas of the World Food Summit – five years later to be held in Rome in November, this year so that it comes into effect and it becomes possible to govern the activities of those involved in achieving the Right to food including national, international institutions and private sectors such as TNCs . Lobbying should therefore be done by the civil societies at all levels to this direction.

Agrarian Reform – The Pre-condition for the Right to Food

However, there is no doubt that mere theoretical exercise would not be able to establish the much desired human right to adequate food of the millions. Until and unless the hungry millions would take active initiative themselves, the right to adequate food is not going to be gifted to them by anybody anywhere in this world. To them, right to food means right to productive resources.

I have mentioned earlier also that the human right to adequate food has long been recognized in article 11 of the International Covenant on Economic, Social and Cultural Rights. Therefore, question arises why millions of people all over the world are still suffering from hunger! A couple of months back I had the opportunity to discuss with the Director General of FAO in the meeting of the CFS in this regard and I was told that lack of political will was the main reason for non-implementation of the Plan of Action adopted in the WFS in 1996. We have to keep in mind that core of the problem is that the vast majority of those who are hungry worldwide are peoples and families who live as small peasants and producers of food. The current system of agricultural policies is destroying the livelihoods of these peasants.

To the peasant communities, the right to food means that they have the right to access to the means of food production, in particular land. Each and every State party to the covenants as well as the community of States parties are under an obligation to respect, protect and fulfil the peasants access to productive resources. It does not require to be mentioned here that only by framing laws be it at national level or at international level, it is not possible to establish the right to adequate food of the millions of peasants. A rigorous act by them can only generate political will among the State parties and to ensure their household food security and eradicate hunger.

To this end, the Genuine Agrarian Reform is the central means for the millions of toiling peasants, women and men to have control over the land, the seeds, water and other productive resources which alone could only enable them to achieve their right to adequate food. Therefore task before the civil society all over the world today is to build up and or strengthen the existing peasant movement as well as to work for international intervention if the right to feed oneself is violated or agrarian reform activists are oppressed anywhere. Lobbying the institutions of the United Nations, the international financial institutions and the national governments both in the South and in the North to put the agrarian reform on their agenda should be one of the major programmes of the NGOs/CSOs in the forthcoming months and years.

It also clearly shows the interdependence of the different groups of human rights.

Agrarian Reform should have Gender Equity

However, in this connection it would not be out of place to mention here that in the 21st century, agrarian reform does not only mean distributing lands. Agrarian Reform is a basic tool to achieve substantial changes in the life of the peasant women and men and turns them into real subjects of the economic, social and political development of society. Women always play a pivotal role in the food production and their right to productive resources and equal opportunities to use and develop their skills must be guaranteed.

It is noteworthy that FIAN, the International Human Rights organization working for the right to food together with various peasant organizations have initiated a Global campaign for Agrarian Reform for Right to Food of the millions.

Emergencies and Right to Food

In the present day world millions of people are denied their right to food suddenly and dramatically threatened by armed conflict and natural disaster. States must guarantee the political and economic rights of those, particularly their right to food within their borders.

States must make greater efforts to prevent and resolve conflicts peacefully, together with donor agencies; they must guarantee food for vulnerable populations including displaced persons and refugees.

Democratization : The Right to Food and WTO

Among the main strategic issues for attaining the right to food, Democratization is one of the key issue to devolve power to local communities, to enable a legislative framework for the flourishing of civil society, and its participation in policy making as well as new forms of international solidarity that support sustainable livelihoods and national democratic processes.

However, it is being noticed with great concern that contrary to the process of democratization, WTO trade policies are increasing the numbers of `unneeded farmers all over the world.' The search for lower cost producers is already driving farmers of the north and south from the land. Further the dumping of cheap imported food causes the destruction of their local markets. The conversion of food from a core principle of human life to purely a trade commodity threatens the foundation of many cultures. Therefore, current pattern of trade liberalization determined by AOA under WTO is detrimental to the democratization process and Right to food of the hungry millions. The NGOs/CSOs everywhere, particularly on the eve of WFS-fyl and Qatar Ministerial meeting should raise demand that WTO should be taken out of Agriculture. The imperative now is to shift to a democratic food system based on sustainable production, conservation and equitable access to resources and right to food for all.

Respected and Dear Friends, very briefly I have tried to present before you some salient points concerning the human right to adequate food. It would be evident from the discussions that there are a number of obstacles standing in the way of achieving the right to food of the millions. These are to be removed and undoubtedly NGOs/CSOs could play a meaningful role in this regard. To ensure human right to adequate food, at this stage the main tasks before us as I have understood are as follows :

(1) To make lobby for adoption of the international code of conduct on the right to food by the UN General Assembly to govern the activities of all State actors and other relevant actors to end hunger and malnutrition.
(2) Advocacy for progressive land legislation at the national level and to initiate campaign for Genuine Agrarian Reform with gender equity.
(3) To call for a right approach to development work.

(4) Greater efforts to prevent and resolve various conflicts peacefully.
(5) To develop public opinion to take WTO out of agriculture.

Let the hunger debate be the human bridge between Rome and Qatar

Thank you !

REFERENCES

International Code of Conduct on the Human Right to Adequate Food.
Profit for Few and Food for All.
Rome Declaration.
The Right to Food – In Theory and Practice

4

Food Security : Empowerment through Access to Resources : A Case from Nepal

Sarba Raj Khadka
Executive Director, Rural Construction, Nepal

Global Scenario

As stated at the Rome Declaration on World Food Security and the World Food Summit Plan of Action – *"Food security, at the individual, household, national, regional and global levels – exists when all people, at all times, have physical and economic access to adequate, safe and nutritious food to meet their dietary needs and food preferences for an active and healthy life."* In this regard, they had emphasized for concerted actions at all levels. It was realized that each nation must adopt a strategy consistent with its resources and capacities to achieve its individual goals and, at the same time, cooperate regionally and internationally in order to organize collective solutions to global issues of food security. They had proclaimed that in a world of increasingly interlinked institutions, societies and economies, coordinated efforts and shared responsibilities are essential.

Another point that was highlighted and claimed essential at the summit was eradication of poverty to improve access to food. It was proclaimed so because the vast majority of those who are undernourished either cannot produce or cannot afford to buy enough food. "They have inadequate access to resources and/or means of production such as land, water, inputs, improved natural disasters, climate related ecological changes and environmental degradation have adversely affected millions of people. Although food assistance may be provided to ease their plight, it is not a long-term solution to the underlying causes of food insecurity. It is important to maintain an adequate capacity in the international community to provide food aid, whenever it is required, in response to emergencies. Equitable access to stable food supplies should be ensured", as is stated in Rome Declaration.

However, whatever efforts have been made at any levels of its effectiveness, the number of chronically undernourished people, according to the latest estimates in 2000, indicates that 792 million people in the developing world and 34 million in the developed world (total 826 million) remain undernourished as of 1996-98. Even though the regional level picture has altered little since the previous years, the trend in the decline in undernourishment observed in the first-half of the nineties (an average 8 million reduction each year), was interrupted in 1998.

Thus, the past declining trend was already far below the rate required to reach the Summit target, and the recent slowdown means that the rate of decline will have to be even higher in future years to compensate. New projections for 2015 and 2030 show that the reduction in the number of undernourished persons in the developing world by 2015 would still be far short of the World Food Summit goal, although the projection is now somewhat more optimistic than at the time of the Summit. According to these latest projections, the number of undernourished in the developing world could fall to around 580 million by 2015. However, the Summit target of no more than 400 million persons undernourished would only be reached towards 2030.

Country Scenario

Economic Base

Nepal is a land-locked mountainous poor country with a per capita income of only US$ 220. About 90 per cent of the population still lives in rural areas. Agriculture has an important role in the economy and society. It is the important source of mass employment. 81 per cent of the economically active population is employed in mainly subsistence agriculture sector. Agriculture sector generates about 42 per cent of the GDP (HMG/N, 2001). The unemployment and underemployment rate in Nepal is around 52 per cent.

According to the recent government report, the percentage of the people under the absolute poverty line stands at 38. The government through its ninth Five-Year Plan (1997-2002) has targeted to reduce this figure from 42 to 32, however it does not seem to have materialized when there is only one more year to complete the plan period. The total population of the country as recently estimated is 23.22 million.

TABLE 4.1 : Population below poverty line

Geographical Regions	Population below the poverty line (%)		
	Total	**Poor**	**Very Poor**
Himal	56.00	23.3	26.7
Hill	41.00	21.3	19.7
Plain or Terai	42.00	28.7	13.3
Urban and Rural Area			
Urban	2300	13.2	9.8
Rural	44.00	26.4	17.6
National average	42.00	24.9	17.1

Source : District Development Profile of Nepal, 2001. Informal Sector Research and Study Centre, Kathmandu, Nepal.

TABLE 4.2 : Land use pattern in Nepal

Land use type	Area (ha)	%
Cultivated land	2,968,000	20.2
Non-cultivated land	9,980,000	6.8
Forests	4,269,000	29
Shrub land/degraded forests	1,559,000	10.6
Grass land	1,745,000	11.8
Others	3,179,100	21.6
Total	14,718,100	100

Source : State of the environment, Nepal (agriculture and forest), His Majesty's Government, Ministry of Population and Environment, Kathmandu, Nepal, 2001.

Since agriculture is the mainstay of Nepalese economy, majority of the people have to depend on the land resource. Out of the total area 14,718,100 hectares in Nepal, the area available for cultivation accounts 3,966,000 hectares (27 per cent). Out of this, only 2,968,000 hectares are recently under cultivation and rest is still under other uses.

Land Distribution Pattern

Land distribution pattern in Nepal is skewed. Consequently, a large mass of the people have limited access to productive land resources.

TABLE 4.3 : Land holding situation in Nepal

Size of land holding (ha)	Himal or high mountains		Hills		Plains or Terai		National total	
	Farm family (%)	Land ownership (%)	Farm family (%)	Land ownership (%)	Farm family (%)	Land ownership (%)	Farm family (%)	Land ownership (%)
< 0.1	5.5	0.5	7.0	0.5	9.7	0.4	7.5	0.4
0.1 – 0.2	11.2	2.4	10.6	2.0	8.0	1.0	9.6	1.5
0.2 – 0.5	26.4	18.2	30.8	13.4	21.6	12.4	26.7	9.4
0.5 – 1.0	29.0	30.0	29.0	26.4	21.6	12.4	26.0	19.2
1.0 – 3.0	16.3	35.9	21.2	42.4	32.9	44.3	25.5	43.0
3.0 – 5.0	1.1	5.9	1.6	7.6	5.7	17.3	3.2	12.6
> 5.0	0.5	7.1	0.5	7.7	2.8	19.4	1.5	13.9

Source : His Majesty's Government of Nepal, High Level Commission on Land Reform, 2052.

It is heartening to note that about 70 per cent of the total farm families hold less than one ha of land that has to support their family throughout the year. This accounts 30.5 per cent of the cultivated area. Whereas, about 14 per cent of the cultivated land is under the control of merely 1.5 per cent of the families. It shows that the poor have limited access to the productive land resources. This implies that only a small segment of the population controls most of the land resource and opportunities. This has serious repercussion in the rural poor, particularly on employment, wage labourers, and their participation in the development process. The inequitable land distribution and access to productive resources in the rural setting is also one of the major causes of poverty, food insecurity and rural unemployment. The national average of land holding size is 0.95 ha.

Food Situation

Food occupies a very significant role in process of economic development in Nepal. Production of foodgrain is the major source of livelihood. However, after more than four decades of planned economic development endeavour with heavy emphasis and priority in agriculture development, Nepal's foodgrains production is falling short to feed her every-growing population. Food grain growth rate in Nepal has not been keeping with the population growth rate. The per capita foodgrain production has decreased from 376 kg in 1974-75 to 277 kg. In 1991-92. The production growth rate of foodgrain over the period of 1980-81 to 1990-91 have been 2.3 per cent per year, the population growth rate for the same period is accounted for 2.5 per cent per annum resulting per capita foodgrain availability shortfall by 0.2 per cent.

Nepal, which was recognized as a foodgrain exporter during the eighties ha lost its self-sufficiency in foodgrain production and now became an importer. Nepal is presently at crossroad facing food security challenges at the national level in general and at the local level in specific. Food shortage, especially in the remote mountains and hills, has become the persistent problem.

TABLE 4.4 : Edible cereal production and requirement in Nepal

Description	Production Year (MT)			
	1995-96	1996-97	1997-98	1998-99
Total production	3,913,878	3,972,587	4,027,348	4,099,597
Total requirement	3,948,229	4,079,135	4,178,072	4,285,868
Balance	-34,351	-106,548	-150,724	-186,271

Source : Central Bureau of Statistics (CBS), 2000

TABLE 4.5 : District wise food balance sheet

Year/No. of districts	Description	Mountain (No of districts)	Hill (No. of districts)	Plain (No. of districts)	Nepal (No. of districts)
No of districts		16	39	20	75
1985	Food deficit distribution	13	34	6	53
	Food surplus distribution	3	5	15	22
1995	Food deficit distribution	16	33	6	55
	Food surplus distribution	-	6	14	20

Source : District Development Profile of Nepal, 2001. Informal Sector Research and Study Centre, Kathmandu, Nepal

TABLE 4.6 : Nepal's Comparison of Food Availability, Prevalence and Depth of Undernourishment and Access to Food (1996-98)

Region, Sub-region, Country	Food Availability	Prevalence of Undernourishment		Depth of Under-nourish-ment	Access to Food
	Average per capita dietary energy supply 1996-98 (kcal/day)	Proportion population undernouri-shed 1996-98 (%)	Number of undernouri-shed 1996-98 (Million)	Average food deficit per person 1996-98 (kcal/day)	GNP per capita 1996-98 (constant US $)
Develo-ping World	2716	18	791.9	255	1205
Asia and the Pacific	2791	17	515.2	263	866
Nepal	2390	28	6.2	270	219

Source : Assessment of the World Food Security Situation, Committee on World Food Security, Twenty-Sixth Session, Rome, 18-21 September 2000.

Access to Resources and Entitlement

People who do not have an adequate standard of living are the most vulnerable in society and are also the ones who are unable to claim the right to adequate food. The UN Committee on Economic, Social and Cultural Rights (CESCR, 1991) has defined vulnerable or disadvantaged groups as *"landless peasants, marginalized people, rural workers, rural unemployed, urban unemployed, urban poor, migrant workers, indigenous people, children, elderly people, and other especially affected groups"*. The overriding concern is how these vulnerable groups can be ensured for the satisfaction of basic needs (adequate food, clothing, and housing)? In practical terms, the right to an adequate standard of living including food — first is "entitlements". Entitlement refers to the bundles of resources such as stocks, assets, claims and incomes, which give people access to food. Entitlements in relation to access to food and starvation emphasizes the relationship between persons and the commodity (the food) not just the supply of the commodity. In order to understand hunger and the starvation, it is necessary to go into the structure of ownership by persons of food as a commodity. There could be five major types of entitlement relations : *trade-based entitlement, production-based entitlement, own-labour entitlement, social security entitlements and inheritance and transfer entitlements.*

An entitlement approach has been suggested to deal with the problem of hunger and starvation. This approach requires a shift in thinking from *what exists to who can command what.* The entitlement approach, should be incorporated into human rights thinking because it provides a link between the analysis of how various development processes affect people's command over food and food producing resources in different ways, and the right to have a command at all. Concretization of the entitlements helps to develop some indicators needed to assess the impact on household food security of macro-economic or social changes taking place at a distant place.

The right to productive resources or the property serve as a basis for entitlements. First, ownership of land for the landless makes it possible to cultivate food required for the family. Second, ownership of productive assets makes it possible to produce commodities, which can be exchanged for goods required to satisfy basic needs. Property distribution is, however, uneven and can exclude many from productive assets necessary for their basic needs.

The next level of entitlement is right to work or gainful employment. The right to work becomes an essential element in ensuring necessary entitlements. Work entitlement is the most common way of assuring an adequate standard of living including the right to adequate food. This is possible only when there is access to work under condition of human dignity and when the income derived from work is sufficient to ensure an adequate standard of living.

In the context of empowerment of people through increased access to productive resources leading towards self-sufficiency in food, the current development model seem failing, at least for the people who are still at the bottom of the economic ladder.

Who to blame in terms of Access to Resource to ensure Food Security?

There are a number of causes of food insecurity. Some times, it is difficult to separate one cause from the other, as they are very much intricate and complex. Therefore, some of the most prominent issues and concerns around food security in the country (and region) are enlisted below :

(a) Conventional development paradigm to ensure food security

State policy (SAP, legal reforms, land reform, engagement in international financial institutions and WTO, etc.).

Inventions and inducement of green revolution technology (HYV, chemicals, cropping intensity, market facilitation, tools, irrigation, agriculture credit, etc.).

Population management (birth controls, resettlement, health services, awareness, etc.)

Resource management (exploitation techniques of natural resource base, financial resources, technical inputs, bio-diversity management, access to resources, etc.)

Miscellaneous

(b) Results of the Conventional Development Endeavours

As a consequence of Green Revolution in the 1970s, small-holder based agrarian structures all over the world were dismantled to pave the way for the new production regime; large numbers of agriculture workers (mostly women) were thrown out of work, small and subsistence farmers that comprised a large number of the food producers were passed over by the new technology, increased indebtedness with decrease in food production; increased land degradation and increased loss of bio-diversity as a result of continuous mono cropping practices, etc.

Further deprivation and marginalisation of the disposed people.

Increased threat to food security.

TABLE 4.7 : Some Facts of Nepal in relation to Agricultural Development and Food Security (an example)

Parameters	1975	At present	Remarks
Extent of use of chemical fertilizer	800 g/ha	24,000 g/ha	Increase by 2,900%
Average price of the chemical fertilizers	NRs. 3,000 per metric tonne	NRs 10,000 per metric tonne	Increase by 233%
Extent of use of chemical pesticides	11 gram/hectare	142 gram/hectare	Increase by 1,200%
Cereal productivity	2 metric tonnes/ha	2 metric tones/ha	No increase
Population (estimate)	11,555,983	23,000,000	Increase by >99%
Availability of per capita foodgrains per annum	376 kilo gram	277 kilo gram	Decrease by 26%
Food budget	Surplus of 300,000 metric tonnes	Deficit by 186,271 metric tons	Decrease by 486,271 metric tonnes
Extent of desertification	0 ha	10,000 ha	Tremendous increment

Source : Permaculture Postal Net (bimonthly), year 1, number 3, Jeshta/Asar 2058 (2001).

Loss of livelihood options of the indigenous people, small holders, women and children.

Increased insurgency and civil strife.

Sovereignty of the State and the people is under constant threat.

Environmental degradation (land, water, forest, air, etc.).

Genetic degeneration and extinction of bio-diversity.

Increased dependence on external forces and agencies.

More profit rather than life sustenance (marketization of the life supporting resources and systems).

Human rights of the people are grossly ignored and violated.

Promotion of technology and continuous degeneration of indigenous knowledge and traditional skills.

Ever widening gap between the 'haves' and 'have-nots' (rich are becoming richer and richer whereas poor are falling behind the ladder of the so called economic prosperity).

Stunted access of the dispossessed people to the power politics.

Continuation of vicious circle of poverty and hunger.

Necessary Strategies for Food Security

Following actions are desirable :

1. Establishment of enabling environment (political, economic and social)
2. Necessary departure from the current development paradigm, which has jeopardized the livelihood bases of the people: People must be at the centre of development. All development models should practice bottom up approach rather than conventional top down model. All developmental efforts must prioritize that livelihood as the driving core factor not profit. Concrete strategies must be formulated to protect and promote indigenous knowledge and traditional skills of the people that are based on the local resources. No patenting but promoting livelihood supporting life forms with a view of improving bio-diversity and adequate resource base. The women are suffering the most as a consequence of conventional development programmes,

therefore, concrete action and result-oriented policies must be developed to mainstream gender aspects with due recognition of the role of women in all economic activities.
3. Empowerment of local communities to manage the common property resources (e.g. land, water, forest, fisheries, mangroves, pastures, etc.) in a sustainable manner
4. Strengthening of people's struggles at all levels: Not only the localized struggles but also the transnational movements are necessary to fight against the anti-people policies of the international financial institutions, WTO and transnational corporations.
5. Ensuring equitable access to productive resources : Revolutionary land/agrarian reform programmes that ensure every household to have access to the productive resources. This reform must ensure right to the tiller. On the other hand, financial resources must be availed at local, national and international levels to promote food self-sufficiency at individual as well as household level.
6. Joint monitoring of democratic governments at local and national levels
7. Cancellation and/or substantive revision of the anti-people conditionalities of WTO, TRIPS, WB, IMF, etc.
8. Full compliance with the international UN summit commitments, covenants and conventions as the signatory party.
9. Allocation of resources and distribution of the produce must be based on the principle of social justice.

Access to food and food producing resources to all is the fundamental principle of social justice. *The truth is that there is enough food to everybody's need but not to any one's greed.* But, the other truth is that one-fifth of the world's population suffer from hunger and starvation in certain quarters of the world, whereas tremendous amount of surplus food is being either fed to livestock or wanted in storehouses of rich countries. The same situation prevails within the countries where large masses of people have faced acute food insecurity. Interestingly enough, when those, who are in control of food producing resources and food production and distribution processes, talk loud about food insecurity and its impact on resource poor hungry and marginalized people, is nothing more than shedding crocodile's tears and a mockery of social justice.

The simple question is, if developed nations, international institutions and the national ruling elites are so concerned with food insecurity, then why food security for all has not become the fundamental measure of development policy, a policy based on the principle of social justice? Why development policies were not pursued from the framework of social equity, agrarian reforms, decentralization and democratic control of food producing resources and other redistributive measures? Why development policies were pursued only from the framework of market driven growth and trickle down paradigm, which, in fact, marginalized resource poor people and created food insecurity to a large masses of ordinary people.

Selected Cases of Empowerment through Access to Resources

(a) Land Resource

Since Nepal is predominantly an agriculture-based country, the importance of access of people to land resource is unquestionable. However, owing to lack of commitment in the part of the State and low level of people's struggles to compel the State to provide assurance for the equitable allocation of the land has remained far from being materialized. Even though the State had enacted Land Reform Act nearly four decades ago (i.e., 1961), the implementation part has remained ineffective. The result, is, about 70 per cent of the farm families hold only 30.5 per cent of the cultivated land area ranging from 0.1 to 0.5 ha of holding size whereas 1.5 per cent of the farm families have a control on 13.9 per cent of the total cultivated area, the holding size varying from 5 hectare to several hundred hectares. On top of this, above 1.17 per cent of the people are landless.

In fact the glaring inequalities in terms of landholding and access to land are not only a unique case of Nepal but is also common in most agrarian economies of the developing world. In a recent study on land, Ghimire (1999) states :

"In Asia, 37 and 36 per cent of the rural households in the Philippines and Indonesia (Java only) are totally landless. Bangladesh and India have nearly the same proportion of the landless people. In Latin America the rate of total landless being 77 per cent in Dominican Republic, 41 per cent in El Salvador, 39 per cent in Brazil and 37 per cent in Mexico. In Africa, there exists a conspicuous land inequality in South Africa and Zimbabwe due to an oppressive colonial legacy. In Egypt, 29 per cent of the rural population is totally landless, whilst in Morocco 33 per cent".

According to Ghimire, the problem is even more acute when the near landless population is considered. For example, among the South Asian countries, 55 and 78 percent of the rural population in India and Bangladesh hold less than one hectare of land respectively (*ibid*). Therefore, 'land to the tiller' has long been an important issue of agrarian movements in developing countries as demand for social justice and economic rationality in existing property and production relations. As a result, throughout the history of rural social movements, land issues had been focus of the various agrarian movements in South Asia as an issue of social justice and equality. The Faraizi, Indigo and Pabna movements in 19th century Bengal (Choudhary, 2001), Tebhaga, Telangana and Naxalbari movements in 1940-1970s in India (Rao, 1979 reprint 2000 and Sundaraya, 1979) and *Jhoda* and *Sukumbasi* movement in 1970s and 1980s in Nepal (Ghimire, 1992, Blaikie, Cameron and Seddon and Seddon, 1987) are a few examples of agrarian movements where land rights were the key issues in their struggles. However, almost all these movements were ruthlessly suppressed by the political regimes.

To obliterate the wide disparity on land holding among the farm families and force the government to revise the Act and implement it effectively, different movements of the people had taken place in Nepal even in the recent past. It is a truth that unless the marginalized communities have access and control over the productive resource (in our case, the land) there is no question of sustainable access to food and enhancement of food security. Some of these movements have gained certain level of achievements, for example, the continuous struggle of the

Kamaiya (debt bonded agricultural labourers) in co-operation and co-ordination with different mass based organizations, NGOs, inter-governmental organizations, human rights organizations, etc. had compelled the government to abolish the Kamaiya system in 17 July 2000. However, the struggles are still going on to ensure the liberated Kamaiya families to land entitlement for their suitable social and economic rehabilitation. Some efforts from the government are underway in bits and pieces to provide small pieces of land to the liberated Kamaiyas.

The Kamaiyas (who have already possessed some land resource and who are devoid of any) are struggling for the adequate piece of land so that their family food needs are met, at the least.

TABLE 4.8 : Number of liberated Kamaiyas and their Distribution by Districts

Districts	Land and shelter-less	With land and shelter	Total
Dang	175	230	405
Banke	165	736	901
Bardiya	2,692	1,281	3,973
Kailali	2,647	2,477	5,124
Kanchanpur	2,453	482	2,935
Total	8,132	5,206	13,338

Source : Kantipur daily, 20 August 2001 (based on the information provided by the Government of Nepal)

The above table suggests that there are a number of liberated Kamaiyas that are land and homeless. The situation of other Kamaiyas is yet not known. Because the government has reported in its previous report that there are 15,151 Kamaiya households. However, the estimates of the Kamaiya households by the NGO communities are almost double to the government figures.

(b) Forest Resource

Increased access to the forests through the enactment of appropriate legislation (forest act 1993 and forest rules 1995) and forestry sector master plan 1997 have resulted some positive impact on empowering people to manage the forest resource on their own. Within the broad framework of the policy, legislation and master plans, some activities introduced in the forestry sector have been proved successful.

One of the successful examples is the formation of community forestry management groups and strengthening their access to the forest resource. At present there are a number of community forestry user groups in the country that have control over the forest that is being managed by them.

Enhanced food security and economic benefit to the local people through access to forests; an example of community managed forest:

Located at about 30 km east of Kathmandu valley in Dhulikhel Municipality, the 21.5 ha Gaukhureshwor forest was handed over to the community forestry user group in December 1995. The forest is dominated by Chilaune (*Schima Wallichii*) and Katus (*Castanopsis tribuloides*), and provides habitat for jackal, leopard, jungle cat and squirrel. Thirty-five households are managing the forest. Extensive forest management practices have increased quantity of leaf litter (raw material for farmyard manure), fodder, agricultural implements and water. It has contributed to increasing soil fertility, and crop and livestock products, thereby enhancing income of the users that has contributed towards food security.

The users get seasonal employment in the forests in nursery, plantation, weeding, value added processing of Argheli Lokta (*Edigworthia popyrifaba*) and Alainchi (*Amomum subulatum*). The user group earned about NRs 252,000 during the period of three years (1996-97 – 1998-99). Part of this income was used for supporting foodgrains to the victims of natural disaster.

The forest has also contributed to increasing greenery, reducing soil erosion and landslides, enhancing drinking water source and promoting eco-tourism. Besides cash income and contribution to environmental conservation, a study has concluded net saving of 3.625 hours per family per day after the formation of this community forestry user group resulting to over 46,309 thousand hours of saving a year for total households. At the rate of 8 hours working day, and NRs. 75/day, the monetary value reaches NRs. 434,150 a year. Thus saved time could be used for other livelihood and income generating activities.

Although small in size, this ensured access and contrôl over the forest by the users has a great potential for additional economic benefits to local people and for environmental conservation.

(*Courtesy :* State of the Environment Nepal, HMG, Ministry of Population and Environment, Kathmandu, Nepal, 2001)

(c) Importance of Access to Financial Resources to enhance Food Security

As described elsewhere in this report, majority of the Nepalese farmers are small holders (<1 ha). And most of the farming is dependent on rainfall (rain fed-farming). Therefore, the cropping intensity is low in most parts. Peasants hardly grow two crops in a year even though there are no other barriers except lack of sufficient soil moisture.

In view of enhancing food security through increased access to financial resources, RRN has facilitated a group of peasant women farmers in Morang district.

Enhanced food security through improved access to financial resource; an example of group financial support

Mrs. Radha Devi Bishwas, a resident of Tankisiniwai VDC-08, Morang is one of the 45 active members of Bauraha Women Group facilitated by RRN to organize in 1995. She lives in a family having six members. Her family had to produce a livelihood from 0.5 ha of land which was cropped twice a year depending on the rainfall. The farm produce was just enough to feed for six to eight months and they had to depend on other income generation opportunities that were very scant.

After joining the group, she received NRs. 10,000 as the support fund under the project provision to invest in production enhancing activities. Part of this amount was spent in installing the shallow tube well that could provide irrigation water during the dry season. It has increased the cropping intensity since they started growing at least three crops in a year. Because the capacity of the tube well was not enough, they grew three crops in half of the available farm. In addition to cereals, the family also started growing vegetables. Now, the family is self sufficient in family food requirement. On top of this, they are also able to produce some surpluses of vegetables that has opened up market access for income. The income thus generated is being used to support their children to school, buy clothes and other household needs.

(*Courtesy:* Integrated Peasant Women Development Programme, Rural Reconstruction Nepal)

REFERENCES

Assessment of the World Food Security Situation, Report of the Committee on World Food Security, Twenty-sixth Session, Rome, 18-21 September 2000.

Central Bureau of Statistic (CBS) Statistical Pocket Book Nepal, Kathmandu : Central Bureau of Statistics, 2000.

District Development Profie of Nepal, Informal Sector Research and Study Centre, Kathmandu, Nepal, 2001.

Ghimire, K. *Land Reform and Peasant Livelihoods : The Social Dynamics of Rural Poverty and Agrarian Reforms in Developing Countries,* Oxford, IT publication, 1999.

Ghimire, K. *Forest or Farm? The Politics of Poverty and Land Hunger in Nepal,* Delhi : Oxford University Press, 1992.

Report of His Majesty's Government of Nepal, High Level Land Reform Commission, 2051 BS.

Report on the FAO – NGOs/CSOs Regional Consultation, Yokohama, Japan, Food and Agriculture Organisation of the United Nations Regional Office for Asia and the Pacific, Bangkok, Thailand, 28-30 August, 2000.

Rome Declaration on World Food Summit, Rome, Italy, 1996.

State of the Environment, Nepal (agriculture and forestry), His Majesty's Government, Ministry of Population and Environment, Kathmandu, Nepal, 2001.

Sharma, S. and M. Thakurathi, A Revisit to the Kamaiya System of Nepal, INSEC, Kathmandu, Nepal, 1998.

The Kantipur national daily, 20 August 2001.

5

Empowerment through Access to Resources

Zafar Ahmad
Unity for Programmed Action in Coastal Lands, Bangladesh

Empowerment and Resource

Empowerment refers to processes aimed at equipping the poor with awareness, skills, resources, and confidence which enables them to take action to improve their social and economic lives. It enables the poor to build up capacities to deal with their problems and to assert their rights within the socio-economic system. The World Bank defines "Empowerment means enhancing the capacity of poor people to influence the State which affects their lives, getting participation in political process and local decision making. It also means removing that work against poor and building the resources assets of poor people to enable them to engage effectively in markets."

According to A.G. Drabek (1997) "Empowerment is the bottom line of development process. The goal of enabling the poor to take control of the decision-making processes, which affects their lives, is paramount ... Civil societies are not just to meet the needs of the poor, but to assist them in articulating those needs; pouring money into dealing with the symptoms of poverty is not enough – it is the underlying problems of poverty which require action".

Resource

Anything human, natural, physical, financial and social which either increases income or reduces expenditure, directly or indirectly is a resource.

These resources are of several kinds:

Human Resources: labour, skills, and good health.
Natural Resources: land, water, fisheries, seeds, sunshine.
Physical Resources: such as access to infrastructure.
Financial Resources: savings and access to credit.
Social Resources: networks, coalitions, contacts, forums which can be used in need, and influence over resources.

The Causes which create Disenfranchisement from Resources

1. Lack of income and assets which causes food insecurity and deprives people of other means of subsistence.
2. Inactivity, passiveness and powerlessness of all forms of institutions in the society.
3. Vulnerability to disaster and shocks, with which they cannot cope with.

The effect upon people who do not have access to resources may be understood by looking at:

1. How many resources they have;
2. How much income they derive from them; and
3. How volatile these earnings are.

The income derived from these resources depends upon access to markets, as well as the global, national, and local influences on earnings in these markets. Returns, however, depend not just on the behaviour of markets, but also on the performance of the institutions of State and society. Access and ownership over resources, and the returns therefrom, has economic worth as well as constituting a political and social force. Access to resources depends upon:

(1) a legal system of ownership;
(2) social norms that define common property resources; and
(3) discrimination on the basis of gender, race, or social status.

Both access to and returns from resources are affected by public and State interventions.

Volatility or shocks on returns are also crucial. Volatility results from market fluctuations, weather conditions and wars, and affects both the value and the returns of resources as it results in a destruction of resources and a depletion of savings.

Lack of Resources and Income therefrom

Having no resources means no income and alternatively, the more prosperous a country grows, the less poor it is supposed to have. Growth decreases income poverty, and a decline in growth increases income poverty. The translation of these theories into action, however, depends upon governance, and sound institutions.

Inactivity, Passiveness and Powerlessness of all forms of the Institutions in the Society.

Disenfranchisement from resources implants passivity, creates inertia, helplessness and hopelessness and makes people victims of exploitation. People are unable to take advantage of new economic opportunities or engage in public affairs, and bureaucracy often works against them. As a consequence many become tied to landowners. In this situation women are doubly disadvantaged as they are discriminated against in the household and in land, labour, and credit markets.

Vulnerability

The most vulnerable members of the population are those tilling marginal land in uncertain rainfall, living in crowded shanties, facing precarious employment, higher risks of diseases, and arbitrary arrest. Women in particular are at risk of being socially excluded and the victims of violence and crime. Low levels of resources make poor people especially vulnerable to negative shocks which can set up a vicious downward spiral such as pulling children out of school, depleting natural resources, sale of land or livestock at low prices and lowering nutritional intake. Civil conflict and wars, economic crises, and natural disasters effect not only their current living standards, but also their ability to escape poverty. Volatile capital flows, global climate change, and arms sales also increases the vulnerability of poor people.

What has been Achieved

WCARRD

The 145 government delegations to the World Conference on Agrarian Reform and Rural Development declared in 1979 that developed and developing countries as well as the international community must contribute to the immense effort required to eliminate rural poverty. In the forward to the WCARRD programme of action, commonly called *The Peasants' Charter,* it is clearly stated that "the rural poor must be given access to land and water resources, agricultural inputs and services, extension and research facilities; they must be permitted to participate in the design, implementation and evaluation of rural development programmes; the structure and pattern of international trade and external investment must be adjusted to facilitate the implementation of poverty-oriented rural development strategies. Growth is necessary but not sufficient; the primary objective should be an improvement in the quality of life of the people; building self reliant institutions for building self reliance in the poor, involving the stakeholder in the planning implementation and evaluation in RD project, and undertaking a total reorientation of macro policies.

WCARRD Programme of Action

These principles are fully reflected in the WCARRD Programme of Action. The Programme set forth the following objectives.

1. The rural poor should be enabled to have access to fixed factors of production in agriculture,
2. The rural poor should obtain access to variable factors of production, i.e. agricultural inputs, markets and services,
3. Priority should be accorded to the generation and extension of technology for small farmers,
4. Importance should be attached to the creation of non-farm employment opportunities,
5. Emphasis should be placed on human resource development, i.e. education, health, nutrition and extension,
6. Women should be enabled to participate equally in development,
7. Rural development should be promoted with the full participation of people, i.e. through active involvement of NGOs, producers' and workers' groups and cooperatives, and
8. Macro policies (i.e. fiscal, price, trade and investment policies) should support grassroots efforts in rural development.

The WCARRD Programme of Action states the primary objectives of rural development as the eradication of poverty, hunger and malnutrition. National development efforts and external assistance must be guided and judged by their contribution to achieving this objective. Essential contributory objectives include growth with equity, national self reliance (especially in food), ecological harmony and the conservation of finite resources.

1996 World Food Summit

More recently, the direct link between resource rights, particularly access to land, overcoming hunger and poverty was emphasised at the 1996 World Food Summit. The Summits of the 1990s examined pending crises – the environment, development, energy and food. Of the many conclusions, the one of most significance is that there are no separate crises. They are all one and the same. The single most important and common cause and effect is poverty, resulting from unequal access and use of resources. If the protocols were blended into one international plan, the call would be for action on the inequitable distribution of wealth, the lack of access by the poor to productive resources, insufficient participation by the poor in decisions which affect their daily lives and the need for reforms in macroeconomic policies that adversely affect the rights of the poor. A review of Summit protocols highlights the re-occurring description of the poor as lacking assets, being vulnerable to agriculture and economic shocks, lacking the capacity (training and knowledge) to participate in decision-making affecting their livelihoods, and suffering from an intergenerational sense of being powerless to change their condition.

Achievement in Opportunities

1. Today, enlightened decision-makers are beginning to understand the interactions between poverty, land rights, the sustainable use of natural resources and economic development.
2. The multiplier effect of investments in agriculture and the rural sector on the wider economy are slowly becoming understood.
3. The productivity and livelihood potential of small holder agriculture, over larger scale and commercial agriculture, is a contributing factor in the efforts to revive agrarian reform.
4. A change is occurring in the culture of excluding the poor, and the poor are gaining access to credit, technology, markets and other productive services.
5. The active participation of the poor in decision making processes and the development of government policies and programmes affecting their communities and livelihoods has increased.

What could not be Achieved

Doubt in Political Commitments

The apparent obstacles in implementing pro-poor policies are often used as an apology for not pursuing reform policies. Even countries committed to improving access to land, water and fisheries and alleviating poverty face machination from the power structure, the vested interests and the landed class. The continuing situation over the last half a century casts grave doubts upon political commitments towards implementing reform.

The last decade has witnessed rapid changes in policies to reduce rural poverty. Greater emphasis has been placed on

(1) the poor's access resources;
(2) territorial control over resources; and
(3) strengthening partnerships.

Very little emphasis, however, has been given to local participation and involving people in mainstream economic activities.

Resource rights and institutions which mediate the access of the poor to resources have been encouraged, and this gives the poor a chance to control organizations which have been formed for their welfare. They are, therefore, allowed the opportunity to look for the alternative actions and analyse the conditions and situations.

Five Institutional Paradoxes

1. The institutions which are supposed to bring changes to the lives of the poor are staffed with people who are not poor.
2. These pro poor institutions receive funds for implementing their agendas from those who do not want to change the *status quo*.
3. These institutions propose changes to representative democracy in order to reflect the interest of the poor majority, however their performance is often minimal. This results in trying to give the poor a piece of the pie without changing the recipe, and often becomes nothing more than a charity bestowed upon the poor by the richer class.

4. Everybody is aware that it is almost impossible to commence a reversal of unjust enrichment under the present Asian social systems, however at the same time they are assuming that it is possible to modify the system to achieve all of the social goals of just society.
5. There is a general consensus that progress depends upon the poor and the institutions working for the poor using their resources and power jointly, however most of the civil society institutions have an undeclared agenda of becoming omnipotent and as such commit few resources for the collective endeavour.

The Widening Disparity

The gap between the rich and the poor is widening and the privatisation of common property land, combined with the expansion of commercial agriculture and water resources, is enhancing the process. This gap in access to productive resources leads to a gap in income and food security. As a result income skewness has doubled during last forty years.

We are living during a time in which the world's population grows by around 250,000 people every day, while the natural resources required to feed them are decreasing at an alarming rate. At present we are losing about 3,000 square metres of forest and 1,000 tonnes of topsoil every second, numerous species of flora and fauna are being wiped out and year after year arable land shrinks by 20,000 hectares. Erosion alone has so far made a billion hectares of soil unusable for agriculture. Funding for international co-operation in agricultural development amounts to less in per capita real terms today than was the case only a few years ago.

People are never the actors

Turning "grass-root development", "self reliance", "participation", "conscientization" and "mobilisation" from rhetoric to reality has to date not been achieved (White : 1998). The goal of assigning to the people not the role of subject, but the role of the actor who defines the goal, controls the resources, and directs the processes affecting his or her life is still far away (Gram : 1983).

Democratisation still a Rhetoric

"The reduction of decision load by sharing it with more people allowing more decisions to be made down below or at the "periphery" instead of concentrating them at the already stressed malfunctioning centre" (Toffler : 1988) remains largely unachieved. "Democratisation, defined in terms of broadly distributed control over political and economic assets and the open flow of information, may for many nations offer the only hope of equitable and sustainable progress". (Korten : 1989).

Dwindling Flexibility

"From relative obscurity a decade ago, civil societies have suddenly found themselves catapulted into international respectability for their presumed capacity to reach the poor and their qualities of innovation and flexibility" (Broadhead : 1997). "Official donors have turned to NGO's out of 'pragmatic considerations' seeing them as 'more efficient conduits for development inputs than the often discredited official agencies.' But the larger they grow the less flexible they are." (Masoni : 1998, p-38).

Seven Horns of Dilemma

The inter-governmental community and the civil society organisations have become involved in debate with respect to several developmental paradigms:

1. Reformist approach for gradual changes or drastic reform.
2. Transformation from the bottom or capturing power and transformation from the palace.
3. Social transformation first or economic transformation first

4. *Ad hoc* sporadic projects or integrated national projects.
5. People should be the actors or scholars should be the actors .
6. Accept foreign funds or deny foreign funds.
7. Work as extension agents of the government or contest the *status quo.*

Collective Action

Civil society organisations should try to galvanise the support of governments and donors together for the poor in getting access to resources. The civil society organisations should try, among other, the following :

Land

1. Establishing independent and accountable Land Commissions with adequate participation by potential beneficiaries;
2. Ensuring the registration of women's names on land records; ensure their rights are enshrined in communal property systems, protect/establish the inheritance rights of widows and daughters and promote representation by women in local decision-making bodies and land commissions;
3. Develop methods to increase financing for land reform and post-land acquisition services including land banks, land for debt schemes and land for taxes; demarcate and protect traditional forms of land tenure such as common property and pastoralist areas;
4. Promote and support improved land management and soil conservation practices;
5. Ensure beneficiary participation in land valuation processes. Reduce leakage and improve service delivery by using rural people's organizations.

Agricultural Production

1. Research and technology systems must be built upon the role of farmers as scientists, as the main source of innovation in

agriculture. Reform macro-economic policies that privilege large-scale farmers;
2. Develop and implement investment plans for improved competitiveness (e.g., agricultural products marketing plan). Package improved production and post-production technologies for staple and high-value commercial crops, livestock and fisheries;
3. Implement certified seed development and propagation programme;
4. Establish *ex situ* and *in situ* germplasm/seedbanks for traditional and indigenous crop varieties; and
5. Develop cost-effective irrigation systems (such as shallow tubewells and portable low-lift pumps) as well as non-traditional systems. Strengthen farmer/fisher-consumer links and encourage consumers to eat locally grown, sustainably produced foods.

Women

1. Ensure that women have equal opportunities with men to own land;
2. The removal of discriminative legislation, policies, or customary practices that deny women the right to access to resources and to sustain their livelihoods; and
3. Women should be enabled to participate equally in development.

Environment

1. A stop to self-destructive agriculture and fishing methods and an end to the conversion of agricultural lands and coastal areas into non-productive land;
2. A ban on the release of genetically engineered organisms and the importation of genetically engineered foods and seeds into our farms and markets; and
3. The adoption of ecological agriculture and sustainable consumption patterns in all countries, North and South, with

opportunities for small-scale production and sustainable rural livelihoods.

Institutions

1. Make State and social institutions work for the interests of poor people.
2. Enhance the formal democratic processes which are part of empowerment.
3. Mobilize poor people in their own organizations to hold State institutions accountable.
4. The promotion of social interaction between individuals and communities will also have an important influence on poverty outcomes.
5. Develop self-reliant and viable agrarian reform communities (ARCs).

Access

1. The rural poor should be enabled to have access to fixed and variable factors of production in agriculture.
2. Promote the rights of artisanal and traditional fishing communities.

Off-farm activities

1. Ensure the poor have access to financial services, the ability to earn income by producing marketable surpluses, accumulate capital and assets, use their own labour and investments to sustain the natural resource base and access non-agricultural livelihood options.
2. Priority should be accorded to the generation and extension of technology for small farmers.
3. Importance should be attached to the creation of non-farm employment opportunities.

Shocks

1. Commitments to, and actual availability of quality and proactive food aid must increase in favour of building local food security. As much as possible, local supplies should be tapped in emergencies so as to reduce dependency on external aid.
2. Community based food reserves must be established.
3. Any insurance and other mechanisms to stabilize farmers' incomes and reduce uncertainty in production must be instituted.
4. Loss of food in transport or storage must be reduced through innovative initiatives.
5. The use of food as a political weapon, such as in food blockades of countries and communities, must be strongly opposed.
6. A modular approach is needed, with different schemes to cover different types of risk and different groups of the population. The tools include health insurance, old age assistance and pensions, unemployment insurance, welfare programmes, social funds, microfinance programmes, and cash transfers.
7. Safety nets should be designed to support immediate consumption needs, and to protect the accumulation of human, physical, and social assets by poor people.
8. Build reserves to cope with drought and preserve their assets during periods of agricultural stress; Introduce disaster mitigation schemes.

REFERENCES

Ahmad, Z. Introduction to New Technology in Agriculture: Resource Allocation and Distribution in an Alternative Framework, Institute of Social Studies, the Hague, The Netherlands.

Bruce Moore, Innovative Agrarian Reform for Sustainability and Poverty Reduction, Popular coalition, 2001.

Chambers, R. *Rural Development: Putting the Last First,* London Longmans. Chamber, R., 1987, Thinking about NGO priorities.

FAO/Netherlands Conference on Multifunctional Agriculture, (1999), People, Land and Agriculture Empowering the Rural Poor to Benefit from the Multi-Functional Character of Agriculture and Land, Maastricht.

Forum on Land, Food Security and Agriculture (11-12 November 1998), Confronting Globalisation, Asserting Our Right to Food, Kuala Lumpur, Malaysia.

Galli R.E. Indigenous NGOs as Strategic Institutions: Managing Relationships. World Development 1999.

Gray, Guy. Development by People: Citizen Construction by a Just World.

Goutel, The meaning of Development, *International Development Review,* Vol. XI, No. 4.

Korten, David C. People Centered Development: Reflections on Development Theory and Methods.

Upholf, N. Local Institutional Development: An analytical source book with cases.

United Nations Conference on Environment and Development (UNCED) (3-14 June 1992), Agenda 21: Programme of Action for Sustainable Development - Rio Declaration on Environment and Development, Rio de Janeiro, Brazil.

White, B. *Rural Development : Rhetoric and Reality,* ISS, The Hague.

World Food Summit (13-17 November 1996), Rome Declaration on World Food Security and World Food Summit Plan of Action, Rome, Italy.

World Social Summit (1995), Programme of Action of the World Social Summit, Copenhagen.

Zafar, A. 1997, *Processes, Policy and Empirical Issues in Rural Industrialisation from a Historical Perspectives.*

6

Role of Civil Society, People's Participation, Gender Equality, Democratization and Food Emergency and Aid

Cyril R. Ekanayake
Sarvodaya, Sri Lanka

The topic as detailed in the agenda titled 'Right to Food' covers five major areas which deal with social aspects of food procurement. These topics naturally involve the infrastructural necessities that have to be developed as a *sine qua non* for achieving food security.

The basic and most important of all needs for human survival is food and clean water. Everyone has the right to secure access at all times to safe and nutritious food and clean water, adequate to sustain an active and healthy life with dignity.

Taking the topics as a whole I would start with "democratization" because I think the other sub-topics can function efficiently, fruitfully and adequately only under a democratic framework. Looking at starvation and poverty globally we can discern that these conditions prevail mostly in lands where democracy as defined to mean the "government of the people, by the people, for the people" does not function or fails function in adequate measure.

In such societies the maintaining of power by the ruling juntas takes priority over all other need. The expenditure incurred in procurement of arms take a major part of the national wealth. The bulk of the food aid is currently consumed by emergencies caused by man made disasters arising from political upheavals and turmoil. The role of the State in this respect is vital in that any effort directed towards agrarian reform and rural development demand strong political commitment which is backed by the people it governs States must guarantee the political and economic rights of the people and also ensure a favourable climate for development.

Next we come to civil society, I personally feel that civil society and people's participation are part and parcel of progressive society. The interaction between these two entities will portend to harmonious living. Civil society is by and large the society in which we work and live. It has its own stratum may be religious, cultural, racial or in a larger measure rural and urban. What is important is that people should be free to group together to collectively work towards the achievement of their desired goals. This is most important in the rural farming communities as self-help during seasonal work-intensive periods becomes essential. This leads to dependency on other members of the community, thus leading a closely knit harmonious society.

Industrialisation and global marketing policies have led to the destruction of the rural small farming community, which is the main sustaining force as regards food. The children of farmers no longer consider it feasible to take the profession of their parents. They are attracted by wage earning opportunities afforded by industrialization. This has led to large tracts of cultivable land being abandoned. It is the duty of the authorities at the helm of society to protect the farmer and make his occupation remunerative and profitable. This only can be accomplished by appropriate legislation and assistance by the State.

The aim of the society should be the achievement of a sustainable society. i.e.

1. Provide all people the opportunity to contribute meaningfully to meeting the need of the family, country and society.
2. Give first priority to meeting the basic need which is food.
3. Live within their means; discourage consumption patterns in food which are alien to them.

We come next to people's participation. People's participation can only be a reality under a society which guarantees political and economic rights of the people. Rural development strategies can realise their full potential only through the motivation, and active involvement of the rural people at the grassroots level. It has to be rightly assumed that the bulk of the rural population is engaged directly or indirectly in the production of food. Hence the need to strengthen them say in the affairs of decision making at all levels becomes imperative.

In order to achieve the full potential of their efforts. The following steps are suggested:

1. Strengthen the active participation of rural people at the grassroots level administration and decision-making process.
2. Encourage and assist the formation of farmer groups and co-operatives self reliance.
3. Encourage self reliance in farm activities.
4. Provide training to group leaders and office bearers of peer groups.
5. Assist capital development by village societies by creation of a favourable credit culture.
6. Development of Entrepreneurship involving agro based industry.

Last but not the least is women's participation. The oft quoted paradigm that women are the weaker sex does not hold water anymore. In the farming communities women are an active agent, the vital role of women in socio-economic life in both agriculture and agricultural related activities has been recognized by U.N. Charter.

In order to develop the full potential of women in the process of food production the following steps are suggested :

1. Remove all barriers preventing the participation of women in social activity.
2. Establish women's organisations.
3. Improve the health and physical conditions of women.
4. Provide training to women in agriculture and agriculture related industry.

The last topic included in the agenda is food for emergencies. The Rome declaration commitment five notes.

"We will endeavour to prevent and be prepared for natural disaster and man made emergencies and to meet transitory and emergency food requirements in a way that encourages recovery, rehabilitation, and development and capacity to satisfactory future needs.

Broadly an emergency could be described an unexpected occurrence needing immediate action. Food emergencies arise from natural and human made disasters.

Natural Disasters

Natural disasters are commonly the result of floods, droughts, typhoons and earthquakes resulting in the disruption of the entire life of the community.

Human-made Emergencies

Human-made emergencies are mainly the cause of civil conflict. These again disrupt the life and peace of the communities.

Prevention of Emergencies

(a) Natural disasters cannot be prevented, but if adequate precautions are taken, the effect of such disasters could be minimized. Some of the measures are summarized below :

(i) Adequate storage of buffer stocks of food items for distribution in emergencies.

(ii) Storage of planting material such as seed paddy.

(iii) The State must take upon itself the responsibility for prevention of emergencies. The establishment of Food departments will ensure quick action to make food accessible to all. They should regularly monitor the food needs in relation to stocks held in store.

(iv) Provision should be made for transport of foodstuffs to effected areas.

(v) A communication network should be established to obtain information regarding affected areas in respect of food needs.

(vi) The State should enlist the co-operation of the NGOs at all times especially in times of emergency.

(vii) Insurance against losses and assistance be provided until the people are able to overcome the difficulties confronted.

(viii) Water supply sources should be restored for farmers to commence cultivation.

(ix) Maintain sufficient outlets for people to purchase food commodities.

(x) In the event of spread of plant or animal disease, adequate action be taken to cordon off such areas for prevention of such disease from spreading.

(xi) Monitoring weather patterns.

(b) Emergencies resulting from man-made actions

Such emergencies are the result of civil disturbances which result from fighting between countries or groups within a country. Such emergencies are difficult to handle, but it should be stressed that it is the duty of a government to see that the majority of the innocent people are not affected.

(1) Government should accept that food is a human right as such there should be no discrimination in the supply of food.

(2) Use of a third party like the International Red Cross or a friendly country to assist in maintaining the supply of essential food supplies.

(3) Clearing of road obstacles to facilitate easy transport of food items.

7

Hunger and Poverty in Asia : Focus on the Rural Households : ANGOC's 200-Village Project

Roel R. Ravanera
Executive Director
ASIAN NGO COALITION for Agrarian Reform and Rural Development (ANGOC), Philippines

Background

The right to food is really no less than the right to life. Few people would seriously dispute the notion of food as a basic human entitlement. Food, like air and water, is indispensable to survival. Hence, on humanitarian grounds, no person should have to go without it. ANGOC's 200-Village Project is built upon this perspective. It is a food security initiative, which aims to generate solid and community-based information for village planning and policy advocacy in promoting household food security in the Asian region. It specifically concerns Asia, where two-thirds (800 million) of the world's poor are found. In the process, it hopes to contribute to poverty eradication by overcoming hunger through community action.

The 200-Village Project is primarily conceived to monitor and determine the extent to which World Food Summit (WFS, 1996) commitments have been achieved at the household and community level. In a statement issued by the NGOs in 1996, and which has become known as the Bangkok Declaration, they called for a food security compact based on the integrity of local farming communities and national food self-sufficiency. As a follow-up to the WFS, ANGOC formulated a strategy for grassroots-based action that adopts the basic principles laid out in the Bangkok Declaration. In 1998, ANGOC put the strategy to work through the 200-Village Project, a combination of community-based projects and complementary initiatives to influence policy at the national, regional and global levels, all working towards improving household and community-level food security in Asian villages.

Project Component

The Project implementation consists of three phases, namely (i) baseline survey and community planning, (ii) community project implementation, and (iii) policy advocacy. The baseline survey consists of data gathering at household, community and national level. As a follow-up phase, Community projects that would address food security will be identified and implemented based primarily on the community planning and baseline survey outcome. Policy advocacy, another major component is a continuing process throughout the Project. Food security monitoring, process documentation, Participatory Rural Appraisal (PRA) processes and case studies will be undertaken across Project phases and will form part of the policy advocacy component of the Project. Major policy advocacy venues are the national and regional summits and conferences such as the World Food Summit, November 2001, WTO/AoA, and World Summit on Sustainable Development, 2002, among others.

Project Status

The 200-Village Project is now being implemented in ten (10) countries, though at different stages, and has already covered 5,640 households in 188 villages. These consist of 74 upland villages, 73 in the lowland and 23 in coastal areas. The remaining 18 villages are upland-lowland-coastal combinations. During the implementation about 125 local NGOs and People's organizations were involved particularly in the household survey and community profiling activities in all the countries covered.

The countries include Bangladesh, Cambodia, India, Indonesia, Malaysia, Pakistan, Philippines, Sri Lanka, Thailand and Vietnam. Selected local NGO networks, namely ADAB, CNAC, AVARD, BINA, SWADAYA, ERA-Consumers, RDF, PhilDHRRA, NNGOC, RRAFA and VACVINA act as Country Focal Points (CFPs), respectively. Japan was included in the initial process but since the household survey is not culturally appropriate in their villages, a case study based on the same framework will be prepared for comparative assessment in the future. Furthermore, there has been a continuous effort to explore the conduct of the Project in Nepal and Laos.

Major in-country activities conducted for the Project include national meetings and workshops on Project concept design and methodology, the household survey, community profiling and village meetings. At the regional level, several meetings were held by the Technical Working Group (TWG) and the Project Advisory Committee (PAC) on the details of the Project design, methodology and management. The first regional meeting was held in December 1998 in Bangkok mainly to consult and orient the CFPs on the Project, to enhance their capability for its implementation and to develop an efficient information exchange mechanism among partners. Also, a Database System was developed to facilitate data processing and analysis. Training in database operation and use was held last on 04 and 05 October 1999 in Tagaytay City, Philippines.

Methodology

In the actual assessment of household food security status, key indicators have been identified, including land tenure and access to food, purchasing power, health and quality of food, community participation and sustainability of agricultural practices. The existing status of household food security is assessed based on the respondent's perception of the sufficiency of regularly consumed food items, which are grouped as staples, vegetables and meat. Households were categorized into four sub-groups corresponding to varying levels of food security. The

"Food Secure" are households that reported sufficiency in all food groups (i.e., staples, vegetables, meats). The "Moderately Food Secure" households are sufficient in at least one food item from each food group, even if other insufficiencies in food items were identified. The "Food Insecure" are insufficient in all food items in one of the three food groups. The "Highly Food Insecure" are insufficient in all food items in two or three food groups. Percentage and correlation analyses were done to assess major trends and the relationship among factors affecting household food security.

Highlights of Findings

Data processing and analysis was undertaken based on the survey results in five countries, which first completed the data consolidation at the national level using the 200-VP database system. The following are selected findings from the household survey in Bangladesh, Pakistan, Philippines, Sri Lanka and Thailand.

General Characteristics of Household Respondents

The survey revealed a very typical profile of a household. On the average, it is composed of 5 to 6 members. More than half (58%) of the members are adults (18 years old and over), 40 per cent are children (aged 1-17), and only a very small proportion are infants. A little more than half of household heads had at most 6 years of formal education, 16 per cent had 10 years and as much as 25 per cent did not go to school at all. Two-thirds of the households have been staying in their present residence for at least 11 years. Most of them own their houses. Electricity and kerosene are common types of lighting facility used and firewood is still the most common fuel for cooking.

The average annual household income in 1998 amounted to $ 1,097.00. Of this amount, 60 per cent was obtained from agricultural sources such as farm production and other farm employment activities. About 34 per cent was earned from non-agricultural work. The remaining 6 per cent was contributed by those received from sources such as pensions, retirement benefits and income of children who work overseas, among others. On the other hand; the average household expenditure was $ 1,075.00. More than half of this (56%) was used to buy food. The other major household expenses are clothing (7%), education (7%) and health (6%).

About 63 per cent of households depend primarily on agriculture. Half of the households surveyed have at least three members engaged in agriculture, which are commonly the head, the spouse and one of the siblings. Considering household heads in particular, most depend on agriculture as a primary and secondary source of income. The same is true for the spouses, although not many of them are engaged in a secondary occupation. Children are commonly employed in non-agriculture economic activities.

Households are predominantly owner-cultivators. About two-thirds of farming households own the land they cultivate. Some 15 per cent and 7 per cent are share tenants and leaseholders, respectively. Of the total number of farming households, 41 per cent still practice traditional farming system, 40 per cent use low chemical input and 19 per cent have shifted to high-input conventional agriculture.

In all countries, majority of the household members (62%) are members of private organizations, followed by those involved in non-government organizations / NGOs (30%) while only a minimal percentage (2%) are involved in government organizations. Credit is the major activity conducted by organizations in which household members are involved. Others include crop production, advocacy campaigns livestock production, post-harvest production, health and nutrition, and the like. Most of the households benefit from their membership in the organizations.

Food Security Status

Based on the methodology described above, households were classified according to level of food security. Pakistan at 81 per cent has the highest proportion of food insecure households. In Bangladesh and the Philippines, the proportion of the food insecure is 64 per cent and 58 per cent, respectively. Thailand has the highest number food secure, with 98 per cent of households belonging to the food secure category. It is closely followed by Sri Lanka with 88 per cent food secure households.

Food Security Indicators

The following statements describe the observed relationships of variables with the household level of food security, following correlation analysis :

- There is a positive correlation between food security and access to land.
- Even among the households who do not own their own land, the food secure groups have better leasehold arrangements than the other categories.
- The predominant modes of land acquisition have been either through purchase or inheritance.
- Relatively fewer food secure and highly food insecure households availed of loans in the past year compared to their peers in the two other subgroups.
- In all five countries, mothers generally eat after the children and fathers have eaten.
- There is a positive association between the level of food security and household income.
- Households with higher food expenditure are more food secure than those that spend less on various food commodities.
- Consumption of good quality food is not necessarily limited to food secure households.
- Food secure households are guided by preferences in choosing food.
- The higher the incidence of disease in the family, the lower the level of household food security.
- Length of membership in community organizations does not necessarily imply higher level of food security.

- Food insecure households have the least participation in community programmes.
- Shifting to high-input conventional agriculture is not a guarantee for food security.
- For resource-poor farmers, shifting to high-input conventional agriculture is of a viable alternative. The situation requires a shift towards a more sustainable farming system utilizing local resources.
- Food secure households are more optimistic than the food insecure ones regarding the availability of sufficient staple food for the household in the coming year.
- Likewise, food secure households are more confident of their capacity to avail of a sufficient supply of staple food.

SUMMARY AND CONCLUSIONS

In 2000 the World Bank (WB) reported that as many as 1,198 million people in developing and transition economies live with less than a dollar a day; 2,801 million were living on less than US$2.

Findings from the 200-Village Project survey confirm this scenario. In five Asian countries, namely, Bangladesh, India, Pakistan, the Philippines and Thailand, five- to six-member rural households earn an average of 3.0 US$ a day. Eighty per cent of this is cash income, while the rest is received in kind.

These income levels, including the slightly elevated ones, have consigned the majority of Asian rural households to a state of chronic food insecurity. In fact, 26 per cent of the surveyed households are not merely food insecure, but highly so. Hence, the survey confirms what experience has always borne out: households with higher incomes are more food secure. In three of the five countries, the correlation between the level of food security and household income is significant. In Bangladesh, 59 per cent of households characterized as food insecure belongs to the two lowest income groups (i.e., up to $1,000 per year).

Declining incomes from agriculture and related industries are primarily to blame. The survey shows that agriculture is still the main source of livelihood, contributing 60 per cent of household income. In many cases, agriculture is also a secondary source of income, for most household heads and for their spouses.

The basic factors affecting food security are highlighted in the results.

Access to land

There is a positive correlation between food security and access to land. The food secure group has the highest number of owner-cultivators and the least number of share tenants and lessees. And where they do not own land, food secure households almost certainly have better leasehold arrangements than food insecure ones. On the other hand, the food insecure households are almost invariably share tenants or lessees, and only rarely are they owner-cultivators.

Productivity

There is a positive correlation between food security and agricultural productivity. Hence, the current low levels of farm productivity would explain the incidence of food insecurity. In all five countries, a larger percentage of households classed as food secure (albeit in varying degrees) harvested an average not about 3,500 kilos or more of rice per hectare than food insecure ones. However, shifting to high input agriculture does of guarantee food security. The fact that majority of the food insecure households practice traditional agriculture would seem to make a case for improvements in agricultural technology. Asia's farmers cannot hope to augment their incomes, much less thrive in the globalized trade of agricultural goods, given their present practice of agriculture. However, this does not imply that high-input conventional agriculture is the answer. While the survey does show that farmers engaged in high-input conventional agriculture are relatively better-off compared to other households, the former group's better financial situation may have preceded, rather than resulted from the shift in farming practice. For instance, it is more than likely that the households engaged in conventional agriculture already owned "good farm land" to begin with, as the hybrid varieties perform best in irrigated fertile lands. They would also have the capacity to buy expensive external inputs. However, what is disturbing is the fact that as much as 37 per cent of these supposedly well-off farmers are food insecure in varying degrees.

Access to Credit and Markets

The lack of access to needed services like credit is another factor that accounts for declining incomes in agriculture. The survey shows that food secure households are also those that are better able to avail of credit, either for farm or non-farm expenses, or both.

In Pakistan and the Philippines, for instance, food secure households have the strongest access to credit.

Lack of control over the marketing of their produce is another factor. The survey shows that traditional middlemen, such as retailers, wholesalers and traders, have greater than 60 per cent market share of agricultural products (i.e., rice), while governments and cooperatives are able to buy only 20 per cent of it. This implies a precarious dependence by farmers on these middlemen for the distribution of their produce and their consequent defenselessness against predatory pricing by these third parties.

As the assessment with the community revealed, it appears that future food security is closely bound with improvements in the agricultural industry. Indeed, when the households were asked to name the factors that would ensure their future food security, support to agricultural production and access to land and support services got the highest rank among the responses.

Hence, in seeking to explain the causes of food insecurity in rural households, one necessarily deals with the reasons why agriculture, as practiced by Asia's small farmers, has become unprofitable.

RECOMMENDATIONS

The initial results of the 200-Village Project survey in five (5) countries suggest certain areas for strategic intervention and initiatives designed to address issues at different levels and timeframes, and from different approaches. As stipulated in the project objectives and framework, interventions should be directed both at the community and policy environments. Operationally, these interventions would translate to interrelated activities that include participatory village-level planning, field projects, and policy advocacy.

Pursue Genuine Agrarian Reform

The agenda for policy advocacy is already suggested by the factors cited above. As far as lack of access to land is concerned, policy advocacy should be directed towards the implementation of genuine agrarian and resource reform. The insignificant contribution of government sponsored agrarian reform to land acquisition by the households is a sad testimonial to the ineffectiveness, if not failure of past land redistribution efforts. This should spur the ANGOC Network to renew its efforts in advocating for agrarian reform in the region in order to revive the agrarian reform agenda not only among governments but especially among international development institutions dedicated to truly lifting up the living conditions of poor people in the countryside.

Promote Sustainable Agricultural Practices

Another significant finding from the survey is that improved agricultural productivity is key to ensuring food security. The fact that many of Asia's poors still practice traditional agriculture is perhaps sufficient evidence of this. The challenge to the Network, however, is to successfully promote a form of agriculture that raises farm productivity while keeping inputs to a minimum and to the extent possible, locally available. With regard to farmers' lack of capacity to control the marketing of their produce, policy advocates should urge governments or NGOs improve their share of agricultural trading and thereby mitigate the effects of the pernicious influence of middlemen.

Community Planning and Field Project Implementation

The baseline information gathered can best be used in community-level planning. Getting feedback from the villages is the most basic area of intervention. It will provide leads to higher levels and forms of initiatives, including tools and approaches. At the same time, the process will serve at least two important purposes. One, it would validate findings from collective and varied perspectives from different sectors in the community. These findings would in turn facilitate a more accurate targeting of interventions. Two, the process of exchanging views and information would eventually encourage involvement and informed participation among members of communities.

A valid appraisal of the situation in the household and village coupled with genuine community involvement will ensure that action plans truly address the unique nature of the food security problems in each village.

Implementing field projects would directly improve conditions in the community and at the same time establish key parameters for replication. However, the challenge is to identify distinct and innovative interventions that will effectively reach the rural poor while complementing existing initiatives. Taking off from the concept of food as a basic human right, projects would be designed to meet the basic food needs of each household and therefore would be assessed according to how much they have improved the status of household food security.

In the end, what will set this Project apart from all others is its consistent emphasis on the Asian Rural Household as the beginning and end of all efforts to address the issues of hunger and poverty. ANGOC believes that unless communities have a stake in this Project and are able to take control of the whole process, then this venture will go the way of many failed interventions. In embarking on this community based approach to addressing hunger and poverty, ANGOC gives form-and meaning-to the vision it lives by:

"Vibrant Asian Rural Communities living in harmony with nature as stewards of the Earth, whose members are able to realize their full human potentials, collectively chart their path to development, provide for their present and future needs and equitably share the fruits of their labours in community celebrations of life."

PART – II

Food Security Issues in India

8

FAO and Food Security

Fracois M. Farah
FAO Representative in India and Bhutan

I have great pleasure in welcoming you to this National Workshop on Post-Harvest Management which is being held on the occasion of "World Food Day and Telefood 2001" celebrations. The World Food Day on 16 October is celebrated to coincide with the date of founding of FAO in 1945 and this year is its 56th Anniversary. The mandate of FAO is to raise levels of nutrition and standards of living, improve agricultural productivity and to better the conditions of rural population.

The theme of this year's World Food Day is "Fight Hunger to Reduce Poverty". Almost 800 million people in the developing world remain locked in the desperate cycle of hunger and poverty. While hunger is a consequence of poverty, the opposite is also true. FAO asserts that fighting hunger must be the first step to reducing poverty, as the people are the engine of a nation's growth and food is their fuel.

In India, as elsewhere in the developing world, poverty is mainly a rural phenomenon. Nearly three-fourths of the poor live in rural areas. A large majority of these are dependent on agriculture for employment and income. Agriculture growth thus offers an enormous source for poverty reduction. The green revolution had been India's best success story, but unfortunately people still suffer from hunger amidst plenty of food in nation's stock. This should indeed seem surprising but this tragic reality could not be denied. The mere production of surplus foodgrain does not mean the end of the problem. There are 300 million malnourished people in India who live below the poverty line. The lack of purchasing power makes them suffer from hunger or live on inadequate food. To improve access to food and income, rural areas need investment in health, education, communications and infrastructure, which can provide proper opportunities for gainful employment. A paradigm shift is required for developing agriculture taking into account that it would not only be the source of food and fibre but also must contribute to people's economic growth, poverty alleviation and mass-based self-reliance. This can be realized by making it geographically broad based and dispersed besides encompassing sub-sectors of field crops, animal husbandry, fisheries and forestry. Development of agriculture with value-addition requires agri-support infrastructure, agri-services, agro-marketing and agro-processing. I am sure the theme of this workshop on Post Harvest Management will support these ideas and orient its recommendations towards the objective of reducing poverty in the rural population of India.

9

Food Security in India : Some Concerns

Hemendra Kumar
Chairman, National World Food Day Committee &
Special Secretary, Ministry of Agriculture & Cooperation

At the outset I would like to thank FAO for giving me an opportunity to share my views with you. The World Food Day has special significance for developing countries, many of which are facing severe problems of poverty and hunger. Food Security is a matter, which has been receiving attention of every one and has resulted in World Food Summit five years ago. As far as India is concerned we have achieved food self-sufficiency and have a large buffer stock of almost 60 million tonnes of foodgrains. However, at the same time we have about 26 percent of the population below the poverty line. In terms of absolute numbers, this means that almost 260 million persons are below the poverty line in the country. A large proportion of this population lives in rural areas. It is estimated that almost 193 million persons out of the 260 million persons below the poverty line live in the rural areas. Agriculture provides the source of livelihood to most of these persons.

Indian agriculture has progressed remarkable during the last few decades and there has been all-round growth in production, whether it is production of foodgrains, commercial crops, horticulture, livestock or fisheries. However, the post-harvest losses in the agriculture sector are still very high. No precise estimate of post-harvest losses in the crops has been made recently, but it is estimated that this will be of the order of 10 per cent. In case of horticulture crops it is estimated that the losses would be anywhere between 20-40 per cent. Experts tell us that these losses could be brought down to about 5 per cent. The financial implication of the post-harvest losses cannot be visualized easily through the percentage figures alone. It would be not an exaggeration to say that the post-harvest losses are enormous and take away large amount of money from the pockets of the cultivators. Take the example of cereals. It is estimated that the value of production of cereals in the year 1999-2000 was approximately Rs. 856 billion. The reduction in post-harvest losses by 5 per cent would mean an additional income to the farmers of approximately Rs. 43 billion, i.e., Rs. 4,300 crores. In case of pulses the corresponding figures are Rs. 125 billion and Rs. 6 billion respectively. The total value of oilseeds production is about Rs. 245 billion and a 5 per cent reduction in post-harvest losses would give an additional return to the cultivators of about Rs.12 billion. I would not like to go into the statistical figures for other agricultural produce, but would like to mention the figures for fruits and vegetables. It is estimated that the value of total output of fruits and vegetables in the country is approximately Rs. 560 billion. If we assume that post-harvest losses in this sector is about 20 per cent and it is possible to reduce these losses to 5 per cent, it would mean a generation of additional income to the cultivators of about Rs. 84 billion. Evidently, the farming community of the country is losing a sizeable amount of money because of high post-harvest losses. It is not only a loss to the farming community but also a loss to the economy. In this background, post-harvest management assumes special significance.

Obviously different agriculture produce require different post-harvest management practices to produce losses. There may not be a common prescription for all the crops, fruits, vegetables, spices, etc. But there are a few general issues, which have relevance for most of the agricultural produce. Sometimes the linkages between production practices and post-harvest losses are ignored. Agricultural and horticultural produce, in general, are like living organisms which breathe. The produce continues to have changes even after the harvest till these reach the consumer or the processor. Moisture plays an important role in determining the keeping quality of agricultural produce. Therefore, the season of harvest becomes important. If harvesting is done during rains, the moisture content is high and the keeping quality deteriorates, increasing the post-harvest losses. Use of balanced nutrient is another factor which has an impact on the keeping quality. Experts tell us that use of nitrogen higher than what is required and lower availability of potassium; calcium and zinc increase the post-harvest losses. The incidence of pests and diseases leads to post-harvest losses in terms of quality and quantity. Then we have varieties in crops, which give, output which are less prone to post-harvest losses. The point that is being made here is that when we discuss the issue of post-harvest management with a view to reduce the post-harvest losses, we should also take into account the pre-harvest factors which have a bearing on the post-harvest management in general and losses in particular.

Let us have a look at the post-harvest management practices, which the farmers are adopting at present in the country for cereals and other crops. There is very little mechanization at farm level. Only limited number of farms, confined mostly to Punjab, Haryana and Western U.P., utilize machines like combines for harvesting. Indian farmer, by and large is still using the traditional practices, which are not suitable for the safety of grains and are time consuming. These practices like manual harvesting, winnowing, threshing, heaping and sweeping, etc., lead to heavy losses. After harvesting, the usual practice is to collect the grains in heaps on the ground till it is taken home or to *mandi.* The heaped grain is vulnerable to insects, moisture, rodents, etc.

Proper drying of grains is important for minimizing post-harvest losses. In India, drying of grains is usually done using the sunshine. If rains follow the harvesting immediately, drying poses problems and excess moisture is left in the grains. Unless the moisture content comes down to a reasonable level, storage becomes a problem. Excess moisture can lead to problem of aflatoxin. Absence of facilities for scientific storage of grains is one of the major factors for high percentage of post-harvest losses.

The Indian farmer stores grains to ensure food supplies to the family and to serve as saving for meeting future need for cash, goods or services. Some quantity is used as seed. It is estimated that nearly 70 per cent of the production is retained at the farm/house level where considerable loss in terms of quality and quantity takes place.

The transportation of grains by traditional methods of bullock carts and tractor trolley also lead to wastage on the way. Movement of grains from *mandis* to large silos/godowns is generally in bags which sometimes require unpacking and rebagging. In the process wastages occur. Even transportation by railway wagons, which are usually general purpose wagons, leaves much to be desired. Then there are losses during storage in silos/godowns. Even the distribution process of foodgrains involves wastage as bagging, rebagging, handling, transportation etc. are involved.

The Government has recognized the important role of agricultural machinery and equipment in modernizing post-harvest operations. The ICAR launched All India Coordinated Research Project on post-harvest technology in 1972. The Coordinating Cell of the project is functioning at the Central Institute of Engineering and Technology, Ludhiana. Several low cost new technologies and equipments have been developed at Central Institute of Agricultural Engineering, Bhopal, State Agriculture Universities and IITs. Mechanisation of post-harvest operations is not easy in our conditions as almost 80 per cent of the farmers are small and marginal with less than 2 ha holding. The country has to go a long way to catch up with what has been achieved in developed countries.

For storage of agriculture produce, a three-tier system exists in the country, i.e. national/State level, district level and village level. The FCI, Central Warehousing Corporation, State Warehousing Corporations and Cooperatives play major roles in creation of storage capacities. It is estimated that the country has storage capacity of about 800 lakh MT. I would not like to go into details of the storage system, but would like to briefly mention about the rural storage facilities. The government has recognized the need for promotion of construction of rural godowns for scientific storage of grains. This will minimize storage losses, enhance holding capacity of farmers and avoid distress sales by farmers. It is proposed to subsidise construction of small rural godowns, partially funded by bank credit/cooperative credit. The godowns will be constructed on scientific lines and operated commercially. Another feature of the proposed scheme is that agriculture produce kept in the godowns will be eligible for pledge loan.

Post harvest management of fruits and vegetables has some unique features as these are perishable products. Moreover, these have a more pronounced market orientation than other agricultural produce. Quality, grading, packaging, off season availability, etc, become more important. India grows a large variety of fruits and vegetables under different agro-climatic conditions. There are a large number of pre-harvest and post-harvest management practices, which, experts tell us, can yield better returns to the cultivators. I shall mention a few without going into details.

Starting from varietal selection for higher yields, better keeping quality, slower ripening and better processing quality, one can mention pruning and thinning to increase fruit size, use of balanced nutrition, proper irrigation, pre-harvest chemical treatment, harvesting at proper maturity and time, are some of the pre-harvest factors which have a bearing on post-harvest returns. Experts also tell us that curing, degreasing, precooling, washing and drying, sorting and grading, disinfestations, post-harvest chemical treatment, waxing, pre-packaging in plastic films, proper packaging and transportation and scientific storage are some of the important post-harvest management practices which can increase the income of the cultivators of fruits and vegetables. Use of irradiation technology can suppress sprouting and increase shelf life. Gradually the adoption of suitable post-harvest management practices is becoming popular amongst the cultivators but still a lot of work is required to be done.

The Government has set up National Horticulture Board to promote commercial horticulture. Its operation covers creation of infrastructure for post-harvest management and processing. The National Horticulture Board along with other Departments/Agencies of the Government helped in creation of several infrastructure facilities for post-harvest management.

These include plastic crates, grading/packing centres, pre-cooling units, cold storages, auction platforms, transport and other facilities at airports etc.

The Government took a decision sometime ago to promote construction of cold storages as it was found that adequate storage capacity did not exist. A credit linked back-ended subsidy scheme was introduced and implemented through NHB and NCDC. I am happy to mention here that the scheme has been a great success and the targets have been exceeded. It is expected that within a short period of two years an additional capacity of 16 lakh MT would have been created. There is a separate component in the scheme for promotion of construction of small storage capacities especially meant for onions.

I am not going into the issues related to processing of agricultural produce. It is well known that only a small percentage of agricultural produce are processed. Fruits and vegetables especially, which are perishable; suffer post-harvest losses because of inadequacy of processing facilities. Moreover, processing adds value-increasing returns to cultivators. Absence of processing means lower returns to the cultivators. Many a time the processing industry helps the cultivators in adopting modern pre-harvest and post-harvest management practices. This helps both the industry and the cultivators. Absence of strong marketing infrastructure also increases post-harvest losses. This needs considerable strengthening.

I would like to conclude here and say that we have to go a long way in promoting adoption of modern post-harvest management practices. This post-harvest losses are very high and concerted efforts have to be made to persuade the farming community to adopt such practices, which would cut down the losses. Our extension agencies may have to be given reorientation for this purpose. NGOs, farmers associations, food processing industry can also play a significant role. As regards transportation, handling and storage losses, apart from private sector the designated government agencies have to adopt corrective measures.

10

Indian Agriculture – New Dimensions

Dr. Panjab Singh
Director General, Indian Council of Agricultural Research

India has made impressive strides on the agricultural front during the last three decades. Much of the credit for this success should go to the several million small farming families that form the backbone of Indian agriculture and economy. Policy support, production strategies, public investment in infrastructure, research and extension for crop, livestock and fisheries have significantly helped to increase food production and its availability. During the last 30 years, India's foodgrain production nearly doubled from 102 million tones in the triennium ending 1973 to nearly 203 million tones (mt) in the triennium ending (TE) 2000. Virtually, all of the increase in the production resulted from yield gains rather than expansion of cultivated area. Availability of foodgrains per person increased from 452 gm/capita/day to over 476 gm/capita/day, even as the country's population almost doubled, swelling from 548 million to nearly 1000 million.

Increased agricultural productivity and rapid industrial growth in the recent years have contributed to a significant reduction in poverty level, from 55 percent in 1973 to 26 per cent in 1998 (Table 10.1). Despite the impressive growth and development, India is still home to the largest number of poor people of the world. With about 250 million below the poverty line, India accounts for about one-fifth of the world's poor. Child malnutrition extracts its highest toll in this country. About 25 per cent children suffer from serious malnutrition. More than 50 percent of the pre-school children and pregnant women are anemic. The depth of hunger among the undernourished is also high.

TABLE 10.1 : Number and percentage of population below poverty line in India

	Rural		Urban		All India	
Year	No. of persons (million)	per cent of persons	No. of Persons (million)	per cent of persons	No. of persons (million)	per cent of persons
1973	261	56	60	49	321	55
1983	254	46	74	41	328	45
1993	213	33	75	32	288	32
1998	170	24	81	30	251	26

Source : R.B.Singh and Praduman Kumar (2001). Unpublished IARI-FAO/RAP study Computed from NSS 38th, 43rd, 50th, & 54th rounds on Household Consumer Expenditure Survey, Government of India.

The agriculture sector recorded satisfactory growth due to improved technology, irrigation, inputs and pricing policies. Livestock, poultry, fisheries and horticulture are surging ahead in production growth in recent years and will have greater demand in the future. Industrial and service sectors have expanded faster than agriculture sector resulting in declining share of agriculture in national accounts. Despite the structural change, agriculture still remains a key sector, providing both employment and livelihood opportunities to more than 70 percent of the country's population, who live in rural areas. The contribution of small farmers to the national and household food security has been steadily increasing. The water availability for agricultural uses has reached a critical level and deserves urgent attention of all concerned.

India has high population pressure on land and other resources to meet its food and development needs. The natural resource base of land, water and bio-diversity is under severe pressure. Food demand challenges ahead are formidable considering the non-availability of favourable factors of past growth, fast declining factor productivity in major cropping systems and rapidly shrinking resource base.

Vast uncommon opportunities to harness agricultural potential still remain, which can be tapped to achieve future targets. There are serious gaps both in yield potential and technology transfer as the national average yields of most of the commodities are low, which if addressed properly could be harnessed.

Concentration was on enhanced production of a few commodities like rice and wheat, which could quickly contribute to increase total food and agricultural production. This resulted in considerable depletion of natural resources and the rainfed dry areas having maximum concentration of resource poor farmers remained ignored, aggravating problems of inequity and regional imbalances. This also led to a high concentration of malnourished people in these rainfed, low productive areas. This era also witnessed rapid loss of soil nutrients, agro-biodiversity including indigenous land races and breeds.

The agriculture policy must accelerate all-round development and economic viability of agriculture in its comprehensive term. Farmers must be provided the necessary support, encouragement and incentives. It must focus both on income and greater on-farm and off-farm job and livelihood opportunities. Education, skill development, livestock, extensive irrigation, diversification, strengthening institutional and infrastructure support will have tremendous impact on rural employment opportunities and the reduction of hunger and poverty. The new policy dimensions which are necessary to accelerate agricultural growth, reduction of poverty and hunger, and help to lead hunger free India.

Fighting Poverty and Hunger

Nearly one-fourth of India's population, 251 million out of nearly one billion, is below the poverty line (Table 10.1). One hundred seventy millions of the poor, 68 percent, are rural and the remaining 32 percent are urban. Number at the national level in rural areas has decreased after 1983; the number of poor in the cities has been increasing. This is essentially due to migration of the destitute from villages to cities. There are serious implications of this trend on feeding the cities and food security of urban people, urban poverty and environment. A question may be asked as to whether the rural settings and opportunities could be improved for securing livelihood security and consequently rationalizing the migration to the cities.

More than half of the landless people are poor. The poverty got significantly reduced from 54 per cent in the landless group to 38 per cent in the sub-marginal group (Table 10.2). Even a small piece of land, less than 0.5 hectare, can greatly reduce both poverty and hunger[1]. The incidence of hunger and poverty gets reduced, as one is able to meet even part of his/her dietary energy requirement through growing his/her own food. Land is the main asset for livelihood security.

TABLE 10.2 : Incidence of hunger and poverty by farm size in rural India

Land class	Percent of population	
	Hungry	Poor
Landless	49	54
<0.5 ha	32	38
0.5-1 ha	24	27
1.0-2 ha	17	19
2.0-4 ha	12	14
>4ha	12	13

Source : R.B.Singh and Praduman Kumar (2001). Unpublished IARI-FAO/RAP Study Computed from NSS 50th round on Household Consumer Expenditure Survey, Government of India.

TABLE 10.3 : Distribution of undernourished and poor below poverty line by farm size groups - Rural India

Farm size	Undernourished			Below poverty line			
group	1983	1988	1993	1983	1988	1993	1998*
Sub-Marginal	48.6	46.9	49.6	41.6	46.8	50.9	49.7
Marginal	17.4	19.5	20.6	18.4	20.7	20.0	20.8
Small	15.9	16.6	15.9	18.6	17.7	15.4	16.5
Medium	11.2	11.0	8.3	13.3	9.9	8.4	9.2
Large	6.9	6.0	5.6	8.2	4.9	5.3	3.9

* Based on thin sample

Source: R.B.Singh and Praduman Kumar (2001). Unpublished IARI-FAO/RAP Study Computed from NSS 38th, 43rd, 50th, & 54th rounds on Household Consumer Expenditure Survey, Government of India.

[1] Energy intake below minimum energy requirement (cal/person/day). Three-fourth of recommended calories (2400/person/day) for rural India that is 1800 kcal/person/day is used the threshold level. An average individual has an intake below this level (the threshold) is undernourished because they do not eat enough to maintain health, body weight and to under take light activity.

As seen from Table 10.3 about half of the sub-marginal farm population is poor and undernourished, and most disturbingly, their number is growing. If we have to meet the target of the World Food Summit 1996, to reduce by half the number of hungry people in the world by 2015, the Prime Minister's call for doubling food production and making India hunger-free in 10 years, highest attention must be given to the sub-marginal farm group for raising their income and employment. The sub-marginal farmers are net buyers and need cash to buy the food available in the market. Their only earning source is to sell labour and/or undertake diversified productive farm activities. A question may also be raised whether a landholding less than half hectare (sub-marginal farmers) can generate income above the poverty line and meet the minimum dietary energy requirement for the whole family ? The reply to this question must be "yes". Now question that arises is how to do it? Important socio-economic factors are identified which may go long way in the reduction of poverty and hunger for small holders.

Livestock's have the highest effects on reducing poverty and hunger. In rural India, 43 percent of the people who do not own even a single livestock are malnourished. Addition of one cattle or one buffalo to their assets reduces the hunger prevalence by 16 and 25 percentage points, respectively (Table 10.4). Only 14 percent of the people who owned one cattle and one buffalo were malnourished. In urban areas also, the addition of one cattle or one buffalo had significant impact on reduction of proportion of malnourished people.

Literacy has a very high impact on poverty alleviation as well as on hunger reduction (Table 10.5). The illiterate people, whether urban or rural, are the most poor and malnourished. In urban areas the impact of literacy on poverty is the highest. Education, even above primary level, is extremely effective in reducing both poverty and hunger. Graduate and technical education is, of course, the most important instrument for reducing both poverty and hunger. But, its impact is most visible on poverty reduction. Therefore, the educational policy of the country must be geared to remove illiteracy as soon as possible, as 50 percent of our people are still illiterate. Free education up to eighth standard couple with mid-day meal in the schools will go a long way in reducing both poverty and hunger and will thus help build a strong India. Further, this move will greatly reduce the violation of child labour rules and will offset some of the non-tariff restrictions imposed by developed countries on exports from developing countries on the grounds of use of child labour.

TABLE 10.4 : Impact of livestock on alleviation of hunger and poverty in India

Livestock	Percent of population			
	Rural		Urban	
	Hunger	Poor	Hunger	Poor
None	36	28	43	55
Cow	31	25	29	42
Buffalo	26	18	20	33
Cow & buffalo	14	8	7	04

Source : R.B.Singh and Praduman Kumar (2001). Unpnblished IARI-FAO/RAP Study Computed from NSS 50th round on Household Consumer Expenditure Survey, Government of India.

TABLE 10.5 : Impact of literacy on alleviation of hunger and poverty in India

Literacy level	Percent of population			
	Malnourished		Below poverty level	
	Rural	Urban	Rural	Urban
Zero	36	28	43	55
Below Primary Level	31	25	29	42
Above Primary Level	26	18	20	33
Graduate and Technical	14	08	07	04

Source : R.B.Singh and Praduman Kumar (2001). Unpublished IARI-FAO/RAP Study Computed from NSS 50th round on Household Consumer Expenditure Survey, Government of India.

New Policy Dimensions

Empowering the Small Farmers

Contributions of smallholder in securing food for growing population have increased considerably even though they are most insecure and vulnerable group in the society (Singh and Kumar, 2001). Off-farm and non-farm employment opportunities can play an important role. Against the expectation under the liberalized scenario, the non-agricultural employment in rural areas has not improved. Greater emphasis needs to be placed on non-farm employment and appropriate budgetary allocations and rural credit through banking systems should be in place to promote appropriate rural enterprises. Specific human resource and skill development programmes to train them will make them better decision-makers and highly labour productive. Human resource development for increasing productivity of these small holders should get high priority. Thus, knowledge and skill development of rural people both in agriculture and non-agriculture sectors is essential for achieving economic and social goals. A careful balance will therefore need to be maintained between the agricultural and non-agricultural employment and farm and non-farm economy, as the two sectors are closely inter-connected.

Raising agricultural productivity requires continuing investments in human resource development, agricultural research and development, improved information and extension, market, roads and related infrastructure and efficient small-scale, farmer-controlled irrigation technologies, and custom hiring services. Such investments would give small farmers the options and flexibility to adjust and respond to market conditions.

For poor farm-households whose major endowment is its labour force, economic growth with equity will give increased entitlement by offering favourable markets for its products and more employment opportunities. Economic growth if not managed, suitably, can lead to growing inequalities. Agrarian reforms to alleviate unequal access to land, compounded by unequal access to water, credit, knowledge and markets have not only rectified income distribution but also resulted in sharp increases in productivity and hence need to be adopted widely. Further, targeted measures that not only address the immediate food and health care requirements of disadvantaged groups, but also provides them with developmental means, that is access to input, infrastructure, services and most important, education, should be taken up.

Identification of need-based productive programmes is very critical, which can be explored through characterisation of production environment. We have to develop demand-driven and location-specific programmes to meet the requirements of different regions to meet the nutritional security of most vulnerable population in the rural areas. Improved agricultural technology, irrigation, livestock sector and literacy will be most important instruments for improving the nutritional security of the farm-households. Watershed development and water saving techniques will have far reaching implications in increasing agricultural production and raising calorie intake in the rainfed areas. Livestock sector should receive high priority with multiple objectives of diversifying agriculture, raising income and meeting the nutritional security of the poor farm households. Need based and location-specific community programmes, which promise to raise nutritional security, should be identified and effectively implemented. Expansion of micro credit programmes for income-generation activities, innovative approaches to promote family planning and provide primary health services to people and livestock and education should enhance labour productivity and adoption of new technologies. Development of the post-harvest sector, co-operatives, investment on road, education, research and development should be an investment priority. A congenial policy environment is needed to enable smaller holders to take the advantage of available techniques of production, which can generate more incomes and employment in villages. For this poor farmer needs the support of necessary services in the form of backward and forward linkages. Small-mechanised tools, which minimise drudgery and does not reduce employment, but only adds value to the working hours are needed to enhance labour productivity. Special safety nets should be designed and implemented for them. Can agricultural co-operatives internalise and galvanize these marginal and excluded people? Off-farm employment provided through co-operatives will go a long way in pulling them out of the State where poverty breeds poverty. Therefore, investment in the empowerment of the small landholders will pay off handsomely. Create rural centres of production and processing by masses through co-operatives or empowerment of Gram Panchayats to promote co-operatives. This will improve efficiency of input and output marketing and give higher income. There is need to disseminate widely post-harvest handling and agro-processing and value addition technologies not only to reduce the heavy post-harvest losses but also improve quality through proper storage, packaging, handling and transport. Panchayatiraj institutions and co-operatives can play significant role in all these directions. Giving them power over the administration, as contemplated under the 73rd and 74th Amendments of the Constitution has not been implemented seriously so far in any of the States.

Bridging Yield Gaps

Potential yield (average yield of last 5 years of 5 best entries in AVTII of All India Coordinated Trials) and National average for various crops are given in Table 10.6. Yield gap as computed by percentage difference between potential and achieved (national average of farmer's) yield reveals the bridgeable gap, which are quite high ranging 45 to 85 per cent. Thus there is ample scope for improving average yields. At the national level, 19 to 55 percent of the potential yield is achieved. The yield gap was highest for sorghum (81 per cent) followed by maize (72 per cent), rice (70 per cent), wheat and brassica (48 per cent) and minimum for pigeon pea. The vast yield gaps exist in two-third cropped area. This can be bridged by (i) extending the area under suitable high yielding varieties; (ii) increasing the use of organic fertilizers and fertilizers based on soil test results, (iii) timely planting under quality and treated seed, (iv) ensuring desired plant population, (v) strengthening agricultural services, including appropriate processing and timely disposal of surplus production, and (vi) ensuring efficient use of irrigation water.

TABLE 10.6 : Yield gap of crop in India

Crops	Potential yield (Kg/ha)	National Average (Kg/ha)	Yield potential	
			Tapped (per cent)	Un-tapped (per cent)
Rice	4877	1903	30	70
Wheat	4960	2582	52	48
Maize	6022	1729	29	71
Sorghum	4437	842	19	81
Pearl millet	2755	779	18	72
Brassica Juncea	1631	853	52	48
Pigeon Pea	1549	703	55	45

Potential yield is the average yield of 5 years (1996-2000) of 5 best entries in AVTII of All India Coordinated Trials.

Arresting Deceleration in Total Factor Productivity

Public investment in irrigation, infrastructure development (road, electricity), research and extension and efficient use of water and plant nutrients are the dominant sources of TFP growth. The sharp deceleration in total investment and more so in public sector investment in agriculture is the main cause for the deceleration. This has resulted in the slow-down in the growth of irrigated area and a sharp deceleration in the rate of growth of fertiliser consumption. The most serious effect of deceleration in total investment has been on agricultural research and extension. This trend must be reversed as the projected increase in food and non-food production must accrue essentially through increasing yield per hectare. Recognising that there are serious yield gaps and there are already proven paths for increasing productivity, it is very important for India to maintain a steady growth rate in total factor productivity. As the TFP increases, the cost of production decreases and the prices also decrease and stabilise. Both producer and consumer share the benefits. The fall in food prices will benefit the urban and rural poor more than the upper income groups, because the former spend a much larger proportion of their income on cereals than the latter. All the efforts need to be concentrated on accelerating growth in TFP, whilst conserving natural resources and promoting ecological integrity of agricultural system. More than half of the required growth in yield to meet the target of demand must be met from research efforts by developing location specific and low input use technologies with the emphasis on the regions where the current yields are below the required national average yield.

Literacy had a positive and significant relation with crop productivity and a strong link exists between literacy and farm modernisation. Literacy emerged as an important source of growth in adoption of technology, use of modern inputs like machines, fertilisers, and yield. Recognising that in the liberalised economic environment, efficiency and growth orientation will attract maximum attention. Literacy will play a far more important role in the globalise world than it did in the past. Contribution of literacy, through TFP, will be substantial on yield growth and domestic supply. As future agriculture will increasingly be science-led and will require modern economic management, high return to investment on education is expected.

The investments that are good for agricultural growth -- technology and its dissemination, rural infrastructure (roads), education and irrigation -- amount to a 'win-win' strategy for reducing rural poverty by also increasing the non-farm economy and raising rural wages. Creating infrastructure in less developed areas, better management of infrastructure and introduction of new technologies can further enhance resource productivity and TFP. Generation and effective assessment and diffusion of packages of appropriate technologies involving system and programme based approach, participatory mechanisms, greater congruency between productivity and sustainability through integrated pest management and integrated soil-water-irrigation-nutrient management, should be aggressively promoted to bridge the yield gaps in most field crops. Besides this, efforts must be in place to defend the gains and to make new gains particularly through the congruence of gene revolution, informatics revolution, management revolution and eco-technology.

Many observers have expressed concern that technological gains have not occurred in a number of crops, notably coarse cereals, pulses and in rainfed areas. Recent analysis on TFP growth based on cost of cultivation data does not prove this perception (Table 10.7). In all the 18 major crops considered in the analysis, several States have recorded positive TFP growth. This is spread over major cereals, coarse grains, pulses, oilseeds, fibres, vegetables, etc. In most cases, in the major producing States, rainfed crops also, showed productivity gains. There is thus strong evidence that technological change has generally pervaded the entire crop sector. There are, of course, crops and States where technological stagnation or decline is apparent. The States of Assam, Bihar, Madhya Pradesh, Himachal Pradesh and Karnataka have lagged significantly in terms of technological change. Public research has also lost out by failing to integrate research and marketing. These are the priorities for present and future agricultural research. Farming system research to develop location specific technologies and strategy to make grey areas green by adopting three-pronged approach -- watershed management, hybrid technology and small farm mechanisation will accelerate growth in TFP. It is necessary to enlarge the efforts for promoting available dry land technologies. Promoting efficient fertiliser practices, improving soil-testing services, strengthening distribution channel of critical inputs specially quality seed and development of physical and institutional infrastructure will help resource-poor farmers.

Accent on Post-Harvest Management, Value Addition and Cost-Effectiveness

Post-harvest losses generally range from 5 to 10 percent for non-perishables and about 30 percent for perishables. This loss could be and must be minimized. Let us remember, a grain saved is a grain produced. Emphasis should therefore be placed to

TABLE 10.7 : Total Factor Productivity trends for crops in selected States

Crop	TFP trend		
	Increasing	No change	Declining
Paddy	Andhra Pradesh, Orissa, Punjab, Tamil Nadu, Uttar Pradesh, West Bengal	Assam, Haryana	Bihar, Karnataka, Madhya Pradesh
Wheat	Haryana, Punjab, Rajasthan, Uttar Pradesh	Madhya Pradesh	
Sorghum	Andhra Pradesh, Maharashtra, Karnataka	Madhya Pradesh, Rajasthan	
Pearl millets	Gujarat, Haryana, Rajasthan		
Maize	Madhya Pradesh	Rajasthan, Uttar Pradesh	
Barley	Uttar Pradesh	Rajasthan	
Chickpea	Haryana	Rajasthan, Uttar Pradesh	Madhya Pradesh
Black gram	Maharashtra	Andhra Pradesh, Madhya Pradesh, Uttar Pradesh	Orissa
Moong	Madhya Pradesh	Andhra Pradesh, Rajasthan	Orissa
Pigeon pea	Madhya Pradesh	Gujarat, Uttar Pradesh	
Groundnut	Andhra Pradesh , Karnataka, Maharashtra, Orissa	Gujarat, Tamil Nadu	
Rapeseed& Mustard	Rajasthan, Uttar Pradesh	Assam, Haryana	Punjab
Soyabean		Madhya Pradesh	
Sugarcane	Bihar	Andhra Pradesh, Haryana, Karnataka, Maharashtra, Uttar Pradesh	
Cotton	Gujarat, Haryana, Tamil Nadu	Andhra Pradesh, Karnataka, Madhya Pradesh, Maharashtra, Punjab	
Jute	Assam, Bihar, West Bengal		Bihar
Onion	Maharashtra	Himachal Pradesh	
Potato	Uttar Pradesh	Himachal Pradesh	

Source : Praduman Kumar (2001). Unpublished IARI study. Based on cost of cultivation data, DES, Government of India.

develop post-harvest handling, agro-processing and value-addition technologies not only to prevent the high losses, but also to improve quality through proper storage, packaging, handling and transport. With the thrust on globalization and increasing competitiveness, this approach will improve the agricultural export contribution of India, which is proportionately extremely low. Cost-effectiveness in production and post-harvest handling through the application of latest technologies will be a necessity. The agro-processing facilities should preferably be located close to the points of production in rural areas, which will greatly promote off-farm employment. Such centres of processing and value addition will encourage production by masses against mass production in factories located in urban areas. Agricultural cooperatives and Gram Panchayats must play a leading role in this effort. In doing so, the needs of small farmers should be kept in mind.

Increased Investment in Agriculture and Infrastructures

The public investment in agriculture has been declining and is one of the main reasons behind the declining productivity and low capital formation in the agriculture sector. With the burden on productivity-driven growth in the future, this worrisome trend must be reversed. Private investment in agriculture has also been slow and must be stimulated through appropriate policies. Considering that nearly 70 percent of India still lives in villages, agricultural growth will continue to be the engine of broad-based economic growth and development as well as of natural resource conservation, leave alone food security and poverty alleviation. Accelerated investment are needed to facilitate agricultural and rural development through:

- Productivity increasing varieties of crops, breeds of livestock, strains of microbes and efficient packages of technologies, particularly those for land and water management, for obviating biotic, abiotic, socio-economic and environmental constraints;
- Yield increasing and environmentally-friendly production and post-harvest and value-addition technologies;

- Reliable and timely availability of quality inputs at reasonable prices, institutional and credit supports, especially for small and resource-poor farmers, and support to land and water resources development;
- Effective and credible technology, procurement, assessment and transfer and extension system involving appropriate linkages and partnerships; again with an emphasis on reaching the small farmers;
- Improved institutional and credit support and increased rural employment opportunities, including those through creating agriculture-based rural agro-processing and agro-industries, improved rural infrastructures, including access to information, and effective markets, farm to market roads and related infrastructure;
- Particular attention to the needs and participation of women farmers; and
- Primary education, health care, clean drinking water, safe sanitation, adequate nutrition, particularly for children (including through mid-day meal at schools) and women.

The above investments will need to be supported through appropriate policies that do not discriminate against agriculture and the rural poor. Given the increasing role of small farmers in food security and poverty alleviation, development efforts must be geared to meet the needs and potential of such farmers through their active participation in the growth process.

Government should facilitate and support community level action by private voluntary organizations, including farmers groups aimed at improving food security, reducing poverty, and assuring sustainability in the management of natural resources. In addition, governments should enhance efforts to ensure good nutrition and access to sufficient food for all through primary health care and education for all.

Modern biotechnology tools, genetic engineering, as well as conventional breeding methods are all expected to play important roles in the generation of higher yielding, pest and stress resistant varieties of rice, wheat, maize and other cereal crops. The availability of genetic innovations in developing countries will depend on continued high levels of investments in agricultural research, both at the international and the national levels. Free and unhindered access to germplasm to breeders worldwide is absolutely crucial to the rapid dissemination and adoption of improved germplasm. This free movement and the dissemination of modern biotechnology innovations to developing countries are hampered by increased patent protection and private sector investments. There is an urgent need to address this problem of free access to technology in the future.

Increased attention will also have to be given to development of sustainable systems that protect the natural resource base. Recent evidence of resource degradation and declining productivity in some intensively cropped areas is of particular concern. Also population driven intensification of agriculture without the use of external inputs, is leading to a serious problem of mining soil fertility

Sustaining global food supplies will depend on continued high levels of investments in research and technology development. It is essential that research capacity have to be increased substantially. In addition to investments in research, infrastructure investments, particularly in irrigation, transport and market infrastructure development are equally important for sustaining the productivity and profitability of food crop production. Mobilize the best of science and development efforts (including traditional knowledge and modern scientific approach) through partnerships involving national and international research institutions, NGOs, farmers' organizations and private sector in order to tackle the present and future problems of food security and production.

Donors and Government must urgently increase funding for agricultural research targeted at the needs of the rural and urban poor, and every effort must be made to ensure the free flow of information, technology and germplasm so that a proper sustainable agriculture can be achieved.

11

Food Security or Crisis?

Dr. Sarala Gopalan
Former Secretary to Government of India
Department of Women and Child Development

The crisis in Food Security dominated our efforts of Development Planning in India after the achievement of Independence. Famines and scarcity in the previous decades resulted in hunger and death. The reliance on heavy imports to augment supply of foodgrains emptied our coffers. Self-sufficiency in food production became an urgent goal of our Five Year Plans. The thrust of the Food Policy in India included the following :

(i) increasing food production ;
(ii) maintaining buffer stock to tide over crop shortages and to maintain stability of inter seasonal prices;
(iii) achieving regional balance in production and distribution of foodgrains;
(iv) maintaining stocks of foodgrains to meet the requirements of the Public Distribution System (PDS); and
(v) increasing nutrition standards of the vulnerable sections of the society by distribution of foodgrains at affordable prices through the PDS and wage employment programmes;

After half a century of planning and completion of Nine Five Year Plans, we have achieved food security at the national level, in the sense we produce enough to meet the demand in the country for the burgeoning population. Starting from a level of foodgrains production of 50.82 million tonnes in 1950-51, we touched 208.87 million tonnes in 1999-2000. This ensures availability of foodgrains of 181 kg per capita per year. We have however not achieved food security at the household level, guaranteeing access to adequate food on a daily basis. We have also not achieved nutrition security for all persons in the country. This is the essence of the crisis in food security that the country is experiencing as of now.

The major reason for this situation is our inability to eradicate poverty among the people, which occurs in varying proportions in different regions of the country, and different periods of the year. Poor "governance" further compound the situation. Our national food security effectively remains illusory, and food crisis a haunting reality accompanied by malnutrition, morbidity and death. In this perspective the current situation of burgeoning stocks that overflow the food storage godowns is ironical. The daunting task before the country now is one of ensuring regular access to food for all, rather than of creating statistics of average availability.

Food Production

The analysis of the Ministry of Agriculture on the rate of growth of food production, particularly foodgrains is that it has been declining since the increases during the green revolution period. The details of production and the rate of growth are presented in Table 11.1. The growth rates of foodgrains production in different States during the last decade are presented in Table 11.2. The significant factor that stands out about our rate of increase of food production is that the green revolution boosted the production of wheat and rice in certain regions of the country with increased investment in irrigation facilities. The neglect of efficiency in the production of coarse grains which continues to be the staple food of large masses of people in different parts of the country has resulted in their having to shift to wheat or rice from their preferred cereal. The production of pulses has also not been adequate to meet the demand in the country resulting in lower per capita availability of pulses -- 34 grams per day (1996) as against 60.7 grams in 1951.

TABLE 11.1 : Production and Growth Rates of Some Major Commodities

Commodity	Production (Million Tonnes)				Growth Rates (per cent per annum)					
	1949-50	1979-80	1989-90	1998-99	1979-80 to 1989-90			1989-90 to 1998-99		
					Area	Prod.	Yield	Area	Prod.	Yield
Rice	23.54	42.33	73.57	86.99	0.45	4.29	3.82	0.49	1.70	1.21
Wheat	6.39	31.83	49.85	72.78	0.57	4.24	3.65	1.64	3.64	1.96
Coarse Cereals	16.83	26.97	34.76	31.46	(-)1.19	0.74	1.84	(-)2.36	(-)0.48	1.63
Pulses	8.16	8.57	12.86	14.81	0.15	2.78	2.63	(-)0.22	0.75	0.65
Foodgrains	54.92	109.70	171.04	203.34	(-)0.11	3.54	3.33	(-)0.18	1.80	1.42
Oilseeds	5.23	8.74	16.92	25.21	2.45	5.75	2.93	1.27	3.06	1.93
Cotton	2.75	7.65	11.42	12.18	(-)1.32	2.19	3.56	2.71	2.22	(-)0.47
Sugarcane	50.17	128.83	225.57	295.73	1.89	3.73	1.81	1.81	2.90	1.08
Milk	17.00*	30.40	51.40	74.70	-	5.39	-	-	4.78	-
Egg (Million nos.)	1832*	9523	20204	32.50	-	7.81	-	-	5.13	-
Fish	0.75*	2.34	3.68	5.26	-	4.78	-	-	4.70	-

* Relates to 1950-51

Source : Ministry of Agriculture; Quoted in Mid Term Appraisal of Ninth Five Year Plan 1997-2002.

TABLE 11.2 : Growth Rates of Foodgrains Production in Different States During Nineties (1990-98)

>2.5 per cent	1.5-2.5 per cent	<1.5 per cent
Mizoram	Meghalaya	Goa
Rajasthan	Madhya Pradesh	Assam
Manipur	Uttar Pradesh	Jammu and Kashmir
Nagaland	Punjab	Tripura
Haryana		Tamil Nadu
Karnataka		Andhra Pradesh
Bihar		Himachal Pradesh
West Bengal		Arunachal Pradesh
Gujarat		Sikkim
		Orissa
		Kerala

Based on Production Estimates.
Source : Mid Term Evaluation of the Ninth Five Year Plan.

Some of the possible reasons for decline in the growth rate in agriculture in the nineties identified in the mid term evaluation of the Ninth Plan are :

- "Low public investment in irrigation and poor maintenance of rural infrastructure, specially canals and roads.
- Decline in investments in rural electrification, and in its availability. This has vastly affected production in eastern India, where huge groundwater potential remains untapped.
- Rising level of subsidies for power, water, fertilizers and food are eating into public sector investments in agriculture, besides inducing inefficient use of scarce resources, such as water. This further aggravates environmental problems leading to loss of soil fertility and groundwater, which in turn reduces returns on capital. Farmers then demand further subsidies to maintain the same level of production.
- Inadequate credit support.
- Continuing imbalanced use of N,P,K fertilizers, (which was 8.5:3.1:1 in 1998-99 as against the desirable norm of 4:2:1) and increasing deficiency of micro nutrients.
- Stringent market controls on foodgrains that suppress their profitability. In the face of pressure from WTO, it is feared that if domestic market reforms are not carried out soon, it would create a situation that an opportunity to capture world markets would be converted into a threat to the future

growth of Indian agriculture. The classic case is that of sugar where imports were opened at zero duty when controls on domestic markets remained.

- Growth in total factor productivity (TFP), which is a measure of technical change, seems to be decelerating, suggesting a decline in the force of technology.
- Demand constraints: slow growth of urban economy, restriction on exports, lack of land reforms, failure of poverty alleviation schemes, slow growth in rural wages.
- Controls on agro-processing industry."

Per Capita Availability

The slowing down of the growth rate in agriculture for the reasons identified above, raises important concerns for survival of the people. The most important is the decline in the per capita availability of foodgrains per year from 186 kg to 181 kg. The decline in the area under coarse grain production, and total production has deprived the poorer sections of their preferred cereal. This leads to decline in the daily per capita energy availability in rural areas from 2268 K calories in 1972-73 to 2158 K calories in 1993-94 as shown in Table 11.3. At the same time, the per capita monthly expenditure on the broad group of food items in rural areas has increased manifold (Table 11.3). The empirical fact is also that the composition of the food basket varies with increase in incomes, and one should not be bothered about decrease in cereal consumption if it is compensated by increase in non-cereal food consumption in calorie terms. However, this trend may add to the calorie costs and therefore to the expenditure burden especially of the poorer sections. This in turn may result in cutbacks on calorie consumption by the poor leading to malnutrition, which is not desirable, particularly in a situation of chronic energy deficiency.

TABLE 11.3 : Indicators of Poverty, Income, Availability of Food and Per Capita Monthly Expenditure on Food for Different Years

Year	Percentage of population below# poverty line	Per capita income at current prices (Rs.)$	Availability of foodgrains per capita per year&	Daily per capita energy availability (K - calorie)*	Per capita expenditure on cereals per month (Rs.) per cent	Per capita expenditure on total food per month (Rs.) per cent
1971		720.4				
1972-73		800.7		(R) 2268 (U) 2107	17.9 (40.6)	32.2 (72.8)
1973-74	54.93 56.4 (R) 49.0 (U)	963.8	171.1			
1975-79						
1977-78	51.30 53.1 (R) 45.2 (U)	1343.3	166.0	(R) 2364 (U) 2379		
1981		1741.6				
1983	44.5 45.7 (R) 40.8 (U)	2143.3		(R) 2222 (U) 2099	36.3(32.3)	73.7 (65.6)
1980-89						
1987-88	38.9 39.1 (R) 38.2 (U)	4153.7	186.0			
1991		5366.9				
1993-94	36.0 37.3 (R) 32.4 (U)	7698.2		(R) 2152 (U) 2071	68.1 (24.2)	177.8 (63.2)
1995	35.96	10160.3	181.0			
1996		11600.9				

Year	Percentage of population below[#] poverty line	Per capita income at current prices (Rs.)[$]	Availability of foodgrains per capita per year[&]	Daily per capita energy availability (K - calorie)*	Per capita expenditure on cereals per month (Rs.)[per cent]	Per capita expenditure on total food per month (Rs.)[per cent]
1998		14712.4			88.0(22.8)	232.0(60.8
1999-2000	26.10 27.1 (R) 23.6 (U)	16047.4				

[#] Planning Commission.
[$] Economic Survey, 2000-2001.
[&] Ministry of Agriculture.
[per cent] Brij K. Taimni, "Food Security in 21st Century: Perspective and Vision", 2001 (Figures in parenthesis reflect the percentage of the total expenditure)
* *Source:* R. Radhakrishna, Food Security, Nutrition and Poverty in India, (1997-98)

Poverty and Hunger

The data on poverty shows a decline from 55 per cent in 1972-73 to 26 per cent in 2000. Even though the latest data are not comparable with those of 1995-96 due to change in methodology, in a broad manner we have to agree that proportion of the population below poverty line, that is not having income adequate to purchase 2400 calories per capita per day for a family of five is more than a third of the population in the country. On disaggregation on a regional basis, the poverty ratio could be more in some regions. Though the per capita national product has increased from Rs. 254.7 in 1950-51 to Rs. 16047.4 in 1999-2000, against an index of 100 in 1950-51 at 1993-94 prices, it is 276.7 in 1999-2000, an increase of less than three times in real income in 50 years (Economic Survey, 2000-2001).

The real income has therefore not risen as much as it should have for giving access to various essentials of life for all the people. Substantial numbers have much less than the minimum required for subsistence and therefore remain below the poverty line.

The disturbing revelation of this is the fact that we still have population that goes hungry to bed without two square meals a day in different parts of the country in varying proportions. It is as high as 43 per cent of the families sampled in Bihar. The proportion is only 2 per cent in States like Punjab. This is shown in the Annexure Statement. *It is urgent to combat this hunger.*

We have put in place a Public Distribution System with a network of fair price shops. We have devised ever so many programmes for poverty eradication. Yet people do not have adequate purchasing power to access food available even in the PDS network, leave alone the open market. The situation is also one of lack of effective demand, which in the long run could adversely impact on food production. The range of wage employment and self-employment programmes has been wide, some of them including a proportion of foodgrains as wage. The implementation of these programmes is not effective either, not contributing to the upward mobility of people below poverty line and raising questions about the quality of governance.

Food Security Infrastructure

The food security infrastructure of the country consists of the open market and the PDS. The PDS has a network of outlets for distribution of civil supplies, mainly foodgrains and edible oil. Issue of rations to the consumers through the PDS is subsidised by the Government of India. The maintenance of the PDS with the food subsidy has risen from Rs. 2800 crores in 1992-93 to Rs. 14000 in 2001-02. The Food Corporation of India (FCI), a statutory body, makes supplies to the PDS. Procurement of foodgrains is made by the FCI on "Support Prices" fixed by the Government of India from time to time. The design of the PDS/FCI infrastructure has been one of food safety net for the consumer and price stability for the farmer. The PDS has evolved over the years. Initially, procurement by the FCI was to provide food in food deficit areas like Kerala, West Bengal, Karnataka, Maharashtra, Gujarat, Rajasthan etc. Subsequently, the scope of the Public Distribution System (PDS) enlarged to cover more rural areas. Even as of now, the PDS infrastructure does not have universal outreach in all parts of the country. In 1997, the Targeted Public Distribution System (TPDS) was introduced. This was based on a two-tier subsidised pricing structure, one for families below the poverty line (BPL) and the other for those above the poverty line (APL). The APL families were to be given supplies at 100 per cent of FCI's economic costs and the BPL families at 50 per cent thereof. The States were expected to do the identification of the two categories of families based on poverty estimates of the Planning Commission.

The principal problem in carrying out economically viable operations through the PDS/FCI infrastructure has been one of harmonising the interests of the farmers and the consumers. In the face of dynamic agricultural input costs, farmers often argue that support prices are not remunerative enough. For the consumer, accessibility to PDS goods would get reduced if the prices are not advantageous relative to open market prices. Balancing between the interests of the farmers and the consumers as also the Government which has huge subsidy commitments calls for high degree of efficiency in governance and administration.

At present, over 60 million tonnes of foodgrains are in stockpile with the FCI against a buffer stock requirement of 16-18 million tonnes. Offtake has been continuing to be low. There have also been reports at the same time of starvation deaths, especially in Orissa. It is this untenable situation which has become a matter of public criticism and debate. This situation is attributable to the cumulative effect of several factors:

- Frequent upward revision of support prices; (Between 1997-98 and 2000-01, minimum support price for wheat was enhanced from Rs. 475 per quintal to Rs. 580 per quintal by 22 per cent; during the same period the minimum support price for common rice was enhanced from Rs. 415 to Rs. 510 per quintal was also 22 per cent. The revisions took place every year, four times in all).
- High operating costs of the FCI;
- Attendant enhancements in issue prices (prices at which foodgrains are issued to the States);
- Narrowing of gap between open market prices and PDS prices; (According to the Economic Survey of the Government of India, 2000-01, "The economic costs of the FCI incurred for procurement, storage, distribution, driage and wastage of foodgrains have been rising in recent years and are now much above the free market prices").
- Lesser consumer access to PDS due to the price factor;
- Additions to FCI stockpiles and consequent carrying costs;
- Deterioration in quality standards of the stockpiles;
- Serious delays in the identification of BPL families. (Even the judiciary has adversely commented on these delays on the part of certain States).

An analysis of the pre- and post-1997 PDS in selected 1752 blocks has shown that without adequate purchasing power in the hands of the people, access to food security cannot be guaranteed even if it is made available through the PDS channel at subsidized prices. The major limitation of the PDS is that it meets only 20 per cent of the cereal requirement of a family and that too largely in urban areas; secondly, it does not include coarse cereals which people are accustomed to consume in most rural areas of the country. This has been mainly due to the thrust on increasing wheat and rice production, which seems to have resulted in lower productivity and production of coarse cereals. May be the PDS would have served the people better if it had included coarse cereals also in its channel of supply.

We have had problems in ensuring issue of ration cards to all families. We have had problems in avoiding leakages of foodgrains from ration shops on the one side; and lack of purchasing power on the other to avail of the entitlement under the ration card. Sometimes, they do not purchase rations as the quality of the supplies is so bad that they would rather not buy.

Strategies For Guaranteeing Food Security

The former Finance Minister, Shri P. Chidambaram has written recently, (Viewpoint, *India Today,* September 24, 2001) "India and poverty have been allies as long as one can recall. Therefore we know how to deal with poverty and scarcity.........plenty is new to us. Certainly, plenty of foodgrains is a new phenomenon...The procurement, it was justified, was necessary to support the Public Distribution System (PDS) and its network of over four lakh fair price shops. If the PDS justified procurement, then procurement justified the creation of a behemoth called the Food Corporation of India (FCI)." Of course, this statement reflects Shri Chidambaram's outrage. But a message that needs to be taken from this statement is that, at the least, the PDS needs reforms.

"The PDS has remained an expensive and largely untargeted programme and its poverty reducing effects are weak. Structural reforms need to be introduced against the background of the changing agricultural and institutional scenario. Given these changes and the weakness and constraints under which the FCI currently operates, it may be better to phase out Government controls over grain markets as well as procurement operations. The FCI should then be allowed to compete in the market without budgetary support, free from controls, with the added advantage of economies of scale. The new role of the FCI may be to stabilise prices within a range, provide a minimum support price and maintain strategic buffer stock."

We may also look for alternative strategies that would serve poverty alleviation and food security simultaneously as we cannot wait to eradicate poverty before ensuring food security. "Food for work" is a time-tested method of ensuring employment as well as food security in rural areas during lean seasons of agriculture. The food component in wage employment programmes should be made mandatory in pockets of scarcity and poverty. The Panchayati Raj Institutions should be provided with resources and capacity to administer such programmes. An ingenious way of food security adapted in some of the tribal pockets, for example in Orissa, is "grain banks" (The practice of grain being taken as contribution from members of a group and held commonly for lending to the needy persons on demand as loan within the local community; repayment of the loan with interest is also in kind). These need to be introduced along with the popularisation of self-help groups. This system of grain banks maintained by self-help groups has to be encouraged by systematic supply of grains in different regions of the country.

ANNEXURE

Percentage of Families Not Getting Two Square Meals a Day

States	**Total No. of Households ('000s) Projected to 1999**	**States**	**Percent not getting sufficient food**
All India	202947	All India	14
Bihar	17364	Bihar	43
Orissa	7187	Orissa	41
Assam	5643	Assam	35
Tripura	665	Tripura	31
West Bengal	18567	West Bengal	25
Nagaland	294	Nagaland	22
Madhya Pradesh	15425	Madhya Pradesh	21
Goa	316	Goa	16
Tamil Nadu	17935	Tamil Nadu	14
Arunachal Pradesh	240	Arunachal Pradesh	12
Maharashtra	23873	Maharashtra	9
Uttar Pradesh	27612	Uttar Pradesh	9
Andhra Pradesh	18888	Andhra Pradesh	7
Gujarat	11674	Gujarat	7
Manipur	362	Manipur	7
Himachal Pradesh	1191	Himachal Pradesh	6
Kerala	7446	Kerala	6
Meghalaya	399	Meghalaya	6
Haryana	3421	Haryana	5
Karnataka	11639	Karnataka	5
Rajasthan	9299	Rajasthan	4
Sikkim	96	Sikkim	4
Mizoram	196	Mizoram	2
Punjab	4316	Punjab	2
Jammu and Kashmir	1193	Jammu and Kashmir	0
Union Territories			
Andaman and Nicobar Islands	80	Andaman and Nicobar Islands	11
D and N Haveli	33	D and N Haveli	10
Pondicherry	220	Pondicherry	10
Daman and Diu	25	Daman and Diu	4
Chandigarh	208	Chandigarh	2
Delhi	2616	Delhi	2

Source : ORG MARG Survey, 1999.
Quoted from Brij K. Taimni, "Food Security in 21st Century: Perspective and Vision, 2001.

12

Nutrition Security

Dr. Sarala Gopalan
Former Secretary to Government of India
Department of Women and Child Development

Nutrition is a primary requirement for human development. Indeed, it is vital for the development of a healthy and productive human resource.

Today, the nutrition profile of the people of India is marked by high incidence of nutrition disorders in various dimensions – Protein Energy Malnutrition (PEM), Iodine Deficiency Disorders (IDD), Vitamin A Deficiency (VAD), Anaemia, Flurosis, and Lathirism etc. One-fifth of the world's blind, six million, are in India. More than 70 million people suffer from IDD. It has been found that 235 districts of the country are endemic to IDD, that is, where the incidence of the disorder is more than 10 per cent.

No doubt, there have been sustained efforts over the years to address the issues on nutrition in the overall developmental context in terms of several initiatives taken up and interventions made. The focus in the 1950s was on removal of food shortages and increasing food production. With continued nutrition deficiencies and persisting malnutrition, attention was given to delivery of nutrition services, especially amongst poorer sections. In the 1960s, the Applied Nutrition Programme was brought and implementation. A significant feature of this programme was securing community participation for production of nutrition inputs through popularization of kitchen gardens, backyard poultry etc. The 1964 witnessed the creation of the Food and Nutrition Board (FNB) with its itinerant extension service in the 1970s targeted programmes were mounted to address specific nutritional deficiencies and disorders, with pre-school children as the priority clientele. Establishment of the Integrated Child Development Services (ICDS) followed this. The 'services' was integrated in the sense of nutrition being viewed in a holistic manner side by side with health and education. Universal immunization, Oral Re-hydration Therapy (ORT), poverty alleviation, public distribution of food, health, family welfare and adult education were sought to be synergized in implementation. In 1980, a task force of the Planning Commission advised the establishment of a National Nutrition Policy. The principal objectives of the Policy were: virtual elimination of blindness due to Vitamin A deficiency by year 2000; reduction in anaemia among pregnant women to 25 per cent by the year 2000; control of iodine disorders; provision of inputs from related sectors through coordination; and addressing problems of specific groups. The Policy was established in 1993 and in 1995 a Plan of Action followed.

Despite efforts, the outcome has not been adequate. Food Production, which is basic to provision of nutrition inputs, increased significantly – from 55 million tonnes in 1949-50 to over 200 million tonnes in 1998-99. But per capita foodgrains availability has decreased. Average per capita energy intake of 30 per cent of the people who are in the lowest economic bracket is only around 1600 kilo calories per day against the standard of 2200 to 2400 kilo calories. According to the National Sample Survey Organization, the States of Assam, Gujarat, Kerala, Maharashtra, Rajasthan and Tamil Nadu have average per capita energy intake of less than the standard.

Even while overall food production has nearly quadrupled and the growth rate of cereal production has been more than that of the population, pulse production has not increased the same way. There has also been a significant and steady increase in the cost of pulses. Indeed, the "protein crisis" identified as early as the 1950s continues. This crisis is reflected in declining per capita consumption of pulses, especially amongst the poorer sections of the society.

Nor does food availability or stability in food supplies alone guarantee food security at the household level. Individual households need to have purchasing power to access available food supplies. A natural calamity like floods and drought can, no doubt, adversely impact on availability of food supplies and consequently causes food insecurity. That may be a temporary phenomenon. But the real problem concerns chronic food insecurity, which is caused by poverty, attributes of which are lack of assets (land and non-land) and income generating livelihood. Since 1961, food production in the country has grown at the annual average of 2.96 per cent. But the rate of growth of calorie intake and protein consumption has not kept pace side by side. Growth rate of calorie intake has only been 0.45 per cent and of protein consumption, 0.25 per cent. Per capita consumption of cereals has declined in rural areas from 15.35 kilograms per month in 1970-71 to 13.40 kilograms per month in 1993-94. In urban areas, the decline has been from 11.36 kilograms to 10.60 kilograms during this period. According to the National Nutrition Monitoring Board, the proportion of the Chronically Energy Deficient (CED) adults is 48.5 per cent (1996), being the pooled average of eight select States. And in terms of Body Mass Index (BMI) grade, only 53.5 per cent of the adults are normal.

The National Nutrition Policy itself has forcefully articulated how poverty persists as a vicious circle through the debilitating impact of nutrition insecurity. According to the Policy poverty results in inadequate intake of food and more essential nutrients causing undernutrition; physical growth and health deteriorate due to undernutrition; inadequate physical growth and indifferent health reduces working capacity and productivity, apart from causing morbidity; lower working capacity and productivity impacts adversely on earning capacity leading again to poverty and completing its vicious cycle.

Growth of population, diversification of food production, price escalations, diversification of consumption basket due to changes in consumer preferences etc. have contributed to the mismatch between growth of food production and food availability on the one hand and intake of nutrition on the other.

During the period 1972-94, consumption expenditure increased by 1.5 per cent per annum, but cereal consumption decreased by 1.4 per cent (1988-94) in rural areas and 0.9 per cent in urban areas.

Nutrition is not also a mere function of calorie or protein intake conditioned by economic circumstances. It is as well a function of delivery of supportive health measures like provision of environmental sanitation; clean drinking water, deworming services etc. Gastro intestinal disorders caused by insanitary conditions including consumption of unprotected and polluted water adversely impacts on absorption of nutrients.

TABLE 12.1: Distribution (per cent) of 1-5 Year Children (Boys and Girls) by Nutritional Status* (Weight for Age) – Gomez Classification

State	Period	N	Nutritional Grades			
			Normal	Mild	Moderate	Severe
Kerala	1975+	737	7.5	35.7	46.5	10.3
	1988+	882	17.7	47.4	32.9	2.0
	1996+	886	22.2	50.7	25.1	2.0
Tamil Nadu	1975+	1183	6.2	34.2	47.0	12.6
	1988+	3337	8.0	42.0	45.8	4.2
	1996+	819	14.4	49.2	33.5	2.9
Karnataka	1975+	1065	4.6	31.1	50.0	14.3
	1988+	2035	4.8	38.1	48.8	8.3
	1996+	1684	9.4	39.0	45.4	6.2
Andhra Pradesh	1975+	809	6.1	32.4	46.1	15.4
	1988+	2838	8.7	39.5	44.3	7.5
	1996+	1962	7.2	38.1	47.6	7.1
Maharashtra	1975+	760	3.2	25.4	49.5	21.9
	1988+	1666	6.7	38.0	47.5	7.8
	1996+	1015	7.4	35.5	49.5	7.7
Gujarat	1975+	718	3.8	28.1	54.3	13.8
	1988+	1262	7.3	33.9	45.8	13.0
	1996+	647	4.5	31.8	47.0	16.7
Orissa	1975+	371	7.5	35.9	41.7	14.9
	1988+	1175	8.1	34.6	46.6	10.7
	1996+	1651	3.3	42.2	50.4	4.1
Pooled	1975+	6248	5.9	31.6	47.5	15.0
	1988+	13432	9.9	37.6	43.8	8.7
	1996+	8664	8.9	40.6	44.3	6.2

* National Centre for Health Statistics (NCHS) Standards Used.

Source : Report of Second Repeat Survey, National Nutrition Monitoring Bureau, National Institute of Nutrition, Hyderabad, 1999.

Undernutrition is especially devastating in its impact amongst children below 5 years of age. Over fifty percent of these children still have high incidence of malnutrition of the second and third degrees, that is, moderate and severe degrees. According to the survey of nutritional status of rural population conducted in 1996 by the National Nutrition Monitoring Board in select villages of seven States, 91.1 per cent of children below five years of age, suffer malnutrition of various degrees (see Table 19.1).

The proportions of this group of children having mild, moderate and severe malnutrition, respectively, are 40.6 per cent, 44.3 per cent and 6.2 per cent. Malnutrition is also a reason for the prevailing high levels of infant mortality, which are 72/1000 live births at the All India level with 77/1000 in rural areas and 45/1000 in urban areas. Child mortality rate stands at 23.9/1000. Presented in the above table are comparative data of the nutrition status of children below five years of age for the years 1975, 1988 and 1996. (These data have been thrown up by repeated surveys carried out during these years, villages and States being the same).

As may be seen from this table, severe malnutrition declined from 15 per cent in 1975 to 6.2 per cent in 1996. During the same period, moderate malnutrition also declined from 47.5 per cent to 44.3 per cent, though in between, in the year 1988, the decline had been even to a lower proportion of 43.8 per cent. There was an increase in mild malnutrition from 31.6 per cent to 40.6 per cent. This only reinforces decline in the severity of malnutrition. Further the increase in the proportion of normal children was from 5.9 per cent in 1975 to 8.9 per cent in 1996, though this was one percentage point decline from the 1988 level. Kerala has registered the most spectacular improvement in nutrition status of these children. The proportion of normal children rose from 7.5 per cent to 22.2 per cent. The proportion of children with mild malnutrition increased from 35.7 per cent to 50.7 per cent. But there was drastic decline in the proportion of children with severe and moderate malnutrition – respectively, from 10.3 per cent down to 2 per cent and 46.5 per cent down to 25.1 per cent. Tamil Nadu also registered substantial improvement. Gujarat recorded increase in the proportion of children with severe malnutrition.

According to the estimates of the National Family Health Survey children in the age group of 1-4 suffering malnutrition in terms of anthropometric parameters are: "underweight" (weight/age) is 53.4 per cent; "stunted" (height/age) is 52.0 per cent and "wasted" (weight/height) 17.5 per cent (1993). The incidence of these dimensions of malnutrition is significantly higher in rural areas.

Lack of nutrition takes its toll among women as well. More than 130,000 women die each year from causes related to pregnancy and childbirth. One-fifth of these mortalities is caused by anaemia which is due to malnutrition. [It is also lack of nutrition to expectant mothers which contributes to low birth weight of babies (below 2.5 kilograms). And one-third of all infants born in the country have low birth weight].

A very vital support service required for provision of nutrition security especially among the weaker sections of society is the Public Distribution System. There have been serious inadequacies in nutrition delivery to the economically poor. The Public Distribution System (PDS) established in the country early in the 1960s has the twin objectives of securing for the farmers remunerative prices as well as availability of food-grains to the consumers, especially in the poorer sections at a affordable prices. Supply management by procurement from the farmers through the infrastructure of the Food Corporation of India (FCI) has ensured availability of foodgrains even through abnormal years of droughts and floods. But price stabilization has not been successful. Some of the important reasons have been: ever increasing support prices for the farmers which reflect in increasing procurement prices; diseconomies in the procurement operations of the FCI; poor quality control in procurement [dilution of Fair Average Quality Standard (FAQ)]; escalation in open market prices due to stockpiling by the FCI; PDS prices being even higher than such escalated open market prices, adversely impacting on off-take from the FCI and adding to its burgeoning stockpiles; irrational spatial distribution of PDS outlets (lopsided regional distribution and relative concentration in urban areas) etc.

As of now, the Government of India for addressing the problems of nutrition is implementing a number of programmes/schemes. Some of them are collateral programmes, which are in the nature of providing support to direct nutrition-related activities. Several Ministries are engaged in their implementation depending upon their areas of competence. A statement of these programmes/schemes is presented in the Annexure.

It has taken about fifty years for reducing malnutrition of a severe nature to 50 per cent. It is obvious that for reducing it further to zero level, we cannot afford to take an equally long period, especially considering population growth which is projected to grow at the rate of 1.57 per cent per annum during 2001-06 and at 1.5 per cent per annum during 2006-11 and consequent enhancement of the demand for cereal and non-cereal food. The war against nutrition deficiencies, which has been a long haul, hitherto has to be intensified to gain accelerated results. Efforts and investment have to be necessarily substantial. Important measures requiring attention for accelerated removal of nutrition-related problems are:

- improving access to available nutrition inputs by enhancing the purchasing power of the people, especially among the weaker sections through effective implementation of poverty alleviation programmes;
- coordinated and convergent action as between various ministries implementing nutrition-related programmes directly or collaterally;
- making the Public Distribution System work;
- preventive health care, especially in terms of hygiene and environmental sanitation; and
- generation of nutrition awareness.

ANNEXURE

Important Current Government Programmes (Including Collateral Programmes) for Addressing Nutrition Problems

Programme	Description
Integrated Child Development Services (ICDS)	Provides a package of services including supplementary nutrition to control nutritional and health problems; implemented by Ministry of Human Resource Development, Department of Women and Child Development
Administration of Vitamin A	To address blindness among children due to Vitamin A deficiency; a concentrated dose of Vitamin A is given orally every six months through peripheral health workers; implemented by Ministry of Health and Family Welfare.
Distribution of Iron and Folic Acid Tablets	To prevent nutritional anaemia amongst women and children; distribution is done through health centres; implemented by Ministry of Health and Family Welfare.
Pilot Programme against Micro Nutrient Malnutrition	To improve micro-nutrients status among school children, adolescent boys and girls, women of reproductive age and elderly population; implemented in five districts in the States of Assam, Bihar, Orissa, Tripura and West Bengal; implemented by Ministry of Health and Family Welfare.
National Iodine Deficiency Disorders Control Programme (NIDDCP)	To focus on provision of iodized salt consumption; most States have banned use of salt other than iodized salt for edible purpose; over 600 private manufacturers have been licensed by the Salt Commissioner to produce iodized salt; more than 500 of them have also commenced production; about four million tonnes of iodized salt is now being produced; implemented by Ministry of Health and Family Welfare.
National Programme of Nutritional Support to Primary Education	This is a nationwide programme started in 1995 as a measure of contributing to universalisation of primary education and of simultaneously improving the nutrition of children in primary classes. Foodgrains (Wheat/Rice) @ 3 kgs per student per month is distributed based on linkage to attendance to children in primary classes. The stipulation is that the children should put in a minimum attendance of 80 per cent. Previous month's attendance is taken into consideration. All children in the primary classes of all Government, Government aided and local body schools are covered. Foodgrains are given free of cost to implementing agencies. Cost of transport of foodgrains is also reimbursed; implemented by Ministry of Human Resource Development, Department of Education.
National Social Assistance Programme (NSAP)	The NSAP was launched on 15th August 1995 as a centrally sponsored programme with 100 per cent central funding to States and UTs. It has, *inter alia*, a maternity related component namely, National Maternity Benefit Scheme (NMBS). The objective is to give financial assistance to pregnant women of households living below the poverty line; implemented by Ministry of Rural Development.
Annapoorna Scheme	The scheme aims at providing food security at 10 kgs foodgrains per month to all those who, though eligible for old age pensions, remaining uncovered under the National Old Age Pension Scheme; implemented by Ministry of Rural Development.

Accelerated Rural Water Supply Programme	The programme is meant for assisting State Governments in provision of drinking water to all rural habitations in the country; implemented by the Ministry of Rural Development, Department of Drinking Water Supply.
Rural Sanitation	The scheme is for supplementing the efforts of State Governments in providing sanitation facilities to the rural masses. The scheme envisages achievements of at least 35 per cent coverage of rural population by the end of the Ninth Five Year Plan. The scheme has also been restructured so as to be community led and people centered. Rural school sanitation is also a major component, the objective being facilitation, at the entry point, of wider acceptance of sanitation among rural masses; implemented by Ministry of Rural Development, Department of Drinking Water Supply.
Urban Water Supply and Sewerage	The scheme provides assistance and technical guidance to States and Union Territories for formulation of water supply and sanitation programmes through Central Public Health and Environmental Engineering Organisation; implemented by Ministry of Urban Development.
Support to Water Supply Scheme of Major Cities Facing Acute Water Shortage	Scheme is self-explanatory; implemented by Ministry of Urban Development.
Special Scheme for Solid Waste Management and Sanitation	Scheme is self-explanatory; implemented by Ministry of Urban Development.

13

Panchayati Raj and Food Security

George Mathew
Director
Institute of Social Sciences

The term 'Food Security' is of rather recent origin and was first coined in 1974 by the FAO. The World Bank has defined it as "ensuring that all people at all times have both physical and economic access to basic food they need". One of the most recent and comprehensive definition is, however, that of the World Food Summit Plan of Action (1996) which states that "Food Security exists when all people at all times have physical and economic access to sufficient, safe and nutritious food to meet their dietary needs and food preferences for an active and healthy life".

Viewed as such, food security has three main components: availability, distribution, and access. Availability refers to the existence of a level of food production sufficient to feed a given population and distribution means the creation of a delivery mechanism to ensure that the food produced reaches all areas and segments of the population. The issue of access involves both the physical and economic aspects. While the problem of physical access can be resolved through an effective distribution mechanism, that of economic access requires a much more comprehensive approach. Economic access to food would entail mechanism, that of economic access requires a much more comprehensive approach. Economic access to food would entail the availability of food at prices which are within the purchasing capacity of all households.

Panchayati Raj Institutions and Food Security—the Linkage

Panchayats as 'institutions of local self government' at the village, block and district levels have a great role in ensuring food security. The local self-government system is the best instrument to contribute to all the three above mentioned components of food security—availability, distribution and access.

Food Production

Although India has attained a level of food production sufficient to meet the dietary needs of all its citizens, there are areas where the production levels are abysmally low, Wherever Panchayats are empowered they have contributed substantially to increasing agricultural productivity.

As is well known the 11th schedule has recommended vital areas of agricultural operation to be brought under the Panchayats. They are:

(1) Agriculture, including agricultural extension.
(2) Land improvement, implementation of land reforms, land consolidation and soil conservation.
(3) Minor irrigation, water management and watershed development.
(4) Animal husbandry, dairying and poultry.
(5) Fisheries.

Moreover, the Panchayats are entrusted with the responsibility of preparing plans for economic development and social justice in respect of these areas. Evidently, they are also expected to act as the implementation agencies of schemes and plans related to these areas.

Panchayati Raj institutions can serve as an effective medium for bringing about technology transfers in the area of agriculture. Being in close contact with ground realities they can ensure that inputs meet local requirements. Also they can provide valuable feedback for agricultural universities and research institutes to help develop technology and inputs suited to regional variations.

The importance of land reforms in ensuring higher production and thus contributing to food security cannot be overstated. Land reforms provide the rural poor (small and marginalised farmers) with greater income and consequently enhanced purchasing power.

The State of West Bengal is the best example. The land reforms through the famous operation *barg*a was successful because of "pressure from below", i.e., the Panchayati Raj institutions. PRI's in West Bengal were crucial in sustaining grass roots pressure in favour of the reforms during their first term (1978-1983). The extent of land reforms in West Bengal can be gauged from the fact that while Bengal has only 3.5 per cent of the country's cultivable land, it contributed 20.77 per cent of the total ceiling surplus land distributed in the country.

The beneficial impact of land reforms on agriculture is evident from the significant improvement in agriculture production in the post 1983 period, when Panchayati Raj had established itself. If the growth of rice production in West Bengal in 1950-60 was 1.01 percent, it reached 6.41 in 1980-81. A visit to West Bengal countryside is a refreshing experience where one can see the linkage between increased agricultural production, land utilisation and relatively self-content village population dependent on agriculture related activities and a vibrant Panchayati Raj system. Functions performed by line departments are now brought under the Gram Panchayats and in close proximity with community problems, giving space for constructive activity.

Food Distribution

The most potent instrument for distribution and thus ensuring food security in India is the Public Distribution System (PDS).

The targeted public distribution system (TPDS) was introduced in 1997 with the aim of providing subsidised rice and wheat to those most vulnerable to food insecurity—households living below the poverty line (BPL). As there is rampant corruption and "leakages" in the PDS system recently the Prime Minister himself had admitted that the targeted PDS did not seem to be working well in many places and pointed out that limited off take in the States where the majority of our poor live, points to serious deficiencies in the administrative capability of the system. He urged the concerned State governments to effectively remedy this situation at the earliest and identified the greater involvement of Panchayati Raj institutions as a means towards achieving success in the "Food For All" mission.

Greater involvement of Panchayati Raj institutions with the PDS can help in ensuring food reaching the needy and that is why the PDS has been explicitly included in the list provided in the 11th schedule.

In order to actualise this provision there is a need for furthering experiments like that attempted in the Keonjhar district of Orissa. Under section 44(1)(x-3) of Orissa Gram Panchayat Act, 1965; PDS is an obligatory function of the Gram Panchayat. Under this provision it is the duty of the Gram Panchayat, within the limits of funds, to undertake control, administer and be responsible for the PDS in the village. Making use of this provision the Gram Panchayats in Keonjhar were entrusted with the retail of the goods through the PDS by replacing private retailers. Observers argue that this not only helped generate funds for the Panchayats but also brought down corruption drastically by bringing in greater transparency and accountability.

In the case of Rajasthan, the government has been utilising the Gram Sabha as a public forum for selecting people below poverty line (BPL) for the purposes of the Integrated Rural Development Programme (IRDP). Under the "Annapoorna" scheme Gram Panchayats are to identify, prepare and display a list of beneficiaries after wide publicity. It has been observed that the BPL identification process by the Gram Sabha has been generally fair and in conformity with the programmatic guidelines.

The recently published report of the Task Force on Devolution of Powers and Function upon Panchayati Raj Institutions has identified the various functions that can be performed by different tiers of PRIs. The report sought to give concrete shape to activities to be performed by PRIs under the PDS. They are: (i) Availability and movement of essential commodities and demand assessment under the PDS programme; (ii) Transport, storage and delivery system; (iii) Vigilance and enforcement aspects; (iv) Linking PDS with poverty alleviation programmes.

Within these broad activity areas the report seeks to identify tasks that can be performed by each tier. An analysis of these tasks reveals that District Panchayats have been generally deemed to be suitable for performing overall planning and assessment tasks. Thus, for instance, District Panchayat has been assigned the task of preparing a district map of PDS outlets and deciding the opening of new shops. Intermediate level Panchayats can assist in the performance of these planning and assessment tasks by undertaking these activities in the areas under their jurisdiction and also providing a link between District Panchayats and Gram Panchayats.

The task assigned to Gram Panchayats are more related to supervision and control of functioning of Fair Price Shops (FPS). Being closest to the people it is seen as crucial in identifying the beneficiaries as well as eliminating bogus ration cardholders.

The Report of the Task Force contains no major surprises. As early as January 2000, the Ministry for Consumer Affairs and Public Distribution had released a six-point action plan empowering the Gram Panchayats to supervise and regulate the working of Fair Price Shops. The Report of the Task Force is, however, a comprehensive attempt at giving shape to the activities of the PRIs while also delineating the various powers and sources of finance, which need to be devolved with each activity. In that sense the latest report in some ways represents the collective wisdom gained by the fore mentioned initiatives and experiments as well as the critical role of the local self government institutions in this vital area.

Access to Food

Increased income generation amongst the rural poor is a *sine qua non* for ensuring food security. For it is only if the people have adequate purchasing power can they have economic access to the food requirements. The recent starvation deaths in Kashipur, Orissa highlight the disastrous consequences of inadequate purchasing power amongst the rural poor. It also highlights the failure of welfare and development schemes initiated from above without giving power to the people through the Panchayats. The PRIs can help break the nexus between the corrupt local officials and the rural elite by both empowering the weak and marginalised sections of society and bringing in greater accountability and transparency.

As is well known PRIs provide an excellent opportunity for ensuring greater participation of the hitherto marginalised sections of society.

Panchayati Raj institutions can further ensure accountability of Fair Price Shops and the PDS system through effectively implementing the right to information and by conducting social audit.

The former finance minister, Shri P. Chidambaram, has in fact argued in favour of replacing the PDS with "food-for-work" programmes run by Panchayats. These programmes are crucial for ensuring the food security of the rural poor who have neither work nor food. However, in order to ensure that these programmes are effectively implemented Mr. Chidambaram has called for a greater role for Panchayats than that has been hitherto assigned to them. He argued that adequate quantity of wheat or paddy should be transported to the drought-affected areas and the stock should be entrusted to the Panchayats. The Panchayats should then decide what works they should take up and fix the wage for each unit of work in terms of wheat or rice.

Thus, the goals of rural development and food security would be met simultaneously by the Panchayats.

Decentralised Planning—Fortifying Food Security

The preceding discussion highlights the numerous ways in which PRIs can contribute to ensuring food security. These are however unlikely to materialise or lead to long term benefits if unaccompanied by a genuine empowerment of the people at the grass-roots levels. It is impossible to imagine starvation deaths in a community where local bodies have the autonomy and the power to decide their development priorities, projects and their implementation and the entitlements of the poor. For no sensitive community today is likely to condemn its members to starvation. Empowerment of local communities through grass-root democracy, decentralised planning is therefore the best guarantee of food security. The experience of Kerala in the last five years highlights the fact that if there is scientific, participatory planning from below decentralisation is the best means of ensuring the development of the people including enhanced food production.

In 1996 the LDF government in Kerala, for the first time in the country decided to earmark 35-40 per cent of the outlay of the State's Ninth Five Year Plan for the local bodies. Moreover, in order to ensure maximum autonomy for local bodies it decided to provide 75 per cent of the funds in the form of grant-in-aid as 'untied'. The only restriction was that the local bodies should spend at least 40 per cent on productive sector (agriculture and allied activities, industries and self-employment, etc.).

Through people's plan campaign a decentralised approach to planning was developed which highlighted the differences that existed between the people's perception of their needs and priorities and those perceived by a centralised bureaucracy. A comparative analysis of the decentralised plan prepared by the Panchayats with that of the State that existed earlier, reveals the shift in priorities. Local bodies gave a much higher priority to agriculture than the State plan—19 per cent of the local outlay compared to 10.5 per cent in the State plan.

Animal husbandry received a greater share (7.57 per cent) which is significant considering that dairy farming in Kerala is not undertaken on a large scale commercial basis. It was found that ideally it suited the raising of income of small and marginal farmers. Numerous case studies are indicative of how agricultural productivity can be boosted through the efforts of PRIs. For instance, the Kanjikuzhy Panchayat (Alappuzha, Kerala) has successfully revived the traditional vegetable cultivation. The Krishi Bhavan provided technical input and guidance while the Panchayat provided the funds and mobilised the community through an awareness and mass contact programme. The programme was a resounding success. A drop in the local prices of vegetables to the extent of 20-30 per cent was observed during the 3-month harvest period. Similarly minor irrigation projects and other infrastructural support for agriculture received greater attention. This illustrates the priority people place on food security. Thus, given a chance they can to a large extent ensure food security for the local community provided the local government institutions are empowered to plan and execute projects required to meet their needs and priorities.

At the implementation stage, in order to ensure accountability and transparency several measures were taken up resulting in less corruption and "leakages". Thus, decentralisation ensured that development programmes not only reflected people's priorities to a greater extent but also increased their efficacy. This is significant for, as shift in priorities discussed above indicated, food security is a priority area for the people, particularly the rural poor.

Conclusion

The foregoing discussion highlights the potential of Panchayati Raj institutions as a means of ensuring food security for the most vulnerable. The 73rd Amendment and the 11th Schedule have provided enough scope for the PRIs to play a crucial role in ensuring food security; be it by ensuring increased production, better distribution or effective accessibility. Some of the initiatives to actualise this potential have been demonstrated by once deficient State like West Bengal and lately to a great extent by Kerala. However, much more remains to be done. There is a need for a two-pronged strategy. Firstly, it is important to ensure that PRIs get the three 'F's—Funds, Functions and Functionaries. Secondly, it is equally crucial to ensure that PRIs take up village level planning effectively and the State not only approves these plans but gives the local bodies the freedom to implement them. Accountability to the people is in-built in such a system. The experience of Kerala illustrates the positive results of such a strategy. If this twin strategy is adhered to then PRIs can emerge as the vehicle for ensuring food security in India.

REFERENCES

1. Report of the World Food Conference (1974), U.N. Publication, 5-16 November, Rome, Italy.
2. The World Bank, *Poverty and Hunger: Issues and Options for Food Security in Developing Countries*, (1986) Washington DC, USA.
3. *World Food Summit Action Plan* (1996), World Food Summit, 13-17 November, Rome, Italy.
4. *Food Security and Panchayati Raj* (1997), (ed.) Pradeep Chaturvedi , Concept Publishing, New-Delhi. See pp. 267-269
5. Bandyopadhyaya, D. (2000) ; Land Reforms In West Bengal, *Economic and Political Weekly* , May 27
6. *Financial Express*, 25 April, 2001
7. Garg, Saurabh; "Gram Panchayats as Retailers of Public Distribution System Commodities" (2000-2001) *Compass*, Monsoon Issue.
8. *Report of the Task Force on Devolution of Powers and Function upon Panchayati Raj Institutions*, Government of

India, Ministry of Rural Development, Department of Rural Development (Panchayati Raj Division) (2001), Krishi Bhavan, New Delhi, August.

9. *Report of the Task Force on Devolution of Powers and Function upon Panchayati Raj Institutions*, Government of India, Ministry of Rural Development, Department of Rural Development (Panchayati Raj Division) (2001), Krishi Bhavan, New Delhi, August, p. 81-82
10. Chidambaram, P.; "Problem Of Plenty" (2001), *India Today*, September 24.
11. Thomas Isaac, T.M. and Franke, Richard W.; *Local Democracy and Development —People's Campaign for Decentralized Planning in Kerala* (2000), LeftWord Books, New Delhi, pp.205.
12. *ibid p. 8*, pp.206.

Activity Mapping of PDS among the Three Tiers of the Panchayats

Activity	District Panchayat	Intermediate Panchayat	Gram Panchayat
1. Availability and movement of essential commodities and demand assessment under PDS programme	i) To coordinate the implementation and review the availability and movement of essential commodities and assess the demand of additional commodities based on the needs of local area ii) To plan/prepare a district map on PDS outlets and coordinate all schemes under the guidance of the State Government.	i) Assist in monitoring of movement and availability of essential commodities in Intermediate Panchayat Area. ii) Plan/prepare a Block/Samiti map on PDS and to coordinate all schemes under the guidance of DP	i) To supervise issue prices of commodities scale of ration per head per month and frequency of distribution of PDS items during the month. ii) To make answerable FPS to Gram Sabha.
2. Transport, storage and delivery system	i) Assess storage requirements, selection of locations and establishment of new godowns/ware-houses iii) Issue of new ration cards and elimination of bogus cards	i) Assist and to coordinate the opening of FPS in its jurisdiction ii) To assist and arrange transport and storage facilities for timely delivery to fair price shops iii) To assess/ensure the coverage of consumers by FPS specially weaker sections iv) Panchayat level action plan for issuing new ration cards and elimination of bogus cards	i) Assisting in proper distribution of essential commodities by FPS under the overall guidance of IP. ii) Certify proper distribution of essential commodities by FPS iii) Assist in planning and preparation of new ration cards, identification of bogus cards and their elimination iv) Assist in selection of sites/ location/dealers for new FPS.
3. Vigilance and enforcement' Aspects and redressal of public grievances	i) To coordinate action for redressal of public grievances inquiring into matters and taking necessary actions	i) Enquire into public complaints assist in vigilance against hoarding and diversion of the commodities ii) Ensure delivery	i) Assist in constituting village level vigilance committee, inspect FPS, report irregularities and other malpractices

Activity	District Panchayat	Intermediate Panchayat	Gram Panchayat
	ii) Strengthening vigilance on the movement, delivery and quality of commodities	of commodities in remote areas by mobilizing, local resources/finances	
4. Linking PDS with Poverty Alleviation Programmes (JRY, IJRY, EAS, etc.)	i) Assessing demand for food - grain for distribution as a part of wages under JRY, IJRY, EAS, etc. ii) Arrange for transport and supply of required quantity to gram Panchayats iii) Maintain vigilance in the supply and distribution of foodgrains as part of wages	i) Collect demand from GPs for ration to be distributed as part of wages ii) Ensure supply and distribution of required quantity of ration to the Gram Panchayats iii) Monitor movement and distribution of foodgrains to the beneficiaries and report/initiate action against irregularities/ malpractices	i) Assist in assess the quantity of food grain required ii) Assist in procurement and distribution of ration to the beneficiaries iii) Maintaining vigilance on quantity and quality of ration distribution to the beneficiaries iv) Reporting against malpractices/irregul-arities

14

Post-Harvest Management : An Overview

Gopi Ghosh
National Officer,
Food and Agriculture Organisation of the UN

In India, Agriculture will continue to be the backbone of its economy. The green revolution has transformed its agriculture from subsistence farming to production-intensive farming. Over the last five decades, the gross cropped area has gone up by almost a third, production has quadrupled, yield tripled and coverage under irrigation doubled. A point for elation for India has been the increase in food production by 4 times from 51 million tonnes in 1950-51 to over 210 last year. Crop-wise, there were 17 times increase in potato production, 11 times in wheat, 5 times each in oilseed and sugarcane, 4 times each in rice and cotton. India today has become the largest producer of pulses, groundnut, tea, jute, milk and vegetables and the second largest producer of wheat, rice, sugarcane and fruits.

In spite of this all-round growth and achievements, Indian agriculture is faced with multiple concerns and challenges. Productivity has plateaued in the green revolution areas responding less and less to agro-inputs as compared to other areas. Lop-sided development, various structural bottlenecks, declining investment and capital formation resulting in unimpressive infrastructure, growing income disparity, continued resource degradation, and recently the declining of prices and sluggish off-take of foodgrains, are some of the most disturbing trends that affect rural populace.

One aspect of utmost importance will be as how to ensure optimum return for the farmer for his produce. The post-WTO phase has witnessed liberalization of imports by the developing countries on the one hand, and increasing use of sanitary, phyto-sanitary and non-tariff barriers by developed countries against exports by developing countries on the other. Market competitiveness has become a creed as never before. The Indian farmers particularly belonging to the small and marginal category seem to have been placed in an unenviably disadvantaged position when placed alongside the farmers with high-tech, commercial intensive agriculture.

Under these conditions, the potential scope for him to increase his income will be through technology-intensive knowledge-based farming systems accompanied by ample value addition and effective marketing of his produce. The agriculture sector is also witnessing a diversification into horticulture, floriculture, plantation and other crops from which the farmer perceives a better return for his investments and labour. Post-harvest management, agribusiness and agro-processing have therefore become the most important elements in the current context.

Agro-produce is generally characterized by perishability, seasonality and bulk. Highly perishable commodities like fruits and vegetables call for instant post-harvest handling. Production undertaken by a large number of scattered small farmers each having only small quantity of marketable surplus, a cooperative or collective form of agribusiness becomes important—perhaps with contractual arrangement with private sector.

Agribusiness contributes to roughly one-fifth of the export earnings. The major products exported include cereals, tea, coffee, oil cake, fruits and vegetables, sugar and molasses, processed foods, fish products, poultry and diary products and flowers. Out of the total exports of agro-allied products, the share of processed products however constituted only about 8 per cent. Though India's agro-food process industry is estimated at Rs. 75,000 to Rs. 80,000 crores, quantitatively India processes only about 1 per cent of its total agricultural production. Its share in world food processing industry is less than 1 per cent and value-addition to food production is a mere 7 per cent compared to 23 per cent in China, 45 per cent in Philippines and 188 per cent in U.K.

A major issue confronting agribusiness is the enormous wastage and value loss of farm produce due to poor post-harvest handling and management. Wastage ranges from, 20 per cent of total production in foodgrains to 35-40 per cent in fruits and vegetables. The total value loss is estimated to be around Rs. 23,000 crores by way of wastage on farm and along the procurement chain as also intermediary margins. The Economic Survey estimated the revenue loss alone to be around Rs. 3,000 crores. Absence of proper picking practices and handling techniques during on-farm, off-farm and transportation stages together with lack of facilities for grading, pre-cooling, storage etc all add to significant value/revenue loss.

Agribusiness in the country is also typical with the presence of a chain of intermediaries. There are normally 5 to 7 intermediaries between the farmer and the consumer comprising of small farmer, large farmer, commission agent, trader, wholesaler, retailer, consumer as against 2 or 3 intermediaries in the case of United States comprising growers' cooperative/wholesaler/retailer. Similarly, there are also sub-wholesalers and retailers. The result is that the farmer ends up getting only about one-fifth of the consumer price as against upto three-fourth in the case of farmers in developed markets around the world.

With farm gate prices in India being 33.5 lower than those of the U.K. and 66 per cent lower than those of the U.S. India's agro-food processing sector enjoys a competitive edge in the international market. According to an independent study, the opportunity to supply basic food for basic needs to hundreds of millions of consumers, whose requirements are expanding with rising incomes will be worth Rs. 2,25,000 crores by 2005 (a three time increase over the present level of about Rs. 75,000), which is more than the value of India's entire manufacturing industry. The study also concludes that the food industry as a growth segment has a multiplier effect of 2.4, which is much higher than that from industries such as power, transport, telecom etc. This multiplier effect would be generated in other industries like transport, refrigeration, pesticides and fertilizers.

Apart from these, a variety of pre- and post-harvest factors, inadequate infrastructure, general lack of business environment, roads and communication, cargo handling, cold storages, warehousing and cooling facilities, transportation network, material handling systems at sea and airports, integrated marketing efforts with branding, packaging with specific market penetration programme, market development in the rural areas, dissemination of market information etc, will have to be addressed. All these should be ably supported by a real time, on-line demand and user-driven information on cropping patterns, climatic conditions, market opportunities, price movements etc. These measures will not be complete unless there is a cogent agriculture development policy with sub-policies on prices, commodity movements, taxation, agri-credit, agro-marketing, agro-storage and agro-processing, cooperative development including involvement of formal and informal agencies, self help groups, NGOs, private sector, etc.

India will have to mount a multi-level, multi-pronged strategy covering all aspects of agriculture including growth with sustainability, proactive agribusiness policy, copious investment on post-harvest infrastructure, investment on research and development, stress on food quality and safety, reduction of regional imbalances, adoption of management system and decentralization and empowerment of grassroot democratic institutions.

Indeed opening up of the market, liberalization of laws and increasing income levels in the recent years have made agribusiness a lucrative proposition. A new sense of hope is palpable among the various players involved – the farmers, traders, consumers and the government. With tropical location, diverse climate, large arable land (second largest), suitable soil qualities, abundant sunlight, spread of monsoon rains and comparative advantage in the global markets and a receptive and resurgent farming community, India can herald what can be called an "agribusiness revolution" as a successor to the green revolution. The tempo generated already shall not only be sustained but also further built up with active support of the government and non-governmental agencies as well as private sector participation in the coming years.

15

Value Addition due to Food Processing and Income Distribution amongst the Poor

Nayaz Rasul
Additional Industrial Adviser
Ministry of Food Processing Industries

India is a country of continental size with a population of over 1000 million, out of which 350 million live in urban areas. For the latter section, processed foods will become their main stay sooner or later. Global processed food business is around Rs.16,000 billion while India's contribution is Rs. 1400 billion. Food Processing industry has been termed as a "sun-rise industry" and several efforts have been made in the last few years to give a big thrust to this sector. With the liberalisation of the economy in 1991 and globalisation, it was felt that food processing industry would come up in a big way. Sadly the hopes have been belied. During the post-liberalisation period of 1991-2000, Foreign Direct Investment approved in the food processing sector was Rs. 834 billion through 698 collaborations of which 137 were of technical nature and 561 were of financial nature. Unless and until the infrastructure facilities improve, agricultural and horticultural productivity increases, modern post-harvest management of foods are followed and entrepreneurial skills are brought in, the hopes are dim. The food processing industry has been identified as a thrust area for development. This industry is included in the priority-lending sector. Most units of the food processing industry have been exempted from the provisions of industrial licensing with the exception of beer and alcoholic drinks and items reserved for the small scale sector like vinegar, bread, bakery. As far as foreign investment is concerned, automatic approval for even 100 per cent equity is available for majority of the processed food items.

Present Status

Food is provided in abundance in nature for every living being. India produces over 200 million tonnes of foodgrains and about 130 million tonnes of fruits and vegetables. Due to the perishable nature of the fruits and vegetables, the post-harvest losses of these commodities is four to five times higher than foodgrains. The wastage cost of fruits and vegetables is Rs. 23,000 crores per year. In India, fruits and vegetables are generally marketed immediately after harvest and hardly 2 per cent of the production is commercially processed whereas more than 50 per cent of the produce is processed in developed countries. The unnecessary wastage of valuable commodities can be avoided if they are processed in value added products or adequately distributed in different parts of the country. There is a great scope of domestic and export trade by improving the post-harvest distribution and processing facilities of these highly perishable horticultural commodities. India provides great opportunities for investment and growth in agro processing sector. A massive thrust to food processing and other agro based industries will add value to the product thereby increasing the income of farmers, create employment opportunities, diversify the rural economy and foster rural industrialisation. This sector is recognised as having an important role in improving agricultural productivity, reducing wastage of fruits and vegetables, providing better nutrition and improving food availability for the domestic market. The demand for processed food is likely to multiply significantly in the coming years. Rapid urbanisation, breakdown of joint family system, increase in the cost of household labour, increase in number of working women, rise in per capita income have all contributed to the rapid growth and change in the demand pattern. India is one of the biggest emerging markets with a population of over one billion with a strong middle class of over 350 million, food processing can add value and find good business opportunity.

The agro and food processing industry in India is of utmost significance in terms of employment and income generation, poverty alleviation, export promotion and foreign exchange earnings. The growth of processed food sector is expected to make a quantum jump of Rs. 1,75,000 crores by 2005. There is vast scope for improvement in value addition in agricultural products, creation of new employment especially in the small towns and rural areas, improvement in the nutritional status of rural women and the poor and availability of cheaper and better products for the consumers. A well run food processing industry ensures that the producer gets remunerative prices for his product and the consumer pays less for higher and assured quality.

Post-Harvest Technology

The post-harvest technology in the area of fruits and vegetables has to match with the production of this perishable commodity to reach the consumers. It is a great challenge that always keeps the scientists, the technologists and the engineers attentive in looking for innovative methodologies and technologies towards making this happen with cost effectiveness built into it and at the same time encouraging the value addition and the by-product utilisation of these commodities. There is a challenge for quality parameters, which the world is, bench marking for a common harmonisation protocols for the global market. For a successful food-processing sector, various aspects such as quality control, quality system and quality assurance, the constituents of total quality management should function in a horizontal fashion for total success.

These are vital for reaching the world market and realising that India itself is one of the big markets. The process of quality control starts from raw materials, process design, product composition, packaging, storage, distribution, consumer preparation and feedback. It should involve critical points, harmonisation with food loss, and implementation of systems, creative innovation, validation, verification and documentation.

The total quality management requires strategic planning, knowledge, worker management as well as their involvement, constant reorganisation and rewards system based on specific measurements and recycling operation of each quality steps for a total success.

Food Processing Plant and Machinery

Tremendous developments have taken place in Europe, U.S.A., Japan, Australia, New Zealand and in Korea in the area of food processing plant and machinery. This has resulted in the production of wide range of food processing machinery conforming to high sanitary standards. Indigenous machinery needs of the food industry in India is being met by the following categories of equipment manufacturers:

(a) Dairy machinery manufacturers with adaptable technology and design back-up who also serve the requirements of fruit juice processing industries.
(b) Chemical process machinery manufacturers have both indigenous knowhow and global knowhow for the manufacture of machinery for the processed food industry with some modifications.
(c) Specialist manufacturers in areas like sugar manufacture, paddy processing and solvent extraction cater to the needs of primary processing sector.
(d) A small number of fabricators in the small scale sector exists with indigenous knowhow and have evolved their own designs over the years.

Apart from the basic designs for plant and machinery, there is need for R&D inputs in the areas of material of construction, manufacturing processes and instrumentations in order to produce energy efficient machines of high sanitary standards.

Increase in Productivity and Employment Generation

Although India is one of the largest producers of raw materials for the food processing industries in the world, the industry itself is under developed in India. Less than 2 per cent of fruit and vegetable production is processed, compared with 30 per cent in Thailand, 70 per cent in Brazil, 78 per cent in Philippines and 80 per cent in Malaysia. The value addition in food sector is as low as 7 per cent. There is need for increasing food processing from 2 per cent to 10 per cent by 2010. This will require an investment of Rs. 1,40,000 crores in the food processing sector. The investment will generate direct employment for 77 lakhs persons and indirect employment for three crores. This will also reduce wastages by Rs. 8000 crores. Apart from these advantages the value addition of food product will go up from 7 per cent to 35 per cent, which will be reflected, in the corresponding increase in GNP. In this scenario, food processing becomes critical. This will mop up surpluses at farm level and ensure fair price for the producer. This will also ensure availability of the produce at reasonable price for the consumer. The employment generation potential of this sector is much higher than other sectors. 54,000 persons get direct employment per Rs. one thousant crore investment in the food sector as compared to Rs. 48,000 in textiles and Rs. 25,000 in paper industry. There is four-fold generation of indirect employment in ancillary and other down stream activities on account of the investment in food sector. Further, 60 per cent of the employment generation is in the small towns and in the rural areas. Food technology has a special role in India's economy to accelerate the pace of social and economic development, reducing poverty besides increasing and improving food supplies qualitatively and quantitatively. It is imperative that agriculture contributes the main development resource for industrialisation to bring about a purposeful socio-economic transformation. Post-harvest agro food system can be the most vital instrument in this context. Having accepted the fact that agro food system can be an instrument of change in the socio-economic conditions, it is important to examine this system in the context of the changed world order. Overcoming the barriers of world trade has certain ramifications with regard to global competition in respect of quality and cost effectiveness. Indian food industry has tremendous opportunity and challenges to exploit the emerging world's consumer markets for fresh agricultural products provided quality and costs are competitive. Quality in the case of foods is of special significance because food preference are sensitive which also directly affect human health and safety. It, therefore, calls for sound technology and adequately trained personnel in handling food right from raw material through processing, packaging and transport to the consumption point. Presence of environmental contaminants in the products such as metals, pesticides and mycotoxins can be controlled only by modern scientific and technical practices. Safety of food, nutrient content, better quality and packaging are all determinants of saleability of the product. The commodity that is handled in a food industry is a biological material and is subject to biological variations. The type of raw material received in the factory and its cost should be constantly monitored with appropriate knowledge and management technique. A properly trained personnel can use his ingenuity in suitably modifying the processing condition to take care of this biological variation in raw material quality so that a product of consistent quality is assured to the buyer. Catering to the needs of newer and emerging markets for manufactured foods, food ingredients and fulfilling the export commitments will call for innovations. Traditional food technologists have practiced food technology by and large in an imperial manner and the industry can ill afford to put inputs on an empirical basis. Modern food technology imbibes the principles and advancement of all branches of natural sciences including frontier areas of natural sciences. Therefore, a trained personnel is equipped with capabilities to practice food technology in a rational manner and make innovations in the industry. Solid scientific foundation is the secret of any successful process or product.

Achievements in the Food Processing Industry Sector

Food processing involves any type of value addition to the agricultural produce starting at the post-harvest level. It includes even primary processing like grading, sorting, cutting, seeding, packaging etc. The status of the different segments of the processed food sector is summarised below:

Cereals and Cereal Products

Grain Processing Industry

The primary grain processing, particularly processing and milling of rice and wheat has substantial capacity in the country. In the last five years, there has been marginal increase in the number of flourmills adding to the capacity, although capacity utilisation continues to be around 60 per cent. As a result of improved availability of bran from these modern and modernised mills, the processing of bran was 35,000 tonnes during the year 2000.

Rice Milling

In the rice milling, there has not been any significant increase in the capacities in the last five years. There are about 92,000 rice hullers, which need modernisation. The total number of modernised rice mills is 35,000. In addition, there are 13,000 hullers-cum-shellers operating in the country. These modern rice mills and hullers-cum-shellers help in recovering good quality rice bran for oil extraction, which is 35 lakh tonnes. The slow rate of modernisation of hullers is attributed to the compulsory levy imposed by States besides inadequate effort in implementation of modernisation programme in many States and lack of financial resources with the huller mill owners which are mostly engaged in custom milling. To give boost to this sector, the Rice Milling Industries (Regulation) Act, 1958 has been repealed and any person is free to set up a rice mill in the country. Due to demand for sorted, graded and polished rice in the export market, particularly for basmati rice and rise in domestic demand for cleaned, sorted and unit packed rice, a number of units have come up in the last five years to clean, sort, grade, polished and unit packed the mill rice, most of which are export oriented units. Due to depleted buffer stocks and fair domestic availability of non-basmati rice in the current financial year, it may be possible to export 50 lakh tonnes of basmati rice.

Roller Flour Milling

In the wheat-milling sector, the number of roller flourmills has increased to 1000. The roller flour milling industry suffer due to low capacity utilisation, low priority for movement of wheat from wheat growing states to non-wheat growing States, high energy consumption for some of the mills.

Pulse Milling

Pulse milling is a major milling industry in India, next to rice and flour milling. About 15,000 pulse mills are scattered all over the country which has sufficient capacity to mill 20 million tonnes of pulses produced in the country or imported pulses. A pulse processing council has been constituted to look into the problems of this industry and to improve the yield. To motivate the millers to modernise their mills as well as to reduce losses during processing, the Government has formulated a scheme for provision of financial assistance for installation of drier and dust control system by the millers for implementation since the year 1997-98. With better capacity utilisation and availability of cereals, modern industries are coming up in this sector.

Cereal based Products

The bread and biscuits constitute the largest segment with total output of 3 million tonnes per year. The manufacture of bread is reserved for small scale sector. 20 per cent of production is in the organised large scale sector and the remaining 80 per cent is produced in the small scale and unorganised sector. Similarly, in the case of biscuits, the production in the organised sector is 5 lakh tonnes and the remaining 12 lakh tonnes in the small scale sector. The bakery industry in India is the largest among the processed food industries, the production of which has been increasing steadily in the country. Other wheat based products are pasta products, comprising of noodles, vermicelli, macaroni and spaghetti and are gaining popularity.

Cocoa Products

There are 20 units engaged in the manufacture of cocoa products like chocolates, drinking chocolates, cocoa butter, cocoa butter substitutes, cocoa based malted milk foods with production of 35,000 tonnes.

Soft Drinks

The production of soft drinks has increased from 6230 million bottles in 1999-2000 to 6540 million bottles during the year 2000-2001.

Beer and Alcoholic Drinks

There are 36 units manufacturing beer with production of 4 lakhs kilolitres per annum. The production of alcoholic drinks from non-molasses sources is very small in the country compared to the total production of alcoholic drinks. However, with various foreign companies producing non-molasses alcoholic drinks, such drinks are gaining popularity in the domestic market.

Horticulture

The horticulture sector which includes fruits, vegetables, tuber crops, spices, medicinal and aromatic plants, plantation crops has established its credibility for improving productivity of land, generating employment, improving incomes of producers and entrepreneurs and providing momentum to exports. Large scale demonstration of technologies, vocational training to upgrade the skills for effective transfer of technology, post-harvest facility, marketing infrastructure, setting up of collection centres and packing houses at production sites, market information system, linking producers and retailers with networking centres are very essential for the development of processed food industry. Support price for perishable horticulture commodities, establishment of commodity boards and market intervention will bring stability to horticulture. Trade in horticultural commodities needs to be encouraged through relaxation of restrictive regulations. Horticultural bio-technology will receive greater attention in future.

Fruits and Vegetables

India is one of the largest producers of fruits and vegetables. Ideal climate conditions ensure round the year availability of a wide range of fruits and vegetables in large quantities. A thousand mango varieties, a range of exotic bananas, all native to India, a growing mushroom sector, red onions, citrus fruits, guavas, grapes and apples have the possibilities for increased production and export. There are attractive opportunities for entrepreneurs in the field of fruit and vegetable processing. The installed capacity of fruit and vegetable processing industries has increased from 21 lakh tonnes in 1999 to 22 lakh tonnes in 2000. The production of processed fruits and vegetables in the country has increased from 9.8 lakh tonnes in1999 to 9.9 lakh tonnes in 2000. The number of licences issued under Fruit Product Order (FPO), 1955, has increased from 5,198 during 1999 to 5,293 during 2000. India's major exports include fruits, pulps and juices, pickles, chutneys, concentrated pulps and juices, dehydrated vegetables and frozen fruits and vegetables. The average annual growth of processed fruits and vegetables over the last five years is 22 per cent. Our fruits and vegetables are unmatched for sheer variety and quantity making India the second largest producer in the world. Tea, coffee, cashew and cocoa are the major crops accounting for 6 per cent of India's aggregate export earnings. With increasing domestic demand over the last 30 years, production has also increased substantially. The largest tea producer in the world, India continues to be largest consumer and exporter of black tea. Cashew is another valuable crop earning US$ 90 million in foreign exchange. Producing 36,000 tonnes annually, India is the world's leading producer and exporter of cashew kernels. The country accounts for 31 per cent of the world' produce of raw cashew and 48 per cent of the world's export of cashew kernels. Coffee grown in the warmer southern region is among the oldest of India's plantation crop.

Milk and Milk Products

India's successful operation flood programme has put the country on the world dairy map. It has been one of the country's most successful development programmes since independence. A cooperative movement which had a small beginning at Anand in Gujarat now links millions of farmers around the country into 70,000 dairy societies. India with its huge livestock population of milch cows and buffaloes has emerged as the second largest milk producer in the world after USA. At present 46 per cent of the total milk production is consumed as liquid milk and the remaining 54 per cent is used for conversion into milk products. The share of the organised sector which produces western dairy products like butter, cheese, ice-cream, milk powder, condensed milk, malted milk foods and infant food is less than 10 per cent. The processed milk food sector is slowly expanding with new products like casein, lactose, dairy whiteners and different type of cheeses. The National Dairy Development Board, Anand and National Dairy Research Institute, Karnal play major role in the development of this sector and provide vital support to the dairy industry. India's milk production has increased from 78 million tonnes during the year 1999-2000 to 81 million tonnes during 2000-2001. There has been increase in the production of milk powder including infant milk food from 2.25 lakh tonnes in the year 1999 to 2.30 lakh tonnes in the year 2000. The production of condensed milk has increased from 11,000 tonnes in the year 1999 to 11,500 tonnes in the year 2000.

Meat and Poultry Processing

India has the largest livestock population in the world with 50 per cent of the world's buffaloes and 20 per cent of the world's cattle. However, only 4 per cent of the buffalo population and 2 per cent of the cattle population is culled for meat. Goat meat is the preferred choice and India has 1/6th of the total world population. Improvement in livestock strains increase in basic infrastructure and use of latest technology. The production of meat and meat products has shown steady increase and the production of value added meat and meat products is also steadily increasing. The total meat production in the country is 5 million tonnes per annum. The slaughtered rate in relation to the population of animals is 6 per cent in case of cattle, 10 per cent in the case of buffalo, 31 per cent in case of sheep, 39 per cent in case of goat and 99 per cent in case of pigs.

Poultry

The Indian poultry sector has made tremendous progress over the last few years and stands today as Rs. 8,000 crore industry. Growing in size, quality and productivity, the industry has transformed itself from a backyard farming area into one of India's largest food sectors. Changes in food habits, rising acceptability of eggs among vegetarians and a burgeoning middle class with additional purchasing power are the factors which have led to this increase in the demand for eggs. Ranking fifth in the world in egg production, the country produces 33,000 million eggs every year and the rise in demand is 10 per cent per annum. Egg production shows an annual growth of 16 per cent. The poultry sector is growing more rapidly at a rate of 27 per cent per annum. Egg product plants produce whole egg, yolk and albumen powders. There are modern, integrated poultry processing plants functioning in the country though a number of small plants also exists which produce frozen chicken and dressed parts. With the growth of poultry in the country, there has been a sharp rise in the availability of eggs and broilers. With the increased availability of eggs in the country and demand of egg products in Europe, Japan and other countries, a number of processing units have been established. These units are exporting egg products like egg powder, albumen powder and frozen yolk.

Fish Processing

India has the potential to become a major player in the field of marine products. Naturally endowed with a magnificent coastline of over 8,000 km., and exclusive economic zone of over 2 million sq.km., 29,000 km. of rivers and waterways, 1.45 million hectares in reservoirs and 0.75 million hectares in tanks and ponds, India has vast marine and inland resources for fishing. Mostly local fishermen to meet domestic demand have tapped India's coastal wealth. It is only in the last decade that the organised corporate sector has ventured into the processing and export of marine products. It has been a successful operation and export of marine products constituted the largest segment of all Indian processed food exports. Most processed canned marine products and frozen fish are exported to markets in Japan, Europe and USA. India offers a wide range of marine fish including prawns, shrimps, tuna, cuttle fish, squid, octopus, red snapper, ribbon fish, lobster, sardine, cat fish, pomfret, mackerel and countless other varieties. Per capita domestic consumption of fish is only 5 kg. per annum as against the world average of 12 kg. per annum and Japan's average of 86 kg. per annum. 55 per cent of the production of fish in India is from marine sources. Processing of marine products into canned and frozen forms is carried out almost entirely for the export market. In all there are 400 freezing units, 15 canning units, 160 ice making units, 15 fishmeal plants and 500 frozen storage units in this sector.

Consumer Industries

In urban India, a burgeoning middle class and its rising consumerism is reflected in high growth demand for items like confectionery, chocolates, cocoa products, soft drinks, ready to eat foods and mineral water. Several large companies with popular brands directly produce a wide variety of cocoa and non-cocoa based confectionery in India. Chocolate production is growing at the rate of 10 per cent to 15 per cent per annum. Other cocoa based products also have a wide demand. Confectionery items other than chewing gum, chocolates, and toffees are produced in the small-scale sector. Soft drinks have the largest share of this consumer food market. Five billion bottles are consumed every year. Ready to eat cereal foods include pasta products like noodles, macaroni, vermicelli and production capacity in the organised sector is 35,000 tonnes. Ten units with a capacity of 10,000 tonnes produce breakfast foods like cornflakes, oat flakes and pearl barley. New industries are increasingly venturing into this sector to keep up with changing food habits in both urban and rural areas.

Packaging

Realising that packaging is an important link in the entire chain of processing, attention is focused on ensuring high standards. Today the packaging in India has facilitated the extension of shelf life, convenience and availability of quality food products. The packaging machinery manufacturers, packaging material producers and processed food manufacturers are integrating efforts to meet the future needs of rapidly developing domestic and export markets. New forms of packing are being produced. Shrink and stretched films and laminates, thermo form containers, PVC shrink labels, leak proof composite containers, bag-in-boxes, laminated cartons, multi-layer film containers and retortable pouches are packaging materials and forms that are available.

Food Safety and Quality

It is necessary for the Indian food processing sector to become quality conscious and move towards attaining the international quality standards. For introduction of quality systems in the industry, the Government should aim at framing the standards such as good hygienic practices, good agricultural practices, and good environment practices for various industries. These standards should become essential for introduction of quality standards in the form of ISO-9000 and HACCP. For this purpose, a comprehensive exercise for framing the standards for introducing the quality systems in the food processing industries is to be initiated. There is need for launching awareness campaign to create quality consciousness among the food processing industries. This can be achieved by creating a separate institution with the sole objective of creating quality conscious and introducing quality systems in the agribusiness sector.

Present Nutrition Status

In India's concern for nutrition is as old as its civilisation. The concept of health as defined by the World Health Organisation is the "state of complete physical, social and mental well-being and not merely absence of disease or infirmity". Nutrition and health are not synonymous, but without good nutrition, health cannot be maintained. Food has always played an extraordinarily vital role in the rise and growth or the fall and decline of a nation because of its effect on the health efficiency of its population. Despite spectacular increase in the foodgrain production in recent years, the problem of chronic malnutrition continues to exist extensively; especially among children and women because they are caught in the relentless sequence of ignorance, poverty, inadequate food intake, disease and early death. This has led to an increasing awareness among planners about the importance of good nutrition. Today, malnutrition is no longer considered an outcome of food deficiency or a health problem but as a multi-dimensional problem interfacing all efforts of developing human resources. The nutritional status of a nation is closely related to food adequacy and its distribution, levels of poverty, status of women, rate of population growth and access of its population to health, education, safe drinking water, environmental sanitation, hygiene and other social services, while the extent of economic growth form its bed rock. The nutritional status is, thus, as outcome of complex and inter-related set of factors. The nutritional problems of major importance can be classified in three broad groups:

(i) Protein energy malnutrition;
(ii) Micro-nutrient deficiencies; and
(iii) Prevalence of chronic diseases.

The trend in nutritional improvement in India during the last 15 years has been positive, though modest. The fact that the overall nutritional status of children has shown some improvement despite a steep increase in population and that there has been a sharp decline in under five child mortality are by themselves healthy signs. The major gains of sound Government policies on food securities and management of health and nutritional sectors have been complete elimination of famines in the last two decades, rare appearances of classic nutritional deficiency syndromes of cardiac, beri beri, peripheral neuritis, pellagra etc. of 50s and 60s, steep decline in Kwashiorkar of the classical kind and almost disappearance of keratomalacia which was a major cause of nutritional blindness among the children during the 60s.

India is known for its population size and the manner in which it is increasing. The country is also known for its family planning programme, the first and the biggest of its kind in the world. The population has increased from 548 million in 1971 to over one billion in 2001. The population of this size will indeed have a tremendous impact on the benefit of development measures. Food, agriculture, health, education and rural development are some of the important governmental sectors whose development measures are strongly dependent on population size. India's population has been one of the major factors that has mitigated dramatic improvement in the nutritional status of India's population so far.

Marketing of Processed Foods

Food processing sector in India has been characterised by poor marketing, transport and communication infrastructure. The density of markets especially fruits and vegetables are low and facilities for storage, godowns and cold chains are extremely inadequate. Irregular and inadequate power supply, lack of roads, education and health facilities and poor rural industrialisation are the main causes for limited markets for processed foods. There is lack of integration of local markets with national and international markets to support faster and more diversified growth. Maintenance of infrastructure is lacking because of limited and declining public resources and the absence of community involvement in the maintenance of community assets. Feeble cargo facilities at airports and seaports are a further bottleneck to export our perishable food products. The infrastructure for extension of food technology is hampered. In addition, there is lack of organised marketing system for meat and poultry products. An integrated approach has to be adopted to promote the consumption of processed foods in the country. This includes generic advertisement through electric/print media, ensure availability of processed foods in all parts of the country, encourage participation in fairs, exhibitions, conferences in various parts of the country/abroad and ensure level playing field to domestic product vis-à-vis imports. For increasing exports, a long term agri and food export plan with focus on tea, coffee, spices, fish and marine products, rice, wheat, mango, grapes etc. will have to be formulated. Further, in order to tap the growth potential of the food processing industry, which in turn would develop more employment and revenue, there is imperative need for penetration in the market particularly in the lower socio-economic groups and rural India and to realise increase in per capita consumption of processed foods. Special attention will have to be paid for setting up of regulated markets with primary objective to improve market efficiency and equitable distribution of benefits between producers, traders and consumers. This is possible by evolving strategies to strengthen the regulated market yields and equipping them with grading, cleaning and packaging facilities among the market information system. This will also enhance income distribution among the poor strata of the society.

Conclusion

The growth of the food processing industry will bring immense benefits to the economy raising the agricultural yields, meeting productivity, creating employment and raising the standard of large number of people throughout the country especially in the rural areas. Economic liberalisation and rising consumer prosperity is opening up new opportunities for diversification in food processing sector. Liberalisation of world trade will open up new vistas for growth. There is enormous potential in India to make profitable business in food processing. To enable appropriate environment ror entrepreneurs to set up food processing industries, the Central Government and the State governments will have to work in a close interactive manner and evolve joint efforts to provide conducive atmosphere for the production of safe hygienic, healthy and high quality, processed foods conforming to international standards at a competitive and economic costs. This will make available processed foods at a reasonable cost to the consumers as well as stimulate demands in the domestic and overseas markets. Extensive training should be provided to the farmers and cooperatives in the area of post-harvest management of agro produce to encourage creation of pre-processing facilities near the farms which include provision for washing, fumigation, packaging etc. Efforts should be made to encourage setting up of agro processing facilities close to the area of production to avoid wastages and transportation of raw materials to far away places and to ensure increased value addition especially for horticultural produce. Application of biotechnology, remote sensing technologies, pre- and post-harvest technologies, energy saving technologies and technologies for environmental protection should be encouraged. This will reduce poverty by providing opportunity for gainful employment to the rural masses with income distribution among the poor class of society. By adopting these measures, India will become stronger economically, socially and politically among the developing nations of the world as the safe, hygienic, healthy and nutritious food is essential for healthy survival of any nation and its citizens.

16

Post-Harvest Management

Sat Pal Malhotra
Former Senior Commodity Specialist
Commodities and Trade Division, FAO, Rome

India had made great strides over the last four decades in the agricultural sector. Production of foodgrains, horticultural products and other commodities has increased manifolds. However, following the success on the production front, post-harvest management of agricultural produces had yet to make commensurate progress. This chapter deals mainly with post-harvest management problems being faced within foodgrains and horticultural product sectors.

Foodgrains

India has become virtually self-sufficient in foodgrains and also emerged as exporter of wheat and rice. Per capita availability of rice and wheat per day increased from about 280grams in 1967-78 to 450 grams in 2000-01. Acute famines in India have practically been eliminated, thanks to increased food availability at the national level, improved early waning systems and expanding infrastructure for more rapid transport of foodgrains and other products to needy areas. However, the existing post-management system, structures and policies are unequal to new challenges.

Despite government intervention in pricing and procurement of foodgrains, primarily wheat and paddy, India continues to suffer heavily on account of losses and wastages incurred during the post-harvest period. These are more man-made than natural. The losses begin with the arrival of foodgrains in the regulated and wholesale markets and continue till foodgrains reach their destination.

What is contributing to continuing losses and wastages are government policies and their implementation, which even stifle growth and modernization of grain markets and processors. The post-harvest losses for foodgrains, according to the World Bank Study[2], are estimated to be 7 per cent to 10 per cent at the farm to market level and another 4 per cent to 5 per cent at the market and distribution level. For the system as a whole, the losses equal to 12 million to 16 million tonnes of grains – all grains – per year including 3-4 million tonnes of wheat and 5-7 million tonnes of rice. With an average per capita consumption of about 15 kgs. of foodgrains a month, these losses are enough to feed about 70 million to 100 million people, about one-third of India's poor, or the States of Bihar and Haryana together, for about one year.

Indian agriculture is at a critical juncture. The changing character of agriculture especially of the foodgrains sector for instance is creating new demands on the post-harvest management and marketing systems. This calls for adjustments to foodgrains policies. Government of India interventions influence prices, volume, quality, storage, processing and distribution of wheat and rice. The government, through the public procurement, distribution, and buffer stocking programmes, repressed the growth and modernization of private foodgrains marketing, undermining its potential contribution to long-term food security. FCI's procurement and distribution operations under the Targeted Public Distribution System (TPDS) create an extensive public marketing channel, leaving the private sector to function only in FCI's residual market. Illegitimate trade, which flourishes on leakages from government food programmes, however, undermines the effectiveness and raises the cost of the public programmes. Within the residual market, private trade is subject to erratic controls and technical shortcomings. Government of India's foodgrains marketing policies have, despite their original intent, brought into being small-scale and fragmented industries characterized by outdated technologies and associated inefficiencies.

The impact of the Government of India's foodgrain marketing policies is critical on two counts. Firstly, by stunting private trade, it discourages much-needed modernization. Market congestion, heavy handling and storage losses, high transport costs and low recovery rates in processing wheat and rice all reflect marketing and milling infrastructure in dire need of improved technology and infrastructure. Investing in such up-grading however, are unlikely to come from private traders as long as government policies heighten their risks and costs by imposing unpredictable limits on their marketing margins and offer them little or no reward for raising efficiency. Second the fiscal cost of maintaining these policies are high. At the same time that the Government of India's pricing policy in the public distribution system contributes to raising fiscal subsidies, technical and operational inefficiencies in FCI operations drive up its costs and the attendant subsidies.

Storage is yet another culprit for losses – thefts and damage besides leakages. Although there are no detailed national statistics on private sector storage, most of it is known to be small-scale, low-quality structures such as covered and plinth (CAP) storage or covered godowns. CAP storages involve stacking grain in bags in a pyramid shape. This is mostly in private sector paid by various government agencies. This type of storage itself results in estimated 20 per cent losses. Extensive use of covered and plinth (CAP) storage unnecessarily increases losses and increases difficulties in implementing the first-in, first-out principle of inventory management. According to the official information half of the FCI stock is at least 2 years old; 30 per cent between 2 to 4 years old; and some grain as old as 16 years. The loss in value due to quality deterioration and ageing in storage and weaknesses in inventory .monitoring and control raise FCI's operating costs. More importantly FCI has limited incentive to cut costs and improve efficiency as all its financial losses are subsidized by the Government of India.

Also, for the storage industry, unpredictable enforcement of storage, credit and movement controls increases storage costs and uncertainness of throughput and the ultimate value of inventories. A major factor deterring the growth and modernization of the storage capacity is the overall implementation of the Government of India's stabilization programme, which not only reduces returns to storage but also increases uncertainty. In most foodgrain markets, price increases during the season are inadequate to make extended intraseasonal storage profitable.

Moreover, despite tall claims, most of the country's 6,800 State operated wholesale markets or *mandis* are severely congested at harvest time. Every market season there are reports of damage to harvested grains in *mandis* and on farms. More than wheat, it is paddy, which is still being handled in a primitive way. The milling of paddy itself is a problem. Both millers and the States invariably get locked in controversies ranging from quality cuts to pricing. At least 30 per cent paddy continues to be milled with less efficient technology relating to hullers and shellers, which yield a recovery rate of 50 per cent to 68 per cent against optimum of 70 per cent to 72 per cent. This reliance on less technologically efficient hullers and shellers implies that for every 100 kg of paddy, about 4 kg to 20 kg of rice becomes unavailable for direct consumption as it is mixed into the by-products. Unpredictable enforcement of various regulatory controls and of FCI open-market sales leaves operators uncertain about the value of their inventories and inhibits investment in cost-reducing technically advanced systems or various quality-raising options.

Wheat milling is mostly done by less efficient, small-scale operations – about 26,000 *chakkis* – that turn 85 per cent of India's wheat into coarse brown flour. The remaining wheat is processed in 812 roller flourmills whose extraction (60 to 65 per cent) is significantly below international norms (72-75 per cent).

Their finished product has a short average shelf life of about one month, compared to about six months in developed countries, requiring quick sale. Further, the enforcement of multiple regulations by multiple agencies – 18 in Andhra Pradesh, 17 in Uttar Pradesh and 12 in West Bengal – consume both valuable time and unofficial fees required by the inspectors.

With the increase in volume of foodgrains procured by the FCI not only cost has gone up even the FCI's inefficiency has increased. In view of this background, the World Bank has made a number of suggestions in respect of necessary reforms needed to better manage post-harvest handling of foodgrains and efficiently making the operation cost effective. It advocates "private enterprise" rather than pure "government intervention". Private sector involvement will stabilize price line, transportation, and distribution and improve handling, which will cut down on wastages and leakages.

The Planning Commission has suggested radical changes in the food policy and advocated greater role for the private sector and immediate corrections in the distorted PDS. The Tenth Plan Panel had indicated that the challenge was to reduce foodstocks to roughly half of its present level and use it for reducing malnutrition without adversely affecting the farmers. Its suggestions include:

- Amendment to Essential Commodities Act to make it an emergency provision:
- Enactment of an Act to ban controls on movement between States;
- Phase out of all levy or monopoly purchases;
- A policy renouncing the use of export restrictions;
- Lift ban on future trading and stocking of all agricultural commodities and on institutional credit and finance for such activities.

The report of the Plan Panel had indicated that the experience of the PDS was not satisfactory even after a hefty increase in the annual food subsidy from Rs. 2,450 crores in

1990-91 to Rs. 9,200 crores in 1999-2000 and to Rs. 13,000 crores in 2000-01. There is 36 per cent diversion of wheat, 31 per cent diversion of rice and 23 percent diversion of sugar from the system at the national level. In addition the TPDS was not working in the poorest north and northeastern States. The allocation of foodgrain of poor States such as UP, Bihar and Assam have been doubled. But poor off-take by States and even poorer actual lifting by the BPL families, the scheme has not made any impact on the nutrition level of these States.

The Panel had recommended that the Government should put a new system in place. In this connection, it had recommended to increase the issue price to a level which is somewhere between the BPL and APL price, and to make the scheme open to everyone, as it existed before 1997. The price should be above the MSP and about 25 per cent below the prevailing market price. The operation of this scheme could discourage black marketeering and result in reduction of subsidies. The savings on this account could be targeted to poorest areas—where poverty level is more than 40 per cent—by doubling the number of old age pensioners, increasing the amount from Rs. 75 to Rs 200 per month and replacing employment assurance scheme by food for work where Government of India's contribution should be 5 kg per day per worker in place of cash[3].

India's Ninth Five Year Plan — 1997-2000 — as well as the current Tenth Plan indicates a readiness on the part of the government to move toward greater market competition, to minimize controls and to use external trade more extensively in managing grain surpluses and shortages. Unfortunately, precious little is being done at the ground level to implement the urgently needed reforms which would improve efficiency of foodgrain marketing system, thereby improve the FCI's efficiency and effectiveness, upgrading market infrastructure and support services; and improve targeting and delivery of safety nets, particularly, the Public Distribution System.

A mere 10 per cent reduction in food subsidies could generate fiscal savings of as much as Rs. 900 crores per year.

Simply cutting the FCI's operational costs by 10 per cent could save as much as Rs. 650 crores per year. Improved private efficiency that reduces physical foodgrain losses alone by a third could generate financial savings of as much as Rs. 280 million and make available additional half a million tonnes of foodgrains per year. Since Punjab's contribution to the central foodgrain pool is the maximum, that State should take the lead in improving its *mandi* board functioning rather than let the board continue "looting" the farmers without providing corresponding facilities in the *mandis* by introducing new technology which maintains quality.

It is interesting to observe that at the Chief Ministers conference held in May 2001, the Central Government tried to sell the idea of decentralized foodgrain procurement to the States. The conference, however, ended in a stalemate. Dominating the Centre's suggestion was the nightmarish accumulation of stock in the Central pool. The main factors for this gargantuan stockpile include: (i) the Central Government's policy of fixing unduly high support prices for wheat and rice and (ii) the drastic fall in offtake following the policy of dual pricing for below poverty line and above poverty line consumers. However, at the Conference these key factors remained undiscussed. Overall, there does not seem to be an adequate realization that unless the basic issues are tackled urgently, the whole system of public distribution itself, both at the wholesale level and retail level, would be in serious jeopardy.

The central Government is currently carrying a high stock of 46 million tonnes of foodgrains, which are three times the recommended norms for security stock. The storage capacity of the FCI is strained to the limit and vast amounts of wheat are stored under cover and plinth in the open. Consequently, the food subsidy (of which carrying charges are the major element) had more than doubled from Rs. 6066 crores in 1996-97 to Rs. 13,000 crores in 2000-01. The huge unsold stocks have led to serious strain on the FCI credit limits with the RBI. The outstanding food credit rose from Rs. 10,200 crores on 31 March 1995 to Rs. 21,247 crores at the end of December 2000. In order to permit procurement during the 2001-01 rabi season to proceed, the Central Government had to resort to the unusable step of removing the cap on credit altogether. While stocks of foodgrains were rapidly piling up, off take fell drastically by about 10 million tonnes in 2000-01 due to the introduction of the Targeted Public Distribution System in 1997. The measures were, without doubt well intentioned. They however, produced an unintended effect—they made the PDS structurally unsound both at the wholesale and retail levels. At the wholesale level, the heavy carrying costs of the huge stocks, which FCI has been forced to hold, have made the operations of the FCI totally uneconomic. At the retail level, the drastic reduction in turnover because of the virtual removal of the APL consumers had made fair price shops unviable. Fair price shops have been closing in large numbers even in a State like Kerala where the PDS was at one time a model for the rest of the country.

The present policies on foodgrains are tending to make the delivery system for the PDS structurally unsound and as a consequence a vital element in the food security system is in danger of becoming vulnerable. A reorientation of the policies on cereal prices and in targeted distribution is imperative. However, the first will be politically difficult and the second will be ideologically inconvenient but unless decisive action on both fronts is taken there will be worse nightmares in the days to come.

Horticultural Products

As in the case of foodgrains, India has achieved tremendous progress in increasing production of horticultural products, especially fresh fruits. It has become one of the largest of most varied fruit producing nations in the world. India accounts for 10 per cent of all fruits produced globally. Fruit production in India increased at an average growth rate of 5.5 per cent between 1990 and 1999, while harvested area and yields increased by 3 and 2 per cent, respectively. Fruit production increased steadily between 1950 and 1989 and dramatically increasing over the last decade despite agricultural policies largely focusing on the foodgrain sector. Production increased by 54 per cent, i.e. from 28.6 million tonnes to 44 million tonnes between 1992 and 1999.[4] Fruit tree production contributes 10 per cent on average to the gross value of total agricultural output in India, plus 13 per cent of the export earnings attributable to major agricultural products.

Despite some efforts to better manage supply surplus due to seasonality, an estimated 25 per cent of the total fruit production goes to waste during the post-harvest handling. The ratio of wastage ranges from as high as 40 per cent in the case of papaya, 25 per cent for banana, citrus and grapes to 10 per cent for pineapple, lychee and chico. This vast amount of wastage is due to lack of proper infrastructure, refrigeration facilities and immediate market. Although steps have been taken to improve the overall conditions in fruit industry, India continues to suffer from huge losses due to wastage. Despite the assistance being rendered by APEDA and the Department of Food Processing Industries, under various schemes, currently only 2.5 per cent of the total production of fresh fruits is being processed. These achievements are far from satisfactory. There is an urgent need to minimize the wastage.

There is a considerable potential for growth in the domestic consumption of fresh fruits, particularly in rural areas where current consumption levels are low. However, market infrastructure, transportation facilities and the quality of the product must be improved in order for the industry to capitalize on its potential. For example, consumption of processed fruits, particularly juices, is expected to increase rapidly, with the income growth projection. Fruit consumption in India is projected to increase by 4 per cent per year according to projected growth rates for income, population, as well as in line with trends in food preferences. This would equate to demand for all fruits reaching 66 million tonnes by 2010.[5] India can meet this increased demand by identifying and adopting measures to reduce waste and improve domestic productivity of fruit. Also on the export fronts there seems to be considerable potential for expansion. This requires in addition to financial assistance and promotion of export oriented production (higher quality) better market promotion campaign and most efficient and effective post-harvest management.

REFERENCES

1. Paper presented at the *FAO National Seminar on Post-Harvest Management on the eve of World Food Day 2001*, 15 October 2001.
2. World Bank : India Foodgrains Marketing Policies : Reforming to Meet Food Security Needs : 17 August, 1999 : Report No. 18329-IN.
3. *The Economic Times :* 1 June, 2001.
4. Ministry of Agriculture; National Horticulture Board ; Indian Horticulture Database.
5. Sat Pal Malhotra : Market for Tropical Fruits in India : A paper prepared for the Second Session of the FAO Inter-governmental Group of Bananas and Tropical Fruits, to be held in San Jose, Costa Rica : 4-8 December, 2001.

17

Post-Harvest Management in Horticulture : Emerging Trends

Dr. Susanta K. Roy
Emeritus Scientist
Division of Fruits and Horticulture Technology
Indian Agriculture Research Institute

Horticulture plays a significant role in Indian agriculture. The varied agro-climatic conditions of this region provide great scope to grow a wide spectrum of horticultural crops. India produces about 132 million tonnes of fruits and vegetables and is considered to be the second largest producer in the world. Unfortunately, unlike other horticulturally rich countries, average Indians do not get the basic daily requirement of fruits and vegetables since a considerable amount is lost due to improper post-harvest operations; as a result there is a huge gap between the gross production and net availability. Furthermore, only a small fraction of fruits and vegetables is utilized for processing and export compared to many countries in the world whose position is much below India's production level. It is a matter of great regret that in spite of becoming one of the world leaders in the production of fruits and vegetables our Human Development Index is very low. Therefore, in order to achieve our target of feeding the population as well as meeting the requirements of the processing industry and export trade, only increasing the production and productivity will not be enough.

A lot more emphasis needs to be given to post-harvest management of these highly perishable crops. According to a joint study conducted by the management consultancy firm, McKinsey & Co and the Confederation of Indian Industry (CII), at least 50 per cent of the production of fruits and vegetables in the country is lost due to wastage and value destruction. The wastage cost is estimated to be Rs. 23,000 crores each year.

Attention to the concept of reduction of post-harvest loss of food as a significant means to increase availability was drawn by the World Food Conference held in Rome in 1974. The seventh session of the U.N. General Assembly in 1975 passed a resolution calling for a 50 per cent reduction of post-harvest losses by 1985. In the FAO, food loss prevention became a priority area and an Action Programme became operational in early 1978. The Food Loss Prevention Programme of FAO earlier focused mainly on the durable foodgrains, because of their prominence in our daily diet. However, in May 1980, an Expert Consultation on Food Loss Prevention in Perishable Crops mainly covering fruit and vegetables was held.

This chapter discusses some of the issues that will help in poverty-alleviation, employment generation, environment protection and economic transformation of rural India.

Importance of Fruits and Vegetables in Diet

Fruits and vegetables in general, except for a few, are not considered to be the primary source of carbohydrate, protein and fat. However, some of them with storage roots and tubers are rich in carbohydrate, particularly starch, in amounts comparable to the cereal crops, and the leguminous vegetables supply as much as 14 per cent protein, dry seeds supplying still more. The lipid content in most vegetables is less than 0.1 per cent. Most fruits, vegetables and root crops are rich in minerals and vitamins particularly vitamin C and A (carotene). Fruits and vegetables also contains some other constituents and dietary fibres, which deserve attention.

Primary Processing

Unlike durable crops like cereals, pulses, and oilseeds, perishable fresh fruits and vegetables in our country are marketed immediately after harvesting without primary processing. It has been observed that 10 to 60 per cent of the fresh fruits and vegetables marketed and purchased by the consumers in India are rejected as inedible parts since they are not fit for human consumption. The inedible parts of the fruits and vegetables, which are rejected by the consumers in the metro cities, end up as garbage. On the other hand, in villages or small towns these inedible vegetable parts are utilized by giving as feed ingredients to the domestic animals.

Preservation of Fruits and Vegetables

Fruits and vegetables can be preserved in the fresh form by increasing their shelf life or by processing into different products. The consumption of processed fruits and vegetables is still low all over the world compared to fresh ones but it is progressively increasing and will continue to do so in view of the seasonal availability of fresh commodities. In most of the developed countries consumption of processed products is relatively high. Processing industries are also beginning to emerge and grow in the less developed parts of the world.

Low Cost Appropriate Techniques of Preservation

Most of the commercial methods of preservation are expensive and beyond the means of the common people. Therefore, it is necessary to adopt low cost methods of preservation so that it can reach the grass-root level. In this respect the following techniques are suggested:

Pusa Zero Energy Cool Chamber

Based on the principle of evaporative cooling, a low cost, easily adaptable zero energy cool chamber has been developed by the author. The chamber is made of double brick wall with brick floor and the space between the bricks is filled with sand. The top cover is made of any plant material in a bamboo frame. The chamber is thoroughly soaked with water; once it is saturated it is necessary to water it only twice a day in order to maintain temperature and humidity. Most of the year the chamber maintains a temperature 15^{0} to 17°C less than the outside temperature and relative humidity above 90 per cent. The chamber has been found to be useful for short term storage of fruits and vegetables. The Pusa Zero Energy Cool Chamber will go a long way in preventing loss and will be very useful for rural and poorer sections of our population.

Solar Drying

Vegetables: Most of the leafy vegetables are rich in nutrients and can be preserved successfully by solar energy. A low cost solar drying chamber made of black polyethylene has been found effective in drying most of the leafy vegetables. Even though the drying process causes loss of considerable amount of nutrients a substantial amount is still left in the dried vegetables to meet nutritional requirements. The storage of dried vegetables is of great importance and should be done with great care. Dried vegetables, particularly the leafy ones in the powdered form can be easily mixed with wheat flour in order to enhance its nutritional value.

Fruits: It has often been found that during the session of glut a huge quantity of fruit is piled up in the production centres due to lack of transportation and marketing facilities. In order to avoid wastage the fruits can be solar dried or the fruit pulp can be dried in the form of a fruit leather or slab/bar and can be utilized gainfully for the benefit of local people by packaging and storing them appropriately. A substantial amount of nutrition can be obtained by consuming them during the off-season.

Proper Distribution

In India it is often found that there is a glut of certain horticultural produce in one part of the country while it is scarce in another part due to improper post-harvest management and lack of adequate transportation and storage facilities. This difficulty can be overcome through proper distribution. There is a great scope to increase domestic trade in our country by improving the post-harvest distribution facility of these highly perishable commodities. If the horticultural produces are evenly marketed from the places of abundance to the places of scarcity, not only will the consumers get the produce at a reasonable price but the producer also will not be forced to sell at throwaway prices. In spite of an abundant and varied production base, India's performance in export of horticultural produce has not been encouraging. The low performance of the country in export of horticulture produce is attributable to a variety of reasons. Lack of infrastructural facilities, particularly storage and transportation, results in heavy post-harvest losses, and this coupled with low productivity and high prices of raw materials makes our exports uncompetitive in the international market.

Processing of Underutilized/Indigenous Fruits and Vegetables and Horticultural wastes for Value Addcd Products:

India has a vast resource of undernutilized/indigenous fruits and vegetables, which have established therapeutic and nutritional value apart from excellent flavour and attractive colour. Research attempts will be made for developing new products from these underutilized/indigenous fruits and vegetables both for domestic and export market. Huge quantity of horticultural waste generated in the packing station can be gainfully utilized for making value added products.

Conclusion

To achieve our target of a hunger free India, only increasing the production and productivity will not be enough. A lot more emphasis needs to be given to post-harvest management since there is a considerable gap between gross production and net availability. The success of production lies in the proper distribution of the produce and its subsequent utilization by the consumer, i.e. 100 per cent utilization of the production in one form or the other should be the motto. Employment generation potential in post-harvest handling and processing of fruits and vegetables sector is much higher than other industries. Post-harvest technology is multi-disciplinary in nature. Its success depends on its multi-disciplinary approach. Post-harvest loss reduction is essential to make available more food from the existing level of production. Every percentage loss reduction will save Rs. 230 crores annually.

18

Post-Harvest Management of Fruits and Vegetables

Dr. O. P. Singhal and Dr. D. V. K. Samuel
Division of Agricultural Engineering
Indian Agricultural Research Institute

India is the second largest producer of fruits after Brazil and the second largest producer of vegetables after China. The varied agro-climatic conditions of India provide great scope to grow a wide spectrum of horticultural crops. These crops occupy hardly 7 per cent of the cropped area of the country but they contribute over 18 per cent of the agricultural output and 52 per cent of export earnings of total agricultural produce. Horticulture plays a significant role in Indian agriculture. The production figure of fruits during 1997 is estimated to be over 40 million tonnes and vegetables about 72 million tonnes including potato and onion. It produces about 9.33 per cent and 12.22 per cent of the world's production of fruits and vegetables relatively. It is unfortunate that the fruits and vegetables produced in India are not enough to meet the basic requirement of the huge population of the country. Furthermost, only a small fraction of fruits and vegetables is utilized for processing and export compared to many countries in the world whose position is much below India's production level. In fact, India's share of export of fresh and processed horticultural crops is not very significant mainly because of non-meeting of quality standards, inadequate capacity, inefficient processing, packaging and marketing facilities. India has registered about Rs 450.00 crores worth of export of fruit and vegetable products which is too low looking at the vast potential, if tapped properly.

A considerable amount of fruits and vegetables produced in India is lost due to improper post harvest operations; as a result there is a considerable gap between the gross production and net availability. As per an estimate, 30 per cent-40 per cent of the production of fruits and vegetables in the country is lost due to wastage and value destruction. The wastage cost is estimated to be Rs. 23,000 crores each year. Therefore, in order to achieve our target of feeding the population as well as meeting the requirements of the processing industry and export trade, only increasing the production and productivity will not be enough. A lot more emphasis needs to be given to post-harvest management of these highly perishable crops. Therefore, our aim is to reduce these losses and to do so we must: (a) understand the physiological and environmental factors involved in deterioration, and (b) use those post-harvest technology procedures which will delay senescence and maintain the best possible quality. Fresh horticultural produce are living tissues, which are subject to continuous change after harvest. While some of these changes are desirable, most are not desirable from the consumer's standpoint. Post-harvest changes in fresh produce cannot be stopped, but can be slowed down within certain limits. Fresh horticultural crops are diverse in morphological structure

TABLE 18.1 : Production figures and estimated loss of fruits and vegetables

S. No.	Commodity	Area Million hec.	Production Million tonnes	Losses %
1.	Mango	1.38	10.16	25-30
2.	Banana	0.442	10.32	25-30
3.	Citrus	0.483	4.26	20-25
4.	Apple	0.227	1.32	14-20
5.	Grapes	0.040	0.97	25-30
6.	Tomato	0.420	6.33	15-30
7.	Onion	0.340	3.14	15-30
8.	Cauliflower	0.249	4.46	40-42
9.	Cabbage	0.228	5.31	38-40
10.	Potatoes	1.210	17.65	15-20

(roots, stems, leaves, flowers, fruits, and so on), in composition, and in general physiology. All fresh horticultural crops are high in water content and thus are subject to desiccation (wilting, shrivelling) and to mechanical injury. They are also susceptible to attack by bacteria and fungi resulting in pathological breakdown. Table 18.1. shows the area, production and approximate loss of some fruits and vegetables.

(a) Physiological Factors

Respiration

Respiration is the overall process by which stored organic materials (carbohydrates, proteins, and fats) are broken into simple end products with a release of energy. Oxygen (O_2) is used in this process and carbon dioxide (CO_2) is produced by the commodity. The loss of stored food reserves in this commodity during respiration means: (1) senescence is hastened, (2) loss of food value, (3) reduced flavour quality, especially sweetness, and (4) loss of saleable dry weight. The energy released as heat, know as vital heat, is very important in post-harvest technology consideration, such as the estimation of refrigeration and ventilation requirements. The rate of deterioration of harvested commodities is generally proportional to their respiration rate.

Ethylene production

It is a natural product of plant metabolism and is produced by all tissues of higher plants and by some micro-organisms. Ethylene (C_2H_4) is considered the natural ageing and ripening hormone and is physiologically active in trace amounts.

Generally, (C_2H_4) production rates increase, with maturity at harvest, physical injuries, disease incidence increased temperature and water stress. On the other hand, ethylene production rates by fresh horticultural crops are reduced by storage at the lowest safe temperature for each commodity and reduced O_2 and elevated CO_2 levels around the commodity.

Compositional Changes

1. Loss of chlorophyll (green colour) – desirable in fruits but not in vegetables.
2. Development of carotenoids (yellow and orange colors) – desirable in fruits such as apricots, peaches, and citrus; red colour development in tomatoes is due to a specific carotenoid (lycopene) ; beta-carotene is provitamin A and thus is very important in nutritional quality.
3. Development of anthocyanins (red and blue colours) – desirable in fruits such as apples (red cultivars), cherries, strawberries, jamuns etc.
4. Changes in anthocyanins and other phenolic compounds – may result in tissue browning which is undesirable from appearance quality standpoint.
5. Changes in carbohydrate include
   (a) Starch to sugar conversion (undesirable in potatoes, desirable in fruits),
   (b) Sugar to starch conversion (undesirable in peas and sweet corn) and
   (c) Conversion of starch and sugars to CO_2 and water through respiration. Breakdown of pectins and other polysaccharides result in softening of fruits.
6. Changes in organic acids can influence flavour quality of the commodity
7. Loss in vitamin content, especially ascorbic acid (Vitamin C) is detrimental to nutritional quality.
8. Production of flavour volatiles associated with ripening of fruits is very important to their eating quality.

Growth and Development

Sprouting of potatoes, onions, garlic and root crops greatly reduces their utilization value and accelerates deterioration. Rooting of onions and root crops is also undesirable. Similar geotropic responses occur in cut gladiolus and snapdragon flowers stored horizontally. Seed germination inside fruit such as tomatoes, peppers, and lemons, is an undesirable change from the standpoint of quality.

Transpiration Loss

Water loss can be one of the main causes of deterioration since it results in not only direct quantitative losses but also causes losses in appearance, textural quality and nutritional quality. Transpiration is a physical process that can be controlled by various treatments applied to the commodity (e.g., surface coating and wrapping with plastic films) or by manipulation of the environment (e.g., maintenance of high relative humidity and control of air circulation rate).

Physiological Breakdown

Exposure of the commodity to undesirable temperatures can result in physiological disorders.

1. Freezing injury – commodities held below their freezing temperatures.
2. Chilling injury – commodities (mainly tropical and subtropical origin) held at temperatures above their freezing point and below 5^0 to 15^0C.
3. Heat injury – exposure to direct sunlight or to excessively high temperatures.
4. Very low oxygen (<1%) and/or high carbon dioxide (>20%) atmospheres can result in physiological breakdown of most fresh horticultural commodities.

Physical Damage

Various types of physical damage (surface injuries, impact bruising, vibration bruising, and so on) are major contributors to deterioration. Mechanical injuries are not only unsightly but also accelerate water loss, provide loci for fungal infection, and stimulate CO_2 and C_2H_4 production by the commodity.

Pathological Breakdown

One of the most common symptoms of deterioration results from the activity of bacteria and fungi. Attack by most organisms follows physical injury or physiological breakdown of the commodity. The onset of ripening in fruits, and senescence in all commodities, results in their becoming susceptible to infection by pathogens.

(b) Environmental Factors

Temperature

Temperature is the most important environmental factor that influences the deterioration rate of harvested commodities. For each increase of 10^0C (18^0F) above optimum, the rate of deterioration increases by two- to three- fold.

Relative Humidity

The rate of water loss from fruits and vegetables depends upon the vapour pressure deficit between the commodity and the surrounding ambient air, which is influenced by temperature and relative humidity.

Atmospheric Composition

Reduction of oxygen and elevation of carbon dioxide, can either delay or accelerate deterioration of fresh horticultural crops. The magnitude of these effects depends upon : commodity, cultivars, physiological age, O_2 and CO_2 level, temperature and duration of holding.

Ethylene

The effects of ethylene on harvested horticultural commodities can be desirable or undesirable. Thus, it is of major concern to all handlers of fruits, vegetables and ornamentals. Ethylene can be detrimental to the quality of the most nonfruit vegetables and ornamentals.

Light

Exposure of potatoes to light should be avoided because it results in greening due to formation of chlorophyll and/or solanine (toxic to humans).

Other Factors

Various kinds of chemicals (e.g. fungicides, growth regulators) may be applied to the commodity to affect one or more of the biological deterioration factors.

(c) Post-Harvest Technology Procedures for Management

Temperature Management Procedures

Temperature management is the most important tool that can be used to enhance the shelf–life of fresh horticultural commodities.

Control of Relative Humidity

Relative humidity can influence water loss, decay development, incidence of some physiological disorder, and uniformity of fruit ripening.

Relative humidity control can be achieved by one or more of the following procedures :

1) Addition of moisture (water mist or spray, steam) to air by humidifiers.
2) Regulation of air movement and ventilation in relation to produce load in cold storage room.
3) Maintaining temperature of refrigeration coil to within about 1^0C (2^0F) of air temperature.
4) Moisture barriers – insulation of storage room and transit vehicle walls, polyethylene liner in containers, plastics, films for packaging.

5) Wetting the floor in storage rooms.
6) Crushed ice in shipping containers or in retail displays for commodities not injured by such practice.
7) Sprinkling produce with water during retail marketing – use on leafy vegetables, cool-season root vegetables and immature fruit vegetables (e.g. snap beans, peas, sweet corn, summer squash).

Post-Harvest Management

1. Harvest at proper physical maturity
2. Careful handling to prevent mechanical injuries
3. Use of precooling chamber
4. Control of temperature and relative humidity during storage
5. Atmospheric control by adding chemical additives
6. Proper storage

Value Addition

The income from the export of the vegetables and fruits could be considerably increased by proper selection, grading, pre-treatment during packaging and careful handling during transport.

Waste Management

A considerable amount of waste is generated during the post-harvest handling of the fruits and vegetables, which also need the proper management to prevent further quality, degradation and environmental protection, appropriate technologies are available for handling such kinds of wastes generated.

Conclusion

The above discussion clearly indicates that if timely action is not taken to improve the post-harvest handling system of horticultural crops then obviously the post-harvest loss will progressively increase with the increase in the production of horticultural produce. It has been established that the food loss reduction is cheaper than equivalent increase in food production so far as economy, energy and impact on environment is concerned. There is no doubt that post-harvest food loss reduction is a significant means to increase food availability.

NOTES

Mondhar, S.C. (2000), Future Needs of Mechanization of Horticultural Crops in India.

Pandey, P. H. (1996), Post Harvest Technology of Fruits and Vegetables; Lyall Publication. Ludhiana .

Roy, S.K. (2000), Post-harvest Management of Horticultural Produce – An Overview. "Dissemination of information on low cost storage and Preservation Technologies." Training programme sponsored by Ministry of Food Processing Industries (Government of India) and organized by Div. of Horticulture Technology, IARI, New Delhi, 23-30 April, 2000.

19

Agricultural Engineering towards Food and Nutrition Security

Dr. Anwar Alam
Deputy Director General (Agri Engineering)
Indian Council of Agricultural Research

"Agricultural Engineering" (AE) is an applied engineering discipline with base in agro-biosciences. It has evolved to apply engineering principles and practices to production agriculture, agro-processing and rural living for land and water resource development and their optimal use; increased production and productivity with reduced cost of production; efficient handling, processing and storage of agricultural produce and by-products, agro-industries generating additional income and employment; removal of drudgery and imparting dignity to work; development of infrastructure, rural water supply and sanitation, ultimately improving quality of rural life. Engineering methods were in use in agriculture and allied activities long before the term Agricultural Engineering (AE) came in use as a subject matter mostly derived from civil and mechanical engineering, initially. Dr. Elwood Mead, a leader in land reclamation who later became head of US Bureau of Reclamation is credited to have provided rationale for AE as distinct profession and discipline. When the Land Grant Institutions were established in USA the colleges of agriculture were termed as College of Agriculture and Mechanics Arts. In 1896, the School Agriculture of University of Nebraska listed two courses — AE under Prof. O.V.P. Stout and Practical Mechanics under Prof. C.R. Richard. Later in 1906 a conference was held at the University of Illinois to discuss teaching techniques and to develop instructional materials for the new field of AE in which Prof. C.R. Crane from Illinois, Prof. J.B. Davidson from Iowa and Prof. C.A. Ocock from Wisconsin participated. In 1910, Iowa State College was the first to confer degree of Bachelor of Science in Agricultural Engineering in USA or for that matter anywhere in the world. By 1925, there were 10 institutions conferring UG degrees in USA and PG and Ph.D programmes followed them soon. In 1906, Department of Farm Engineering was established at the Manitoba Agricultural College. It was first in Canada with Prof. A.R. Greig, a mechanical engineer as its head.

Starting in 1942, AE in India has come a long way. It has now 26 institutions that are offering formal education leading to the Bachelors, Masters and Ph.D. degrees in AE. Some of them could be called world class. However, there are weak spots, many institutions unable to maintain themselves and offer incentives for PG programmes. AE is one of the faculties at State Agricultural Universities (SAUs). However, some SAUs have yet to establish faculty of AE. It is aimed to familiarise the scientific community of the activities and achievements in the field of agricultural engineering as it relates to food, nutrition, and environment security. It also offers opportunity to have inputs of thought to strengthen agricultural engineering for our economy, self-reliance, and socio-economic stability.

Scope

Engineering inputs to agriculture are vital in development and harnessing natural resources for agriculture and allied activities, practising cost effective farming through achieving timeliness in field operations, precision in metering and placement of inputs for desired levels of productivity, economy of inputs, and elimination of arduous labour. Economic sustainability and profitability does not come merely through more production and high productivity. Agriculture is largest private sector enterprise of India and it is forcefully influenced by forces of marketing domestic as well as global level, factors of demand and supply, quality, product recoveries as raw materials and so on. Vulnerability of agricultural produce and by-products to market price fluctuation is closely associated with their perishability, specially if the post-harvest management infrastructure is weak. If perishable products like fruits or vegetables do not reach to a remunerative market in time at right stage of maturity and acceptance in the market adopting pre- and post-harvest practices — harvesting, prepackaging, packing, and transport in a manner and an environment that allows requisite time for transport, marketing and distribution before reaching to right maturity/ripeness, they do not fetch due dividends.

India has long tradition of agriculture and livestock husbandry. Harappan civilization flourished basically on crop cultivation, pastoral livestock husbandry and crafts. They not only domesticated plants and animals and improved them but also developed tools, implements, post-harvest equipment and wheeled transport. These over ages have gone through refinement in geometry, used of appropriate wood, and metals phasing out gradually neolithic tools of stone and bone as copper, bronze, iron and steel were developed. The Harappan technology had remarkable resilience lasting over four thousand years. Its inadequacies became apparent only with the population explosion, industrial revolution coming up with steam engines, IC-engines, and electrical motors which could do jobs at much competitive cost hitherto done by men and draught animals. In spite of that, the traditional indigenous farm equipment have not lost their relevance for marginal farms below one ha. Muscles have reserve capacity several times larger than normal loads for a few seconds. This enables draft animals to carry out operations with much lesser average horse power than otherwise needed by electro-mechanical sources.

Mechanisation of agriculture became an imperative during 20th century globally especially the second half. It requires intensive use of commercial energies diesel and electricity. Punjab, agriculturally leading most State of the country, during

1965-66 to 1979-80 post-Green Revolution period achieved an annual growth rate of 12.5 per cent in foodgrains, during this period, total energy consumption increased at the rate of 26.6 per cent with conventional animate non-commercial energy uses remaining almost static but the commercial energy uses increased at the rate of 89.3 per cent per year. Energy has become an important cost component in agriculture. Incidentally, petroleum is the largest import bill of India thus compulsions to conserve commercial energies supplementing and substituting with new and renewable sources of energy. Therefore it has become an other important area of R&D for the agricultural engineers.

Agricultural engineers have been using mathematical modelling and simulation of agricultural production and post-production processing processes as total for optimisation, economy of time and effort. However, revolution in information technology (IT) has added to their role in development use and maintenance of hardwares and softwares, portals, databases and data warehousing for agriculture and rural development.

Agricultural Engineering Education

Allahabad Agricultural Institute (AAI), an affiliated college of the Allahabad University, now a deemed university, has the distinction of starting a course leading to the degree of Bachelor of Science in Agricultural Engineering (a two-year course) in 1942, for the first time in India and for that matter in South Asia. Prof. Mason Vaugh is considered father of AE in India. Ten years later in 1952, as per Dhar Committee, the Indian Institute of Technology (IIT), Kharagpur, the first IIT of the country, started B.Tech. (Agric Engg.), a four-year programme, an important landmark in the development of AE education in India, soon after (1956) it started PG programme also for the first time in India, and yet another important landmark when it awarded the first Ph.D. degree in Agric. Engineering in India in 1965.

R. Radhakrishnan Committee recommended establishment of Rural Universities, a concept that gained momentum. Indo-US Joint-Team came up with the recommendation of establishment of SAUs in each major States on the pattern of American Land Grant Colleges integrating teaching, research and extension. GB Pant University of Agric and Technology (GBPUAT) as the first SAU of India, structured itself — with Agricultural Engineering and Technology as one of the faculties, starting UG programme in 1962. Subsequent SAUs created faculties or College of Agricultural Engineering such as Punjab Agricultural University, Rajasthan Agricultural University (the then University of Udaipur), Orissa University of Agric & Technology. Agriculture being the State subject, variations appeared. Maharashtra State with four SAUs established Colleges of AE in only two SAUs namely MPKV Rahuri and PKV Akola initially. Madhya Pradesh established Jawaharlal Nehru Krishi Vishwa Vidyalaya, (JNKVV) Jabalpur (1964) with only two faculties namely Faculty of Agriculture and Faculty of Veterinary Science, Agricultural Engineering remained a Department under College of Agriculture till the Faculty of Agricultural Engineering started in 1967. Likewise Rajendra Agricultural University, Samastipur; Marathwada Agricultural University, Parbhani; Andhra Pradesh Agricultural University, Hyderabad; University of Agricultural Sciences — Bangalore/Dharwad; Bidhanchandra Krishi Vishwa Vidyalaya, Kalyani; Haryana Agricultural University, Hisar; and Kerala Agricultural University, Thrissur; started College of AE many years after their establishment. By this time SAUs, as a result of two wars and resultant inflation, had begun to experience financial constraints which resulted in half-hearted approach, poor infrastructure, inadequate faculty and staff, and insufficient operational grants.

Start of M. Tech. and Ph.D. programme at IIT Kharagpur and subsequently at IARI, AAI and SAUs have enabled considerable self-sufficiency in human resume development in AE in India. Faculty improvement under TCM and USAID assistance provided large number of faculty members to have foreign PG/Ph.D degrees and exposure. By 1997, there were

10,686 graduate agricultural engineers, 2351 with Master Degree and 330 Ph.Ds that had passed out from 26 institutions that have formal education at programmes in AE in India. There is annual induction capacity of 850 for Bachelors Degree, 335 for Masters Degree and 85 for Ph.D of which 506, 95, 27 respectively pass out each year (1996).

Advances in Agricultural Engineering

Activities of AE are organised generally into four major areas namely Soil and Water Engineering, Farm Implements and Machinery, Post-Harvest Engineering and Technology, Energy and Power. With phenomenal growth in IT, the Information System Development is a new emerging area in AE. Initially the R&D activities were empirical in nature but with time analytical base has been widened; automation and controls, computer aided designing, mathematical modelling and simulation techniques are being increasingly applied. Developments in bio-sciences have also added new vistas in AE activities. Agricultural Engineers are increasingly addressing to bio and food engineering, environmental safety and ecofriendliness of agricultural systems and their hardware, agricultural equipment and agro-processing enterprises, consultancies, banking etc.

Soil and Water Engineering

Land Reclamation and Development

AE started with land reclamation, land and water development, for practicing intensive agriculture and to undertake other allied activities. Independent India was faced with the rehabilitation of displaced people for which massive land reclamation work was undertaken. AE played major role in this exercise removing trees, stubbles, levelling and grading of land, drainage of swampy areas, sinking of bore/tubewells. Imported heavy earth moving machinery were utilised for the purpose which set in motion farm mechanisation in India.

Soil and Water Conservation

AE contributed immensely through mechanical measures in soil and water conservation and watershed development. Design criteria were developed and massive programmes executed involving contour and graded bunds, terracing, land levelling, stabilisation of gullies, installing run off disposal structures. R&D was undertaken on *in situ* and *ex situ* rainwater conservation. Techniques have been developed for sealing farm ponds to conserve stored runoff against deep percolation. Irrigation water conveyance and application through surface irrigation methods were studied and ensuing irrigation water losses were established and ways found out to minimise loss of valuable irrigation water.

Irrigation and Drainage Engineering

Assured irrigation and drainage are essential for realising crop potentials. It also acts catalyst for use of other inputs essential for increased production and productivity. Scientific data base of surface irrigation methods were strengthened and design specifications developed for border irrigation assuring greater uniformity index. Low cost animal drawn equipment were developed for land levelling, grading, making borders and irrigation channels. With mechanisation and wide use of tractors scrapers, levellers smoothers, bund and border makers, ditchers were developed/adopted made available commercially.

Under AICRP on Optimisation of Ground Water Use through wells and pumps, design criteria were developed for construction of dug and bore wells in hard rock areas. Yield of existing dugwells were increased through vertical and horizontal boring. Corrosion and encrustation problems in tubewells were addressed. Also low cost efficient strainers were developed. Considerable efforts were made adoption of engine and electric motor operated irrigation pumps. With the popularisation of centrifugal pumps R&Ds were undertaken to enhance system efficiency developing efficient foot valves, reflex valves and engine safety mechanism etc.

To create better environment from crops and save them from excess water, under AICRP on Agricultural Drainage under Actual Field Conditions, surface, sub-surface, and vertical drainage systems were designed, installed and studied that enable increasing agricultural production from 25-50 per cent, in many cases where due to excess of water crop cultivation was difficult, water levels were brought below the root zone and successful crops taken. Concept of skimming wells, and vertical drainage were successfully tried in containing watertable problem in Punjab where groundwater is generally saline.

Micro-irrigation and Surface Covered Cultivation

Water Use Efficiency (WUE) in Indian agriculture has traditionally been too low. As a result of R&D, there have been definite improvements. But for various reasons WUE continues to be low primarily due to continued use of traditional flooding irrigation. About 88 per cent of the freshwater are currently being used in agriculture. To combat wastage of scarce and valuable irrigation water micro irrigation system at farm level were introduced in 1980. The National Committee on Use of Plastics in Agriculture (NCPA) has played very important catalytic role. In 20 years micro irrigation has picked up which has reached to 2,00,000 ha in 1998-99. R&D under ICAR, AICRP on Application of Plastics in Agriculture is promoting micro-irrigation and surface covered cultivation. There are about 7,00,000 ha under sprinkler irrigation. Ministry of Agriculture, and Ministry of Water Resources are working together to promote the pressurised irrigation systems. They almost double the command area of a water source with yield advantage of 15-50 per cent. Lot of work has been done on establishing consumptive use of water, design, installation and trouble shooting in micro-irrigation systems. AE are involved in installation, marketing and management of micro-irrigation system. Micro-irrigation also avoids abuse of excess use of water, water logging or impairment geohydrology as surfacing in Punjab, Haryana and a few other pockets. Efforts are on to make it cheaper and trouble free at the same time to have low cost filtration unit, fertigation equipment and accessories for small and marginal farmers.

Farm Power and Machinery

At the time of independence, India had mostly traditional farm equipment evolved over ages, made by local craftsmen from locally available materials without any standardisation and quality control other than dictates of skills of the craftsmen. The colonial period witnessed famines almost every 12 years, seven of them great famines. It led to institution of Famine Commission, the Cattle Commission (1869), the Conference of Provincial Delegates, Royal Commission on Agriculture (1926) that no doubt led to many legislative and agricultural research and development initiatives. However, agricultural technology remained traditional during the colonial period. Adoptive trials on European technologies on Indian soil were often more directed to marketing those goods in India than to help the Indian farmers. It was more so in the case of farm equipment.

Independent India has witnessed phenomenal growth in agricultural mechanization. Initially efforts were directed to learning farm tradition and to improve traditional equipment. AE undertook massive effort evaluating and adopting improved agricultural implements from Western World. By mid-1960s centrifugal pumps run by engines and electric motors 3-5 HP received farmers acceptance and were the first modern farm equipment to be successfully commercialised in India. Soon after interest in tractors grew and a few Indian companies in collaboration with principals abroad started assembling CKD (completely knocked down) tractors in India and gradually indigenising their manufacture. Today India is largest producer of small general purpose tractors in the world with an annual production of over 2,50,000. It makes virtually most of the farm equipment needed in India including harvester combines. It is now an industrial sector with annual turnover of about 30,000 crore, Rs 20,000 crore crop production equipment and about 10,000 crore post-harvest equipment. However, still the large number of farms specially rainfed small and marginal (below 2 ha) continue to use traditional equipment. There are new emerging trends of marginal farmers becoming part time farmers looking for custom servicing, some are leasing out their lands for greater opportunity which is making *de facto* farming units larger amenable to mechanisation as happening in Punjab and Haryana.

Farm Power

Traditional farm power sources on Indian farms as evolved since Harappan periods are men and draft animals – bullocks, he-buffaloes, camels, donkeys, and other animals. However, now most predominant farm power sources that do tractive and transport, and stationary operations are humans and pair of bullocks. He-buffaloes are widely used in coastal deltaic areas where rice-rice cultivation is common. In hill areas humans are major source of farm power to rationalise use of human energy and that from draft animal power (DAP) sources ICAR has launched AICRP on Utilisation of Animal Energy (UAE) with Enhanced System Efficiency, and AICRP on Human Engineering and Safety in Agriculture (HESA). UAE has studied and established draftability of major draft animals currently in use in India. It is found that draftability of bullocks is about 10-12 per cent of their body weight which can be enhanced by 15-20 per cent i.e. 11.5-14.4 per cent of body weight through improved yokes and harnesses. Camel exert on sustained basis about 16-18 per cent of their body weight. However, donkey is found to have maximum draftability equivalent to 30-35 per cent of its body weight. Animate power can meet the requirement of marginal and small farms but as farm size increases, they start revealing their limitation as they fail to achieve timeliness and economic advantage. Per unit energy animate are too expensive as compared to electro-mechanical source due to their regular feeding and maintenance as well as health care even if not in use. Bullocks are, however, are by-product of dairying/cattle rearing and can survive on crop residues and natural vegetation thus are sustainable and are likely to be in use. DAP reduce dependence on commercial energies of diesel and electricity which account for largest import bill of India.

Agriculture as practiced is very labour intensive. Human labour is steadily becoming expensive with rising labour wages. Besides using labour as beast of burden and forced to do arduous labour is dehumanising. Leaving agriculture excessive labour dependent not only increase unit cost of agricultural produce but also deters rural educated men and women youth taking agriculture for vocation which is not national interest. There are work hazards, disabilities and fatalities involved with farm operation. Therefore, need for rationalisation of use of human energy in agriculture for efficient use and economy, removal of drudgery and minimisation of health hazards, injuries, disabilities and fatalities. Principles of ergonomics are being applied making hand tools and equipment controls compatible with anthropometric peculiarities of agricultural workers, designing out health hazards and bringing in safety measures, design modification that reduce the efforts required, establishing work-rest cycles compatible to physiological responses optimising work outputs with undue fatigue.

Farm power availability has direct bearing on agricultural productivity (Fig 19.1). It is evident farm mechanisation in India initially grew slowly and then accelerated from the Green Revolution period as it was essential for high productivity and optimal use of costly inputs (Table 19.1). Till the late 1960s Indian agriculture remained mainly powered by animate power sources. The availability of tractor power during 1950-1997 increased from 0.006 kw/ha to 0.364 kw/ha a growth rate of over 10 per cent. Tractors are being used 35-40 per cent for on-farm use such as tillage, seeding, interculture, harvesting, threshing

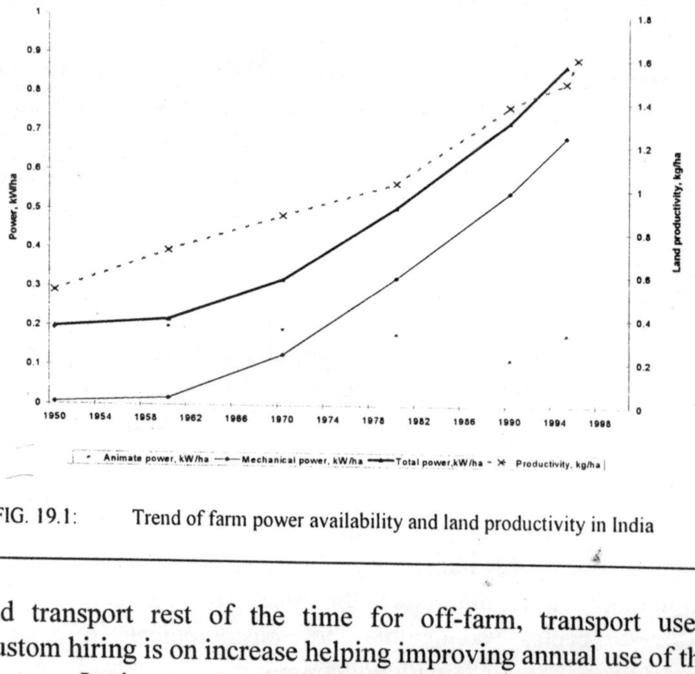

FIG. 19.1: Trend of farm power availability and land productivity in India

and transport rest of the time for off-farm, transport uses. Custom hiring is on increase helping improving annual use of the tractors. In rice growing areas use of power tillers is on increase, owned as well as custom hired. It may be mentioned here that average use of human power in crop production has increased from 723 man-hours (man-h) in 1971 to 769 man-h in 1991 and likely to reach 789 man-h by year 2000 (Singh *et al* 1999).

Farm Implements and Machines

In pre-independent India only traditional farm equipments were in use namely *Desi Hal, Pata* (plank), *Bakhar, Dufan, Tifan, Gorru,* Yokes/ harnesses, and hand tools like spade, *Kudali, Sabal* (crowbar), sickles, *dav,* axe etc. In last 50 years improved tools, implements and machines matching to major sources of farm power – men, DAP, tractors, power tillers, engines, motors have come in use and are commercially available in the markets. Most common are implements needed for foodgrain production for seedbed preparation both under upland and wetland situation; sowing-drilling, planting and transplanting; interculture and fertilizer application, spraying and dusting; lifting conveying and application of irrigation water; harvesting, threshing, winnowing and cleaning; and transport. Table 19.2 to 19.8 gives a list of implements and machines that have been developed and commercialized in India.

TABLE 19.1 : Population growth trends in mechanical farm power sources in India

	1950	1960	1970	1980	1990	1997	2000*	Growth rate (%) Base year 1970
Tractive power (number in million)								
Tractor	0.008	0.031	0.148	0.518	1.222	2.037	2.471	9.84
Power Tiller	-	-	0.003	0.021	0.040	0.085	0.110	12.7
Stationary power (number in million)								
Electric pump	0.020	0.100	1.629	4.330	6.019	8.254	9.525	6.06
Diesel pump	0.083	0.230	1.546	3.101	4.659	5.899	6.465	4.88
Others (number in million)								
Power sprayer/duster	-	-	0.045	0.124	0.200	0.245	0.311	6.66

Source : Singh, *et al.*, 1999.

TABLE 19.2 : Selected Equipment for Seedbed Preparation

S. No.	Name of the Implement	Size, mm	Price, Rs	Work Capacity		Suitability
				ha/h	h/ha	
A. Animal operated						
1.	M.B. Plough	150	400	0.024	40-42	For all Regions
2.	Disc Harrow (4-8 disc)	600-1200	1000-1500	0.18-0.22	5-6	For light soils
3.	Cultivator (3 tines)	300-400	700-1000	0.08	12-14	For light soils
4.	Bakhar	500	400	0.06	16-18	For heavy soils
5.	Helical Puddler	500	800-1200	0.06	16-18	For puddling in all types of soils
6.	Harrow Patela	1500-2000	1200-1500	0.2-0.25	4-5	For collection of trash and planking, all regions.
B. Power Tiller operated						
1.	Rotavator	500-600	15000	0.07-0.09	11-13	All regions
C. Tractor operated						
1.	M.B. Plough	2x350 3x350	10000-15000 20000-22000	0.20-0.25 0.30-0.35	4-5 3-4	All regions
2.	Disc Plough	2x350 3x350	14000-16000 24000-26000	0.20-0.25 0.30-0.35	4-5 3-4	All regions
3.	Disc Harrow (16 discs)	2000	15000-18000	0.40-0.50	2-2.5	All regions
4.	Cultivator(9-11)	2500	12000-15000	0.40-0.50	2-2.5	Lighter soils
5.	Rotavator	1500	40000-50000	0.2	5	All regions
6.	Sweep cultivator	5x500	12000-15000	0.35	3-3.5	Heavy soils

TABLE 19.3 : Selected Equipments for Sowing and Planting.

S. No.	Name of the Implement	Size, mm	Price, Rs.	Work Capacity		Suitability
				ha/h	h/ha	
A. Manually operated						
1.	Mustard seed drill	1 x 600	1000	0.1	10-12	Lighter soils
B. Animal operated						
1.	CIAE 2-3 row seed-cum-fertilizer drill	3 x 225 3 x 300 3 x 450	2500-3000	0.1 0.125 0.155	10-12 8-8.5 6-7	All types of seeds

TABLE 19.3 Contd.

2.	CRIDA drill plough	1 x 225	500	0.04	20-25	All types of seeds
3.	CIAE mustard drill	2 x 450	2500-3000	0.125	8-8.5	All types of soils
4.	CIAE 2-3 row planter	3 x 450	3000-4000	0.155	6-7	Maize, cotton, groundnut and other types of seeds
5.	IISR sugarcane planter	1 x 900	3000-4000	0.125	8	Lighter soils
6.	Potato planter	2 x 450	3000-4000	0.125	8	Lighter soils
C. Power tiller operated						
1.	Seed-cum-fertilizer drill	5 x 225 5 x 300	6000-8000	0.164 0.21	6-6.5 5-5.5	All types of soils
D. Tractor operated						
1.	Seed-cum-fertilizer drill	11 x 225	12000-15000	0.75	1.25-1.5	All types of soils with suitable furrow openers
2.	No-till-drill	11 x 225	15000	0.75	1.25-1.5	For direct sowing of wheat after paddy in rice-wheat cropping system
3	Strip-till-drill	1500	25000-30000	0.25	4-5	For direct sowing of wheat after paddy in rice-wheat cropping system
4.	Sugarcane cutter planter	2 x 900	40000-45000	0.25	4	Suitable for all regions with suitable ridger bodies
5	Potato planter	2 x 600	20000-25000	0.25	4	Suitable for all regions

TABLE 19.4 : Weeding and Interculture Equipment

S. No.	Name of the Implement	Size, mm	Price, Rs.	Work Capacity		Suitability
				ha/h	h/ha	
A. Manually operated						
1.	Grubber	150-200	30-50	0.012	80	Lighter soils
2.	Dryland peg weeder	150-200	250-300	0.025	40	All soils

TABLE 19.4 Contd.

3.	CIAE twin wheel hoe	150-200	250-300	0.025	40	All soils
4.	PAU wheel hoe	150-200	400-500	0.035	30	Lighter soils
B. Animal operated						
1.	Dora	300	500	0.1	10	Heavy soils
2.	Three tined Sweep/ cultivator	600	700-1000	0.2	05	Lighter soils
C. Power tiller operated						
1.	3 tined cultivator/ sweep	1000	5000-7000	0.2	05	All soils, wider row crops
D. Tractor operated						
1.	9-11 tined tiller	2500	12000-15000	0.45	2-2.5	All soils, wider row crops
2.	5 tined sweep	2500	12000-15000	0.45	2-2.5	All soils, wider row crops
E. Self propelled weeder						
1.	CIAE/TNAU Power Welder	500	30,000	0.12 5	8	All soils, wider row crops

TABLE 19.5 : Equipments for Spraying and Dusting Operations

S. No.	Name of the Implement	Size	Price, Rs.	Work Capacity		Suitability
				ha/h	h/ha	
A. Manually operated						
1.	Hand compress-ion sprayer	14 litres	1500-2000	0.095	10.5	All regions
2.	Lever Operated Knapsack sprayer	13-16 litres	1500	0.095	10.5	All regions
3.	Foot sprayer		2500-3000	0.165	6	All regions
4.	Duster	4-5 kg	1000	0.25	4	All regions
5.	Controlled Droplet sprayer	1 litre	1500	0.25	4	All regions
B. Power operated						
1.	Knapsack sprayer cum-duster	5 litres	5000-7000	0.22	5	All regions
2.	Stationary power operated sprayer	5-10 hp	20000	0.35	3	All regions
C. Tractor operated						
1.	Tractor operated sprayer	5000 mm	30000-40000	0.5	2	All regions, wider row crops
D. Self propelled						
1.	High clearance sprayer	10000 mm	200,000	0.5-1.0	1-2	Cotton, potato and other tall crops

TABLE 19.6 : Equipments for Harvesting Operation

S. No.	Name of the Implement	Size	Price, Rs.	Work Capacity		Suitability
				ha/h	h/ha	
A. Manually operated						
1.	CIAE Serrated sickle		25-30	0.008	125	All regions
B. Animal operated						
1.	CIAE groundnut-cum-potato digger	500 mm	2000	0.1	10-12	All regions
C. Power tiller operated						
1.	Vertical Conveyor Reaper	1200 mm	15000	0.25	4	All regions, suitable for paddy and wheat crops
D. Tractor operated						
1.	Vertical Conveyor Reaper	2000 mm	35000	0.4	2.5	All regions, rice, wheat, soyabean etc.
2.	CIAE Soyabean Reaper	2000 mm	35000-40000	0.4	2.5	All regions
E. Self propelled machines						
1.	Vertical Conveyor Reaper	1000 mm	40000-50000	0.25	4	All regions, suitable for paddy, wheat, soyabean etc.
2.	Combine harvester	4200 mm	6-12 lakhs	1.5-2	0.75-0.5	All regions, for paddy, wheat, gram, soyabean etc.

TABLE 19.7 : Equipments for Threshing Operation

S. No.	Name of the Implement	Size	Price, Rs.	Work Capacity Kg./h	Suitability
A. Power operated					
1.	Power operated thresher	5-10 hp	12000-20000	200-500	All regions, for single crop, paddy, wheat
2.	CIAE Multi-crop thresher	5-10 hp	15000-25000	200-500	All regions, wheat, paddy, soyabean, maize, gram, pigeonpea etc.
3.	High capacity multi-crop thresher	15-20 hp	40000-50000	1500-2000	All regions, wheat, paddy, soyabean, maize, gram, pigeonpea etc.

TABLE 19.7 Contd.

S. No.	Name of the Implement	Size	Price, Rs.	Work Capacity Kg./h	Suitability
4.	Tractor PTO operated multicrops thresher	25-35 hp	60000-70000	1500-2500	Wheat, soyabean, maize, gram etc.
5.	Paddy thresher	5-15 hp	12000-25000	200-1000	All regions, paddy
6.	Maize thresher	5-15 hp	12000-25000	500-2000	All regions, maize
7.	Groundnut thresher	10-15 hp	25000	500-1000	All regions, groundnut

TABLE 19.8 : Selected Equipments for Post Harvest Operations

S. No.	Name of the Implement	Size	Price, Rs.	Work Capacity Kg./h	Suitability
1.	Tubular Maize sheller		15	20	All regions
2.	Maize sheller		500	100	All regions
3.	Groundnut decorticator		700-1000	50-60	All regions
4.	CIAE pedal-cum-power operated cleaner-cum-grader		7000	400-600	All regions, wheat, gram, soyabean, pigeon pea etc.
5.	Multi purpose grain mill	2 hp	6000-7000	8-30 kg/ph	All regions, mill-ing of cereals to grit and fine powder and grind-ing of spices.
6.	Power operated dehusker-sheller for maize	2 hp	8000-10000	400-450	All regions, maize
7.	CIAE Daal mill PKV Daal mill	2 hp 2 hp	15000 35000	100 kg 100 kg	All regions, for pigeon pea, green gram and black gram

For seedbed preparation rototilling with tractor mounted rotavator or a power tiller is found time and energy efficient. Under favourable condition seedbed both upland and wetland can be obtained in single pass. However, these are relatively costly and problem of rapid wear of tines needing metallurging and production engineering inputs. There are noise and vibration problems in tractors and power tillers.

Conservation tillage equipment Zero-Till Drill for sowing wheat after rice have been received well in Rice-Wheat agro-ecosystem. It saves 8-10 days in rabi sowing and unit cost of operation reduced by 800-1000 Rs/ha. Raise-bed Planter is an other promising sowing equipment that has been found very useful. It saves irrigation water by 35-50 per cent, helps in control of Phalaris minor and gives about 5 per cent yield advantage. Both of these equipments are currently being promoted in India specially in Rice-Wheat ecology.

Timeliness in harvesting is very important failing which excessive field losses occur and the quality is also adversely affected due to vagaries of nature. As a result of R&D, we have for harvesting improved sickles that reduce effort and increase output by 15-30 per cent. Vertical conveyor reapers (VCR)- self propelled walking type and tractor mounted were developed and introduced in early 1980s and self propelled riding type in late 1990s have enabled mechanised harvesting and winnowing of crops like wheat, barley, rice, soybean, gram etc. Tractor mounted VCRs were introduced in 1982-83 when 30 units were manufactured, in 1983-84 about 300, 1984-85 about 3000 but in 1985-86 it was reduced to 2000 units, the year insurgency in Punjab peaked when farmers found combining convenient, cheaper and less risky.

Power threshers have virtually replaced traditional threshing of wheat, barley, maize, sorghum, pearl millet, gram, blackgram, greengram, rapeseed/mustard, sunflower soybean, groundnut etc. removing drudgery involved with threshing and cleaning of foodgrain crops. Rice and multi-crop threshers are being used for rice where mechanisation has spread.

Combining is becoming popular where labour wages have shot up or there is acute labour shortage. Annual production of combines have reached to about 2000. Combining is cheapest proposition for harvesting and threshing of crops. These normally do not make bhusa. However, straw combines developed in Punjab eliminate this shortcoming. Harvesting of fruits and vegetables, commercial crop like sugarcane, jute and kenaf continue to be manual. With labour wages going up and increased competition due to globalisation there is demand for sugarcane harvesters and cotton pickers which are being addressed under NATP.

Energy Management in Agriculture

Energy in Production Agriculture

Intensive high productivity modern agriculture apart from solar energy, uses large quantities of additional energy inputs in the form of plant nutrients from soil, manures and fertilizers, animate and electro-mechanical tractive power and equipment for field operations, irrigation water and plant protection and growth regulating chemicals. Traditional agriculture with about one t/ha yields used mostly animate (men and DAP) and non-commercial energy inputs (seed, manure, biopesticides). However, it is not possible to achieve high production and productivity without direct and indirect commercial energies. Figure 19.2 depicts nexus between commercial energy and agricultural productivity. For each per cent of increase in agricultural productivity energy input has to increase by 1.7-2.0 per cent, however, commercial energy input component may have to be increased much more. Fig 19.3 presents post Green Revolution trend of energy use and its association with agricultural productivity. During 1970-1993 direct energy (diesel and electricity) use increased at the rate of 8.01 per cent, indirect commercial energy (fertilizer and agro-chemicals) had a growth rate of 5.01 per cent when the total energy increased at the rate 4.38% per annum. During this period foodgrain productivity increased at the rate of 2.39 per cent, for each additional ton of increase in foodgrain productivity on an average about 6.49 GJ of energy was used. It may be added here that this is the situation when only 30 per cent of area has experienced mechanisation. It has been in a way a global trend also.

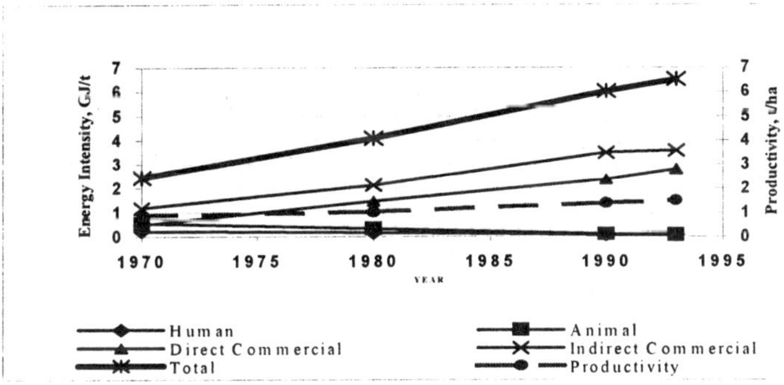

FIG. 19.2 : Trend of Use of Total Energy Intensity in Production Agriculture in India

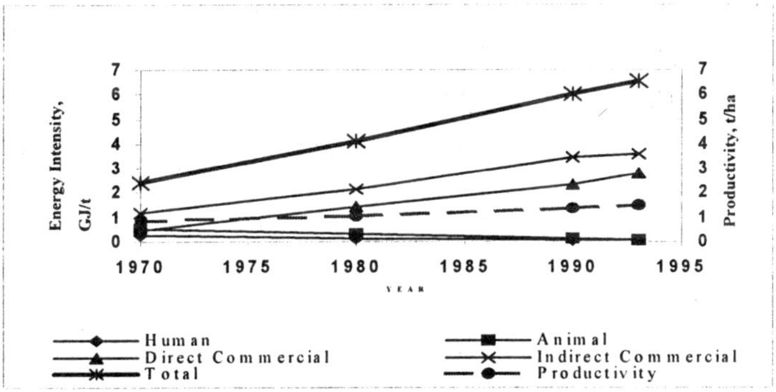

FIG. 19.3 : Trend of Use of Total Energy Intensity in Production Agriculture in India

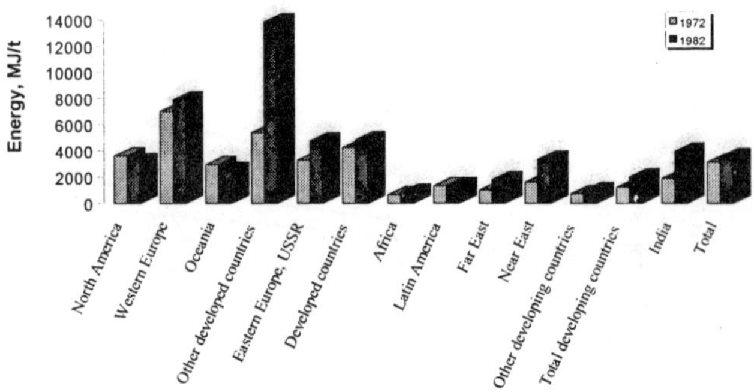

FIG 19.4 : Commercial energy use for foodgrain production in different countries

Fig 19.4 and Table 19.9 depict a global scenario of agricultural productivity and energy use. North America during 1972-1982 increased its cereal productivity from 3.4 t/ha to 3.7 t/ha with a decline in every use per ton, Oceania also had similar trend though at low cost productivity levels, Latin America also had increase in agricultural productivity without increase in energy use. India on the other hand energy use was 1.3 times that of developed countries, which went up further up to 1.8 times with productivity increasing from 1.9 t/ha to 2.3 t/ha. In a globalisation scenario this trend needs to be checked through regular energy audits and adopting energy conservation measures in agriculture.

Energy Intensive Crops and Crop Rotations

Average energy consumption in production of some major crops and crop rotations in India are depicted in Fig 19.5 and 19.6. Sugarcane and potato are the most energy crops. The most energy intensive crop rotations is sugarcane-sugarcane, the next most intensive rice-wheat-maize. The overshoot in energy use in these crops and crop rotations is primarily due to indirect energy uses seed, fertilizer, chemicals etc. Rice-wheat a dominant crop rotation in Indo-Gangetic plains requires less than one-fourth the energy consumed in sugarcane-sugarcane (ratoon) rotation.

TABLE 19.9 : Spatial pattern of use of commercial energy and foodgrain productivity in different countries

Region	Arable area per agricultural worker (ha)		Cereal yield (t/ha)		Energy (MJ/t)	
	1972	1982	1972	1982	1972	1982
North America	64.5	92.0	3.4	3.7	3625	3179
Western Europe	4.6	6.1	3.2	3.8	7022	7908
Oceania	75.4	99.7	1.2	1.3	2953	2524
Other developed countries	1.5	2.1	2.5	2.6	5397	13864
Eastern Europe, USSR	6.0	7.7	1.8	1.8	3310	4742
Total developed countries	**7.9**	**10.6**	**2.5**	**2.7**	4250	4855
Africa	1.6	1.4	0.8	0.9	664	853
Latin America	4.1	4.5	1.5	2.0	1331	1336
Far East	1.0	0.9	1.4	1.8	1021	1793
Near East	2.6	2.4	1.2	1.5	1625	3373
Other developing countries	0.8	0.7	1.9	2.1	760	987
Total developing countries	**1.0**	**1.0**	**1.5**	**2.0**	1247	2020
India					1640	3595
Total	**1.8**	**1.8**	**1.9**	**2.3**	3154	3566

Spatial Variability in Energy Use in Agriculture

India is a big country with wide soil, climate, technological, socio-economic variability. AICRP on Energy Requirement in Agricultural Sector of ICAR has studied energy used in different crops and crop rotations in different parts of the country. There is wide variability. For example in paddy cultivation in irrigated areas total energy use ranges between 16,000 to 1,03,000 MJ/ha while in rainfed areas it is between 6,600 to 8,800 MJ/ha. Direct energy use in irrigated areas accounts for 56-62 of total energy, diesel and electricity depending upon method of irrigation

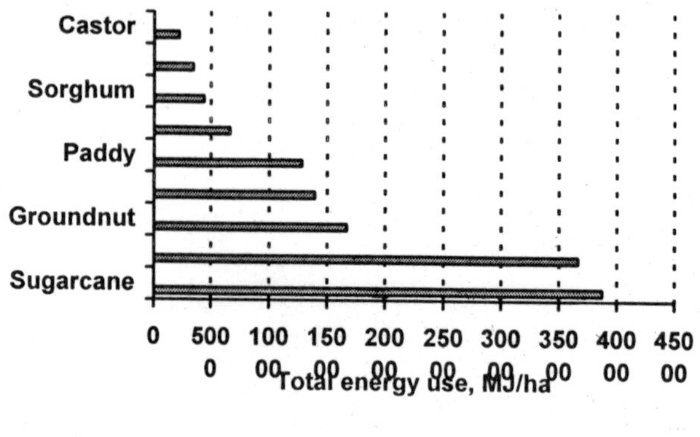

FIG. 19.5 : Average energy consumption in production of major crops in India (1986-88)

amounts to 38-85 of the direct energy use. Fig 19.7 depicts spatial variability in energy consumption and yield of paddy in representative villages in Punjab, Tamil Nadu and West Bengal. In the three States their different level of mechanisation, and energy use and thus different level of productivities. Compared to many countries, Fig 19.8 energy intensity in India is very high. For competitiveness it should be brought down by adopting energy efficient equipment and practices, popularised by extension agencies.

Energy Intensive Unit Operations in Crop Production

Fig 19.9 & 19.10 depict the energy intensive operations in rice and wheat cultivation. Irrigation using groundwater requires maximum operational energy, in rice it is found ranging between 35-90 per cent and in wheat 35-65 per cent. In Intensive agriculture areas like Punjab, irrigation consumes about 51 per cent of the operational energy followed by harvesting and threshing (19%) and seedbed preparation (13%). However, under dryland agriculture seedbed preparation, weeding and interculture, and harvesting and threshing become energy intensive operations.

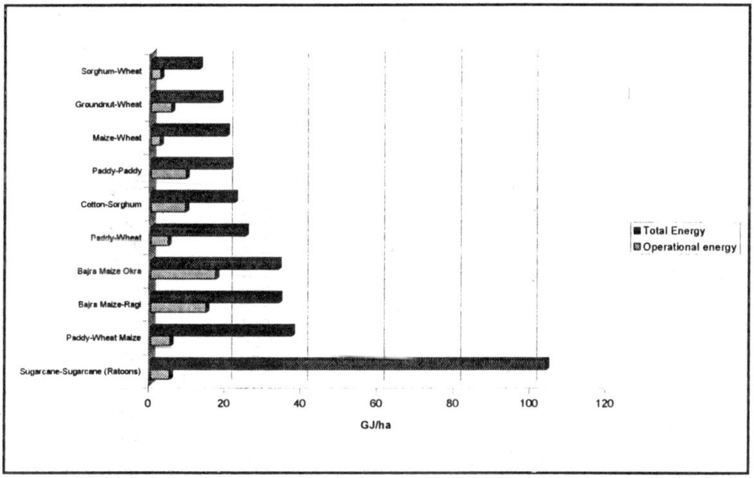

FIG.19.6 : Average energy consumption in major crop rotations in India

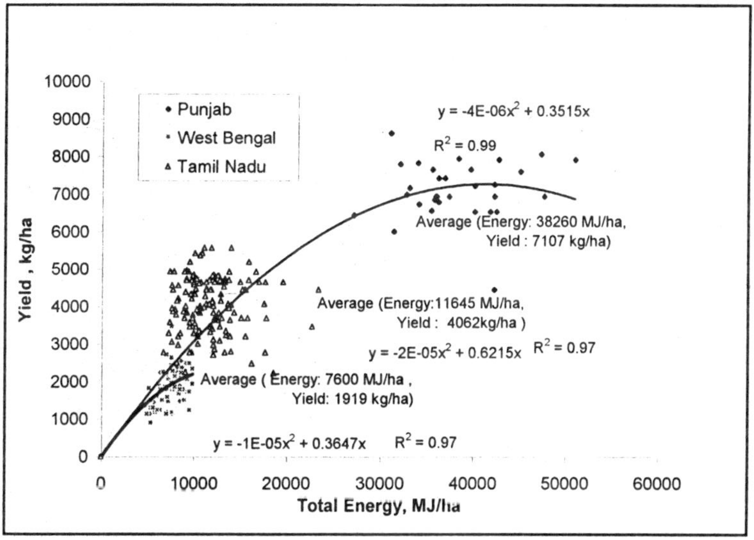

FIG.19.7 : Spatial variation in energy consumption and yield of paddy cultivation in representative villages

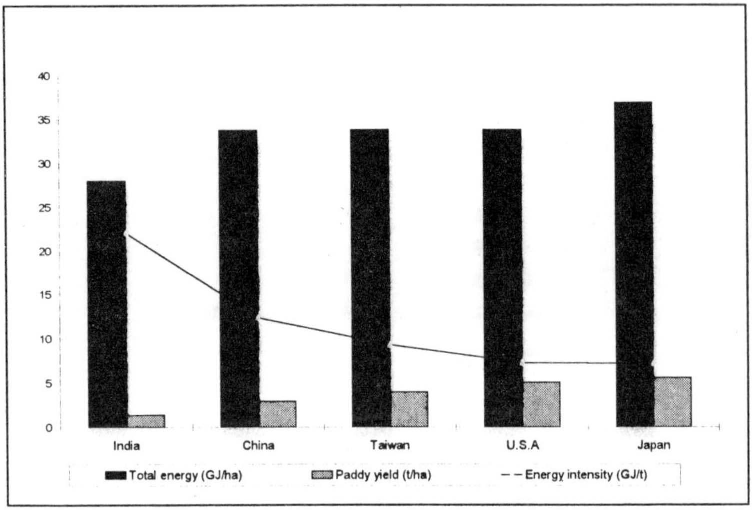

FIG.19.8: Energy use pattern for paddy cultivation in different countries.

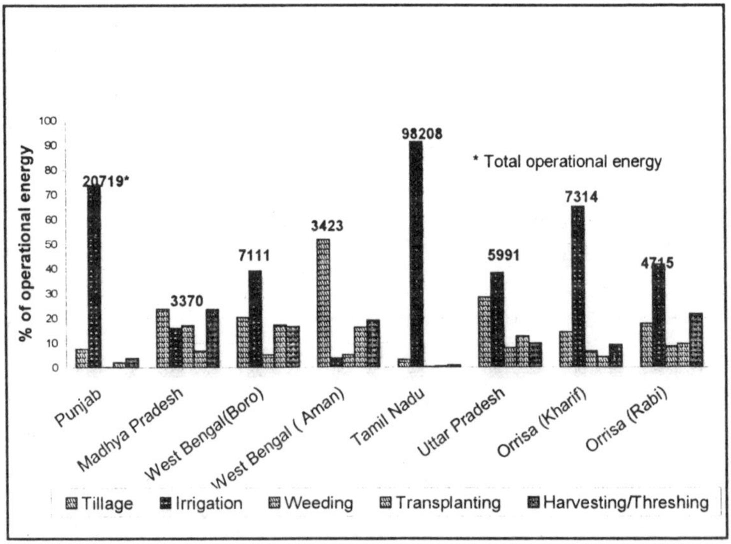

FIG.19.9: Variation in Operation-wise energy consumption for paddy-cultivation in different states

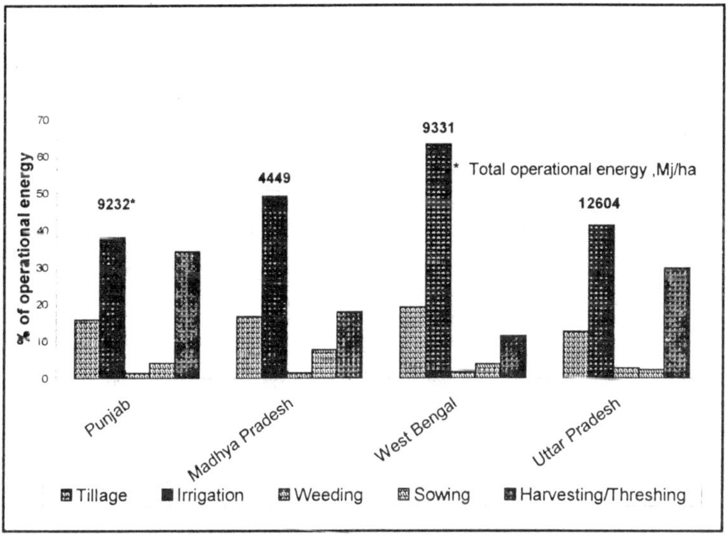

FIG. 19.10 : Variation in operation-wise energy consumption for wheat cultivation in different States.

Groundwater irrigation may take 20-40 times more energy than surface irrigation. However, if sprinkler irrigation system is utilised ratio drops to 3-5 times. If sprinkler is practiced with using surface water energy requirement of sprinkler requirement may 5-12 times than flooding irrigation. Sprinkler irrigation method using groundwater may take 6-7 per cent additional energy as compare to flooding irrigation. It is estimated a 5 per cent increase in water use efficiency reduces total energy use by 4-7 per cent using groundwater, however in case of surface it is 25-163 per cent.

Post-Harvest Engineering and Technology

Agricultural commodities are perishable in nature, some highly perishable like milk, meat, fish, fruits and vegetables and some relatively less called semi-perishable like foodgrains, oilseeds, certain tuber crops, cotton, jute and kenaf etc. Under scientific management losses can be kept low (below 5 per cent) but on-farm situations where infrastructure is poor and farmers are not aware of proper management practices losses can be high. Post-harvest losses in foodgrains are estimated at about 10 per cent level whereas in perishable like fruits and vegetables it is around 20-40 per cent. Milk, meat, egg and fish that receive much more attention also suffer 10-12% losses between production and consumption. Estimated value of post-harvest losses to agricultural produce is about Rs. 76,000 crore. It can be easily reduced to half, that is Rs38,000 crore decentralised addition to rural economy. Post-harvest technology a multi-disciplinary scientific and technological endeavour primarily deals with loss prevention and value addition by extending shelf

TABLE 19.10 : Status of agro-processing industries in India (1995-96)

Operation	Type of Units	Number of Units
Wheat Milling	Atta chakkies (burr and hammer mills)	2,66,000
	Roller flour mills	640
Rice Milling	Hullers	90,000
	Shellers	4,500
	Hullers-cum-shellers	7,000
	Modern rice mill	33,000
Daal Milling	Daal mills	12,000
Oil Milling	Oil ghanies	2,50,000
	Expellers	50,000
	Solvent extraction plants	600
	Oil refineries	200
	Vanaspati hydrogeneration plants	97
Fruit and Vegetable	Jams, jellies, juices, pickles, canning,etc.	6,000
Processing Plants Milk Processing Units	Milk, cheese, butter,etc.	400
Sugar Mill	White sugar mills	400
Agro Processing Equipment	Maize shellers (hand & power operated)	1,12,000
	Sugarcane crushers (i) Animal operated (ii) Power operated	 5,25,000 1,50,000
	Cleaners & graders	2,86,000
	Driers	7,000
	Groundnut decorticators	3,78,000
Storage Warehouse	Godown type structures	3,000

Source : Vision 2020. CIPHET Perspective Plan. CIPHET, Ludhiana.

life and transform the produce into readily usable convenient product. The major post-harvest operations include cleaning, grading, drying, dehydration, dehulling, decorticating, shelling, peeling, grinding/milling, polishing, extraction, expression, curing, treatment, handling, blending, packaging, storage, transportation, dispensing and marketing etc. Status of agro-processing industries in India (1995-96) is given in Table 19.10.

Milling of Cereals

Rice milling has been modernised in India however, hullers continue to be in use. Traditional shelling and polishing of rice (mortar-pestle and *Dhenki*) is virtually replaced by hullers except in remote tribal areas. On an average paddy has 72 per cent rice, 22 per cent husk, 5 per cent bran and 1 per cent germ. Hullers usually give only 50% head rice, shellers about 60 per cent and modern mill 65% in raw milling. In parboiled rice milling the differences narrow down considerably. Advancements have been made in processing and utilisation of husk and bran. There are mini rice mills available on - farm milling of rice that give husk, bran and brokens separately.

Wheat milling is also modernised. For whole wheat flour 'chakki' (burr mill) are commonly used mostly by custom milling where as organised wheat milling is being done in roller mills for refined flour, suji and rawa. There are mini-grainmills available that allow wheat milling at cottage level. Sorghum and other millets need to be pearled before milling. Pearlers have been developed and are available in the market. Snack foods out of cereals traditional as well as modern type are available in the market.

Milling of Pulses

Pulses are major source of protein to vegetarian people. It is one area where impact of GR is not as visible as in other foodgrains. Legumes are usually converted in to daal, decuticled splits in traditional daal mills that do dehusking using carborandom-emery roller. In each pass they produce 1-

1.5 per cent of fines (*chuni*). Pigeonpea may take 3-5 passes to get commercially acceptable daal. There is need to minimise losses in daal milling. Also legumes are difficult to store as a result farmers sell them off immediately after harvest when the market prices are low. On-farm processing of daal makes them available to the rural consumers at the cheapest rate at the same time milling wastes *'chuni', 'chokar'* which are feed concentrate to livestock. To meet this need mini-daal mills have been developed such as CIAE Daal Mill, PKV Daal Mill, PDP-Daal Mill, Pantnagar Daal Mill, CFTRI Mini Daal Mill etc.

Soybean Processing and Utilisation

Soybeans a native of Manchuria is called by various endearing names like 'golden nugget' as they have about 40 per cent protein with very balanced amino acid profile and 20 per cent fat. Under good management up to 3.5 t/ha of soybean can be harvested. Soybeans have been successfully introduced in India and area under soybeans are steadily increasing presently at about 5 Mha with average productivity of 1 t/ha. ICAR established under Indo-US sub-Commission on Agriculture the Soybean Processing and Utilization (SPU) was established at Central Institute of Agric Engineering, Bhopal to process whole soybeans for human consumption for combating protein and fat malnutrition so widely spread in the poorer sections of the society. SPU have developed low cost technologies to have full-fat and partially defatted soy-flour, soy-milk, soy-paneer (tofu), soy-yogurt, soy-ice cream, soy-fortified biscuits, and Indian dishes prepared out of soy-products. Soy-paneer plant costing about Rs. 2.00 lakh can sustain a family. A network for such soy-processing units can be anchor of nutritional security throughout the country.

Oilseed Processing

Oilseed processing in India is 3-tiered Kolhu-Expeller-Solvent-extraction, with residual oils of 10-12 per cent, 5-7 per cent, and less than 1 per cent, respectively. Oilseed cakes are rich in vegetable protein which with proper preprocessing and post-harvesting prophylactics and process adjustment can be used for human consumption. Energy efficient expellers, extrusion-expelling and batch-solvent extraction systems are relatively new introduction. India manufactures semi-automatic and automatic solvent extraction units. Technology Mission on Oilseed brought self sufficiency in oilseeds with integrated approach on increasing production, productivity, processing, and marketing. These gains need to be consolidated in a globalised market scenario. Fats and oils are one of the three macro-nutrients of human diet.

Agro-Processing Centres

Penny saved is penny earned. To help the rural people meet their basic needs of rice, ata, daal and vegetable oil at the least cost, and earn more through value addition AICRP on Post-Harvest Technology (PHTs) of ICAR has developed Model Agro-Processing Centres. These centres at a cost of about Rs. 2.00-2.50 lakh can provide self employment to 3-4 persons besides enabling the rural people having their domestic consumption as well as marketable surpluses primary processed to meet their needs at least cost and market surpluses after value addition and retain milling by-products for their livestock. These are successfully doing custom processing of agricultural produce.

Fruit and Vegetable Processing

India is second largest producer of fruits and vegetables (F&V). However, it is mostly used as table grade and suffers 20-40 per cent post-harvest losses. Fresh F&V are highly perishable, need a cold chain to protect them from qualitative and quantitative damages but available cold chains are too expensive. A F&V may contain 60-80 per cent water therefore their transport is expensive which can be avoided if these are processed in the production catchment. Drying and dehydration are low cost methods of conserving F&V for off-season use and marketing value added products. Quality hygienic pickles and preserves have both domestic and foreign markets. There are about 5000 F&V processing units but so far less than 2 per cent of the F&V are processed and we have very small share in the processed F&V global market.

Jaggery and Khandsari

Jaggery (*'gud', 'khand'*) are traditional sweeteners and have become part of Indian culture. People of Indian origin always look for quality, hygienic nicely packed ethnic food items. Sugarcane and date palm jaggery are one such item. This cottage industry has survived against stiff competition from organised sugar industry. If vacuum pan concentration is allowed, it might do even better. Out of about 250 MT of cane produced 35-40 per cent is used for jaggery products. To provide scientific back stopping to this sector ICAR has launched AICRP on Jaggery. Improved technologies have been developed for traditional jaggery production at the same new products processes like liquid and powder jaggery have been developed and ready for industrial interface for exploitation.

Cotton

Cotton, cotton and blended yarn and fabrics are our one of major exports. Government of India has launched a Technological Mission on Cotton directed to make it more competitive in domestic as well as international markets. Indian cotton bales carry excessive trash (8-12 per cent) compared to some of our competitors (below 2-3 per cent). Pre-cleaners and high capacity gins have been developed and commercialised. With increasing labour wages manual picking of cotton adds considerably to the unit cost of production. Efforts are on to have mechanical cotton pickers/strippers. Cottonseed is rich source of edible vegetable oil. Cotton stalks can be processed into particle board and craft paper for corrugated packaging boxes, Central Institute for Research on Cotton Technology (CIRCOT) of ICAR has the technology.

Jute and Kenaf

Jute has distinction of bringing industrialisation in India. It has traditionally been used for packaging and carpet backing. The synthetics have eroded the traditional markets. At National Institute for Research on Jute and Allied Fibre Technology (NIRJAFT) diversified uses of jute and kenaf have been developed such as utility items using their mini-carding and spinning machine, Caplan blankets, light bags, eco-friendly tea chests, geo textiles. Jute and Kenaf are natural fibres and are eco-friendly except for retting and extraction which release excessive organic loads in retting waters which flow to natural streams and rivers creating hazards to aquatic life and pollution. Ribbon-retting technology has been developed that minimizes pollution due to retting.

Animal Products Processing

India witnessed White Revolution soon after GR. Today, India is largest producer of milk in the world producing about 73 MT annually. About 46 per cent is consumed as liquid milk and remaining 54 per cent is processed. Organised sector processes about 10 per cent producing butter, cheese, icecream, milk powder, condensed milk, malted and infant milk food etc. The remaining 44 per cent is processed into traditional dairy products.

Meat production in India is about 3 MT of which 56 per cent comes from goats and sheep, 26 per cent beef, 13 per cent poultry, and 7 per cent pork. Meat is used mostly fresh. With the popularity of refrigerators, frozen meat is also being used. Modern slaughter houses, a few, have been established. Traditional slaughter houses are also being improved. Meat of culled animals is tough which can be better used processed. However, processed products currently are less than 1 per cent mostly for defence. About 23 billion (2 MT) eggs are produced. Eggs are also used fresh. Egg albumen powder and egg pickles have been commercialised.

Fisheries

India has 7500 km coast line, 28,000 km of rivers and 3 Mha ponds and reservoirs harvesting about 5 MT of fish annually. There are 1,59,481 traditional, 31,726 motorised traditional, 46,916 powered fishing boats and about 256 deep sea fishing vessels. Central Institute of Fisheries Technology (CIFT) has developed totally indigenous energy efficient deep sea vessel. Fish is also used fresh or iced coming from distance. There are 376 frozen fish units which can process 0.544 MT and also there is a dried fish production capacity of 0.3 MT, canned fish capacity is around 0.085 MT, and fish meal production capacity of 0.82 MT deep sea fishing vessel. There are 149 ice factories and 457 cold stores to keep fish. In spite of all this about 10-12 per cent fish are lost and fish in market are found to have high microbial load. Improved modern technologies have been developed for smoked and dried fish, fish curry by CIFT.

Information System Development

Starting under National Agricultural Research Project II (NARP II) and now under National Agricultural Technology Project (NATP) information system is being developed for the National Agricultural Research System (NARS). State

Agricultural Universities, ICAR Institutes, other institutions of higher learning in agriculture, Central/State departments of agriculture, and other line departments, NGOs, private sectors are also investing building IT capabilities. With thrust given to IT in the country India is likely to emerge a world leader in IT software, hardware, and databases and data warehousing. Agricultural engineers are playing important role in IT in agriculture and allied activities. AE as a system man is better suited for the job.

Challenges in New Millennium

In the new millennium agricultural engineers are required to be more creative than ever before for optional use of land and water resources, putting in place environmentally safe, eco-friendly practices. The new millennium has challenges of being globally competitive be it production agriculture or post-harvest engineering and technology to protect and utilize domestic markets and exploit exports markets in terms of unit cost of production, quality of the produce and processed products meeting global norms, if not better.

Soil and Water Engineering

Land and water resources per caput are going to be shrinking steadily and under constant threat of degradation. These have to be conserved. Water so vital for agriculture as a biological industry has to be used most judiciously adhering to evapo-transpiration needs of the crops. Ways and means have to be provided for optimal water use efficiency, method found that removing non-uniformity in water application. Micro-irrigation systems, laser-land levelling have to be made popular. Mechanized plastic lined ponds construction, mechanized raised bed farming under plastic tunnels and mulches at affordable costs have to be made available. System efficiencies of water lifting and application have to be enhanced.

Farm Power and Machinery

Petroleum becoming steadily costly requires that specific fuel consumption of engines used in agricultural tractors, power tillers, stationary and auxiliary engines be brought to international standards else it will erode competitiveness, profitability, and sustainability of agriculture. Indian farm equipment suffer from certain weaknesses like frequent replacement of fast wearing parts, modern metallurgy, surface coating and surface hardening techniques will have to be brought to farm equipment. There are serious noise and vibration problems in tractors and power tillers that need to be tackled. Exposure to global markets demand making farm equipment not only functionally efficient but ergonomically and aesthetically appealing. To counteract the dumping in our markets farm equipment by our competitors we have to constantly strive to reduce the unit cost of farm equipment besides improving quality factors. Creativity needs to be demonstrated in mechanization of horticulture, agro-forestry, livestock husbandry, and aquaculture. There is a persistent demand for sugarcane harvestors, cotton pickers, vegetable planters, transplanters, semi-automatic and automatic nursery raising, mechanized milking, mechanized handling processing and utilization of solid and liquid waste of livestock.

There is talk in certain States about Madagaskar rice cultivation technology which is basically check-row planted rice in which repeated mechanized cultivation is done aerating root zone besides eliminating weed. We have to develop check-row planters and transplanters for crops there is specific advantage.

Fertilizer after irrigation could be most energy intensive input and steadily becoming costly. It is also one of the major factors of water pollution. We need to establish ways and means of application of fertilizer that enhances fertilizer use efficiency like fertigation, slow release fertilizers and equipment to apply them appropriately.

Energy Management in Agriculture

Incorporation of crop residues into the soil specially where mechanized harvesting, combining, has picked up is a challenge. Biomass is a wealth. Incineration of crop residues is not only polluting but loss of economic opportunities. With C-levels in our soil depleting, and rising demand of organic farming we need to have *in situ* and *ex situ* organic manure production. Mechanized composting, as an entrepreneurial activity must be considered. Crop residues can be processed into livestock feed blocks. Advances in biomass conversion technology now enable extracting energy through biological pathway and still have wastes as value added manure.

Animate energy in Indian agriculture is going to be continued feature. It needs to be rationalized and made ergonomically sound, free from arduous labour, and made dignified. New and renewable sources of energy have to be developed and put to conserve costly commercial energies supplementing and substituting them for greater competitiveness.

Post-Harvest Technology

Post-harvest losses are excessive. We have to bring them down. With the available technologies it can be reduced to half and over a long period through pre-harvest and post-harvest management practices brought down to negligible levels. Penny saved is penny earned.

Processes, equipment and entrepreneurships need to be developed for on-farm processing and processed products for domestic needs and fresh and processed products specially fruits and vegetables for export. Modern techniques of modified atmosphere packaging (MAP), controlled atmosphere (CA) storage, cheaper affordable cold chains to handle, transport, store and dispense perishables in hygienic manner without qualitative and quantitative losses. Ultrafiltration, supercritical CO_2 extraction, ultra-high pressure processing, ascepting packaging etc. have to be given a sincere effort and exploited. Food safety, sanitary, and phytosanitary measures have to be developed and put in place.

Agro-processing centre models developed need to be popularized and more location specific packages developed in order to provide avenues for additional income and employment.

Biodegradable plastics, processing of crop residues for craft paper to have corrugated paper packaging boxes; processing of jute and kenaf sticks and whole stems cotton and pigeonpea stalks and other such woody crop residues for paper and pulp products, particle boards and other timber substitutes have to be pushed commercially.

The traditional use of commercial crops are going to be steadily eroded by man-made option therefore to sustain those agricultural commodities constantly new, bulk and highly remunerative diversified uses have to be developed and commercialized like liquid and powder jaggery, gasohol and other liquid fuels, composites and geo-textiles from jute and kenaf, edible grade lac die from lac waste, high temperature insulation lacquer from lac, high value chemicals of pharmaceutical, cosmetics and bio-pesticides.

Information System Development

IT revolution and its penetration in education, distance learning, research and research management, extension and business management is going to have phenomenal growth. Already there is very high demand for expertise, databases, software and hardware personnel. Data warehousing, artificial intelligence and neural networks in decision-making planning and management is going to expand. Opportunity is wide open to agricultural engineers along with others.

20

Engineering Inputs for Sustainable Crop Production

N.P.S. Sirohi
Principal Scientist and
Scientist-in-Charge, Indo-Israel Project
Indian Agricultural Research Institute

Food security, as a global issue, came to the fore in the 1970s, and has been defined in a number of ways since then. The World Bank gave one of the most acceptable definitions of food security as the "access by all people at all times to enough food for an active and healthy life". Thus, food security of a nation encompasses production, post-production management, and consumption of food materials. In our country, while production of foodgrains has reached to an adequate level, the remaining two components of food security are still lacking.

Production of different crops is the first and essential step towards food and nutritional security. From the consumer point of view, an appropriate mix of grains, edible oils, pulses, vegetables and fruits provide the required nutrition. On the other hand, the producer's objective is what to grow and how best to grow to achieve maximum production and resultant profit. Crop production, like any other production process, requires application of technology and management to remain remunerative and competitive. Both of these involve several disciplines of science and engineering.

Till few years back, the emphasis of agricultural sector remained on achieving the targeted production levels mainly in foodgrains. Having attained that, the focus shifted to economics and sustainability of production and associated environmental issues. Today, striking a balance between the farm productivity with minimum environmental impact, and still to stay economically competitive are major challenges for the modern agriculture.

Engineers have a major role to play on the above aspects. To make the technology economically sound and environmentally clean, various components of the production system must be carried with precision and in time. Agricultural engineers have contributed tremendously to achieve the above aspects. Mechanization of crop production and post-production operations, post-harvest and irrigation management are some of the critical areas which have greatly influenced the productivity of Indian agriculture. However, engineering efforts need to get more focussed for continued upgradation and improvement of management practices with respect to critical inputs, like, seed, nutrient, water, chemical and energy.

To make the crop production system remunerative and cost effective, it is important that the application efficiency of inputs is higher with minimum energy requirements. Some of the issues, which need attention of engineers for research and development efforts, could be:

i) Precision Application Devices for Seeds, Fertilizers and Pesticides

Improvement in the efficiency of above critical inputs would result in increased economic benefits but also reduce the adverse environmental impacts. As of now, the application of agro-chemicals is as highly inefficient process mainly due to inadequacies in the design and quality of applicators.

ii) Protected Cultivation of Horticultural Crops

Protected cultivation technology of horticultural crops has great potential to accrue sustained and almost assured economic gains even from small land holdings. A systematic and integrated approach is required to make it cost-effective and successful on large scale.

iii) Sensors and control systems

This may sound to be out of place in crop production situation in our country today. But, there are farmers in several regions who are now practising a high technology and capital-intensive agriculture for upmarkets and exports. In the absence of suitable indigenous hardware support, they have to depend on technologies of foreign origin which would not serve purpose in the long run. It is time that engineers initiate efforts to evolve indigenous hardware and software to attain self-sufficiency in the application of this emerging technology in agricultural sector to become competitive in the global markets.

(iv) Technology for Women Workers

Since women workers provide a substantial amount of labour on small farms, gender issues figure prominently in agricultural production and engineering technology. Studies have shown that whenever alternate source of farm power becomes available, it is usually the man in the family who uses it, leaving the women as disadvantaged and overworked as before. Increasing the efficiency of women workers with reduced drudgery is extremely important from economic and social point of view. Agricultural engineers have to address this issue emphatically by developing suitable technologies.

21

Role of Greenhouse Technology in Food and Nutritional Security of India

Pitam Chandra
National Phytotron Facility
Indian Agricultural Research Institute

Greenhouse technology development in India began in early eighties although the technology elsewhere in the world began about two hundred years ago. During the last two decades, a number of greenhouse structures have been proposed for popularization in India. There has been more emphasis on export-oriented crops. There has been some development of marketing infrastructure including the refrigerated storage facilities at the international airports with the help of APEDA. Liberalization of economy has helped in the import of greenhouse components and planting materials. Government of India has also provided tax incentives on greenhouse equipment imports and subsidies on greenhouse construction. The greenhouse industry experienced a steep growth in the early nineties. But something went wrong and a lot of apprehensions have lately been expressed about the future of greenhouse technology in the country.

The cost of greenhouse establishment has varied from Rs. 1.5 lakhs to 15 lakhs for a 500 square metre unit. Rate of interest on bank loans has been very high. The greenhouse operations have been, in many cases, noted to be highly energy intensive. Above all the greenhouse produce has not met the requisite standards. As a result many commercial greenhouse units have become sick.

Greenhouse technology has a place in Indian horticulture. It could increase the availability of fresh vegetables, fruits and flowers leading to better nutrition and standard of living. However, we need to understand better the greenhouse designs and appropriate environmental control. Energy intensiveness of the greenhouse production system should be reduced and more advantage of the local climatic conditions should be taken.

There have been some efforts to study the failures of greenhouse ventures in India, particularly in the hi-tech floriculture cultivation. It has now been concluded that the reasons have been high cost of installation, high interest rates, high energy requirements, costly energy, over invoicing and lack of honest interest of some of the floriculture units. It is, therefore, necessary that cost effective greenhouse technology be made available to Indian greenhouse growers. The success of greenhouse venture would also depend upon the choice of crops, varieties, appropriate environmental control and market accessibility. The crop, which is economical in a given year, may not be so remunerative next year. Therefore, there should be flexibility in crop selection from one year to another.

Status of Research and Development

Galvanized steel pipe framed greenhouse of quonset shape were developed which had inadequate natural ventilation capacities. Such structures worked well during winter months when the need for ventilation is less. Besides, mechanical ventilation provisions were made. Subsequently, fan-pad evaporative cooling systems were developed for these greenhouses. Several cropping activities, e.g. raising of seedlings, vegetative propagation, off-season vegetable cultivation and floriculture were studied. The greenhouse frames were subsequently modified to provide more height with vertical sides to better utilize the floor space and permit crop growth. Low tunnel fabrication has also been standardized.

Summer cooling of greenhouses was studied in relation to mechanical ventilation rates, exterior shading, and different modes of evaporative cooling. Cooling efficiencies as high as 85 per cent were observed when the relevant parameters were optimized. At any given location the greenhouse cooling is limited to the wet bulb temperature of the ambient air. With 85 per cent efficiency the greenhouse air temperature is expected to be about 2° C higher than the ambient wet bulb temperature. Shading improves the cooling system performance.

Several efforts have been made to develop location specific greenhouses. Large multispan greenhouses have relied upon the ridge ventilation by providing adequate opening at roof level. Saw tooth wave designs have become popular under mild climates; the sidewalls also have openings for natural ventilation. The side and roof ventilation along with fogging/misting is capable of maintaining favourable microclimate in the greenhouse crop zone. Greenhouse heights of 4 to 6 metres have been found to maintain desirable thermal stratification. Bamboo framed rain shelters have been developed for north-eastern region where good quality bamboo is conveniently available at reasonable cost. Design of a naturally ventilated greenhouse using eucalyptus poles has also been developed. In view of frequent electrical power failures, design of a greenhouse using natural ventilation through side openings has been proposed. In the event of power failure, the plastic film from the sides is rolled up. Fine plastic nets on the side prevent the entry of insects. During nights and winters, the sides are fully covered with plastic film. The roof may be shaded from outside to cut down the excessive sunlight, especially during summers. Performance of such a greenhouse needs to be evaluated. A greenhouse for colder regions have been developed which reduces the heating requirements by about 80 per cent. The remaining heating requirement could be easily met through solar energy storage in places where sunshine is readily available. Cost effective greenhouse designs for mild climatic conditions of Pune and Bangalore and cold climatic Kashmir have been proposed by the FAO consultant. These designs are presently under field testing.

There have not been any studies on greenhouse heating in India, though heating has been extensively studies abroad and the availability of fuels for greenhouse heating in India is highly constrained. Greenhouse designs for cyclone prone coastal areas are also to be developed. Energy efficient greenhouses are needed for hot deserts of Rajasthan and Gujarat where water availability is severely limited. As the greenhouse growers become aware of the necessity for optimum climatic control in greenhouses, studies on humidity, light, carbon dioxide and nutrition management will be needed.

Greenhouses in India have been very successfully used for raising seedlings from seeds as well as for vegetative propagation. The seedlings of high quality and take less time in attaining adequate growth. Greenhouse grown seedlings could often permit off-season (early or late) production in open fields. Greenhouses have been used to grow off-season vegetables, e.g. tomato, cucumber, capsicum, summer squash, cole crops, leafy vegetables and okra. The important flowers grown in greenhouses in India have been rose, crysanthemum, carnation, gerbera, lilium, tuberose, gladiolus. Limited trials have also been conducted on some medicinal and commercial plants such as isabgol and betelvine. A good amount of progress is made in the areas of installation and use of low tunnels, cloches and plastic mulching.

Issues

Greenhouse area in the country today is estimated to be only about 800 ha which is negligible in comparison to the greenhouse area in China, Japan, South Korea, Holland, etc. The cumulative area under low tunnels and plastics mulching may not be more than 10,000 ha at present. The question today is whether protected cultivation technology is relevant under Indian conditions? Which specific crops could be grown? What could be the marketing arrangements for the perishable greenhouse produce? What should be the short term and long term policies in promoting this technology?

Greenhouses, low tunnels, cloches and plastic mulching form an integral part of periurban agriculture where agricultural land is limited and demand for certain perishable horticultural produce is very high year round. This technology can be an extremely useful intervention in those regions where the normal growing season is limited to 4-6 months. Horticultural production in the hills of UP, Himachal Pradesh, Jammu and Kashmir, North-east; and even desert areas of Rajasthan, and Gujarat could be expanded for a larger part of a year. This, in turn, should increase economic activities as compared to traditional agriculture and, therefore, it should appeal better to educate these areas. Another aspect of greenhouse technology is that it has greater scientific input for rural youth. Greenhouse crop cultivation is definitely not as drudgery as traditional agriculture is.

Greenhouse crop yields are usually several times higher than those obtained under open field conditions. For example, cucumber yields in greenhouse have been noted to be as high as 200 t/ha. In fact, the cucumber crop in the Indo-Israel demonstration project at IARI performed so well inspite of several teething troubles that the yields could easily be more than 400 t/ha. Similarly, Capsicum at IARI has yielded up to 150 t/ha under greenhouse conditions. These result and those of low tunnels, plastic mulching etc. when viewed in the light of experiences elsewhere in the world, clearly indicate that protected horticulture technology could greatly contribute to the vegetable production in India. With no possibility of bringing additional area under vegetable crops, if a portion of existing area is put under protected horticulture, the per capita vegetable availability in the country could be brought to the recommended level. One million hectares under protected vegetable crops would mean 100 million tonnes of vegetables annually as compared to about 15 million tonnes at present. That is 85 million tonnes of additional vegetables from the same area.

It is planned to bring this one million hectares under protected horticulture over a ten-year period, the annual investment is quite reasonable i.e. Rs. 10,000 crores. The government share would not be more than Rs. 5,000 crores. Private industry partnership could be considered to further reduce this share. The proposition also means 5-10 million additional jobs, reduced migration from villages to cities and from hills to plains. Besides vegetable crops, floriculture, medicinal plants and biotechnology industry also needs greenhouse technology for higher productivity and financial returns.

If the above-mentioned progress has to be achieved the pace of development has to be accelerated. Appropriate greenhouse technology needs to be made available to the prospective greenhouse growers along with adequate financing and marketing arrangements. The following R&D activities are required.

1. Development of location and crop specific greenhouse structures using local materials as far as possible.
2. Development of energy efficient environmental control systems for greenhouses.
3. Integrated nutrient management.
4. Integrated insect and diseases control practices.
5. Breeding of crop varieties suitable for greenhouses.
6. Post harvest practices for greenhouse produce.
7. Entrepreneurial development.
8. Human resource development.

The commercial greenhouse experience in India so far has clearly highlighted the dearth of trained human resource in greenhouse operation and crop management. There is a need to introduce greenhouse technology programmes at undergraduate and postgraduate levels to prepare adequate trained human resource. The initial phase of greenhouse development should focus on the domestic markets. In the process, the greenhouse growers develop adequate expertise to graduate to the level of exporters. Meeting quality standards is essential in export obligations.

22

Food and Nutrition Status in India in 2001 Case Studies from Six different Agro-Climatic Locations

Pradeep Chaturvedi
Secretary General
Indian Association for the Advancement of Science

Background

The objective of the study was to focus on revisiting the areas surveyed in 1992 to study the food and nutrition situation in 2001 and to benchmark the results against the earlier study.

The Regional and Expert Consultations identified the need. A second survey was recommended in the Report of the FAO/WHO Joint Inter Country Workshop. The concept was further supported by the National World Food Day Committee the Ministry of Agriculture and Cooperation, Government of India, at its meeting on April 24, 2001.

Data was collected at the following sites:

i. Plains Singhu Village (Near the Metro City Delhi)
ii. Desert - Madni Village (District Sikar – State of Rajasthan)
- Peepalwas Village (District Udaipur – State of Rajasthan)

iii. Tribal - Raipuria Village (District Dhar – State of Madhya Pradesh)

iv. Hills - Niglat Village (District Nainital – State of Uttaranchal)

v. Coastal - Pallipuram Village (District Ernakulam – State of Kerala)

Primary data was collected for a sample size of 1414 households having a total population of 7519. This data gave an effective insight into the micro-level situation at the *household level – which is considered the smallest unit of food security.* However, to ensure validity and to identify linkage to wider overall situation, secondary data at village level and district level was also collected.

It was decided to collect secondary data also for the village from records and interviews of village chief and other functionaries; and the secondary data for the district which is the smallest administrative level unit controlling the village. This data gave an insight into the demographic characteristics and social development indicators for the environment of the surveyed villages. District records also helped in identifying the infrastructure available for improving nutritional status and the facilities created by the government. Therefore, the analysis will also present the interpretation on the district and village profiles beyond the sample household data.

The analysis is presented, as benchmarked against 1992 situation, to reflect a comparative picture of the developments that have taken place during this period and to recommend future Action Plan.

District Profile

Please refer to Table 22.1 on District Profile.

2.1 Population Growth

The surveyed sites had wide variations in population growth rates (during 1991-2001) and literacy levels. Delhi District registered a growth of 46.31 per cent (highest in the country – mainly because of the available infrastructural facilities that encouraged migration to Delhi); Sikar District 24.11 per cent;

Table 22.1 : District Profile

Particulars	Singhu	Madni	Peepalwas	Niglat	Raipuria	Pullipuram
1. District Name	Delhi	Sikar	Udaipur	Nainital	Dhar	Ernakulam
2. Population of the district (1991)	9420644	1843000	2086000	1540174	1367412	2797779
3. Male population (1991)	5155512	947000	1066000	823798	700952	NA
4.Female population (1991)	4265132	896000	1020000	716376	666460	NA
5. Rural population (1991)	949019	1455000	1690000	1037210	1187702	NA
6.Urban population (1991)	8471625	388000	396000	502964	179710	NA
7. SC (1991)	1794836	258000	139000	243314	731272	NA
8. ST (1991)	0	49000	964000	0	731272	NA
9. District Growth rate 91991-2001)	46.31	24.11	27.37	0	27.29	9.09
10. Projected population 2001	13783344	2287347	2656938	774330	168	1162
11. Density of population (1991)	6352	238	142	170	168	1162
12. Surrounding district	East-Ghaziabad GB Nagar West : Jhajjar North : Sonipat South : Gurgaon, Faridabad	East : Jaipur West : Nagour North ; Jhunjhunun South : Ajmer	North : Rajsamand South : Dungarpur, Gujarat East : Chittorgarh West : Sirohi	North : Almora, South : US Nagar, East : Chamapawat West : US Nagar	North : Ratlam South : Khargaon West : Jhabua West : Indore	East : Idukki West : Arabaian Sea North ; Triture South ; Kottyam
13. Literacy rate	75.29%	42.49%	34.80%	55.10%	34.54%	93.47%
14. Geographical Area of the district (ha.)	147488	774244	1462000	411721	815300	115700
15. Forest (ha.)	1561	59982	391131	300763	119724	0
16. Cultivable waste land (ha.)	10510	9443	134135	26437	53149	0
17. Fallow land (ha.)	12846	76490	84735	5304	6475	0
18. Land put Non-agri. Use (ha.)	72191	32590	156802	2955	115675	38500
19. Barren land (ha.)	9822	18299	358057	8702	0	700

Table 22.1 Contd.

Particulars	Singhu	Madni	Peepalwas	Niglat	Raipuria	Pullipuram
20. Grazing land (ha.)	746	42282	91645	1191	0	0
21. Misc. Tree Crops (ha.0	1267	114	590	16056	0	60700
22. Net Sown Area (ha.)	48349	539044	245000	50313	502785	15800
23. Irrigated Area (ha.)	NA	5421336	92206	30285	232642	NA
24. No. of tehsils/Blocks	2/5	6/8	10/11	6/11	7/13	NA
25. No. of inhab./unihab. Villages	199/10	987/13	2235/13	556	1487	NA
26. Major crops of the district	Wheat Paddy Barseem Jower	Bajara Wheat Gram Pulses Rai & Mustrad	Wheat Maize Jowar Barley Gram	Paddy Wheat Bean Vegetables	Wheat Maize Gram Soyabean Cotton	Paddy Coconut

Source : District Statistical Handbook of Sikar (1999), Udaipur (1999), Dhar (1999), District Census Handbook of Nainital and Delhi.

Udaipur District 27.37 per cent; Nainital District 32.88 per cent; Dhar District 27.28 per cent; and Ernakulam District 9.09 per cent. The exponential growth in Delhi is an example of migration of rural population to urban area. As the State of Kerala has attained a total fertility rate of less than one per cent therefore the growth in Ernakulam is just 9 per cent.

2.2 Literacy Rate

Literacy rate was the highest in Ernakulam at 93.47 percent followed by Delhi at 75.29 per cent. The two districts of Udaipur and Dhar, having tribal villages, recorded literacy rate of around 34 per cent. Sikar has literacy rate of 42.49 per cent and Nainital has 55.10 per cent. Certain observations indicate that districts with higher literacy rates have lower total fertility rate.

2.3 Spread of Nutrition Improvement Programme

The district and village level data also indicates that government has effectively carried the message of balanced diet and nutrition supplementation programmes under anganwadis for primary school, mid-day meal programme and the ICDS programme. Government's schemes of reaching the food to the last, under Antyodaya, has also been widely publicized and implemented.

2.4 Effectiveness of Public Distribution System

The spread of Fair Price Shops is even across the districts and villages. All the villagers are registered to get food-grain under the public distribution system. Only the tax payers are now excluded from taking the subsidized foodgrain. However, it was observed that those above poverty line do not purchase the food-grain because the price at the Fair Price Shop is higher than that in the market. Those below poverty line do not avail of the over subsidized food grain under targeted public distribution system because they have no purchasing capacity to buy their monthly supply at one go. Possibly they would like to buy the foodgrain on a daily basis. Thus, the public distribution system is not effectively reaching food to a group of beneficiary.

2.5 Natural Disasters

Three Districts of Udaipur, Sikar and Dhar faced droughts for a number of years. However, the local capacity to grow their own food helped the poor people to get over the situation. The District of Udaipur suffered a major drop in nutrition energy intake as they were, mainly dependent on cereal crops for their survival. District Sikar was also equally badly affected but because of availability of milch animals and the tradition of not selling milk they were able to survive and maintain their nutritional intake.

3.0 Village Level Analysis

Please refer to Table 22.2 for data

3.1 Comparative Statement on Consumption Pattern and Expenditure

3.1.1 *Shift to More Balanced Diet*

All the six sites surveyed indicate an overall shift from cereal-based diet to a balanced diet, in spite of drought conditions at three of the places, viz, Peepalwas, Madni and Raipuria. The consumption of vegetables and milk and milk products has considerably increased and consumption of cereals has decreased. Singhu village has also shown higher consumption of fruits because of the higher purchasing capacity of the people. A small population in Singhu also showed tendency towards obesity. Most of the foodstuff came from their production. Also in Singhu village it has been noticed that the people have stopped selling milk (that they did earlier) because they have alternate source of income from rentals of their houses. The milk is now consumed improving nutritional intake. However, in case of coastal village of Pallipuram though half the population is involved in traditional fishery the catch is mostly sold and does not add to the improvement of nutrition. The population is generally poor.

Table 22.2 : Consumption of Foodstuff & Expenditure

Site	Foodstuff	Protein (gm)		Dietary Energy (Cal)		Expenditure (Rs.)		Income (Rs.)	
		1992	2001	1992		2001	1992	1992	2001
1. Singhu Delhi	Total	67.02	69.07	2343.00	2289.00	7.03	10.11	12.02	26.21
	i) Wheat & Rice	51.80	42.26	1698.00	1280.00	2.63	2.58		
	ii) Sugar	0.04	0.05	154.00	213.00	0.41	1.25		
HH : 467	iii) Pulses	4.45	6.83	68.00	104.00	0.29	0.66		
Pop : 2391	iv) Vegetables	3.92	3.16	92.00	74.00	1.38	2.00		
Male : 1308	v) Oil & Fats	0.00	0.00	188.00	285.00	1.04	0.58		
Female : 1083	vi) Milk/milk products	6.81	14.36	143.00	301.00	1.28	1.66		
Av.HH Size	vii) Fruits	0.00	1.01	0.00	24.00	0.00	1.12		
: 5.12	viii) Meat/meat products	0.00	1.39	0.00	9.00	0.00	0.26		
2. Niglat, Nainital	Total	74.44	66.12	2191	2192	8.32	7.56	10.66	20.81
	i) Wheat & Rice	45.98	41.63	1557.00	1387.00	2.59	3.30		
	ii) Sugar	0.00	0.03	167.00	129.00	0.44	0.49		
HH : 183	iii) Pulses	10.05	6.03	153.00	92.00	0.66	0.72		
Pop. : 991	iv) Vegetables	4.65	3.04	109.00	71.00	1.64	1.14		
Male : 530	v) Oil & Fats	0.00	0.00	0.00	200.00	0.00	0.70		
Female : 461	vi) Milk/milk products	8.08	13.59	169.00	285.00	1.77	0.43		
Av.HH Size	vii) Fruits	0.00	1.05	0.00	25.00	0.00	0.17		
: 5.42	viii) Meat/meat products	5.69	0.75	35.00	5.00	1.23	0.59		
3. Peepal was, Udaipur	Total	86.09	48.51	2470.00	2127.00	3.34	3.97	3.50	5.68
	i) Wheat & Rice	85.05	38.19	2446.00	1755.00	2.98	1.80		
	ii) Sugar	0.00	0.01	0.00	53.00	0.00	0.18		
	iii) Pulses	0.00	3.83	0.00	60.00	0.00	0.23		
HH : 265	iv) Vegetables	1.04	2.52	24.00	59.00	0.37	0.53		
Pop. : 1298	v) Oil & Fats	0.00	0.00	0.00	127.00	0.00	0.58		
Male : 663	vi) Milk/milk products	0.00	3.28	0.00	69.00	0.00	0.26		
Female ; 635	vii) Fruits	0.00	0.02	0.00	1.00	0.00	0.00		
Av.HH Size : 4.90	viii) Meat/meat products	0.00	0.67	0.00	4.00	0.00	0.38		
4. Madni, Sikar	Total	81.00	80.61	2388.00	2553.00	5.35	10.67	10.14	19.23
	i) Wheat & Rice	70.00	61.10	2034.00	1786.00	2.45	2.36		
	ii) Sugar	0.00	0.03	0.00	122.00	0.00	0.52		
HH : 267	iii) Pulses	2.00	2.67	39.00	41.00	0.16	0.35		
Pop. : 1842	iv) Vegetables	1.00	1.21	27.00	29.00	0.40	0.57		
Male : 946	v) Oil & Fats	0.00	0.00	128.00	251.00	0.88	1.00		
Female : 896	vi) Milk/milk products	8.00	15.48	160.00	324.00	1.44	5.81		
Av.HH Size	vii) Fruits	0.00	0.01	0.00	0.20	0.00	0.01		
: 6.90	viii) Meat/meat products	0.00	0.11	1.00	1.00	0.00	0.05		
5. Raipuriya, Dhar	Total	55.88	61.12	2613.00	2623.00	4.34	9.26	5.54	10.73
	i) Wheat & Rice	45.68	46.95	2418.00	2085.00	2.81	3.97		
	ii) Sugar	0.00	0.03	0.00	126.00	0.00	0.54		
HH : 745	iii) Pulses	3.36	6.33	51.00	96.00	0.22	0.77		
Pop. : 3740	iv) Vegetables	0.18	2.35	4.00	55.00	0.06	0.97		
Male : 1917	v) Oil & Fats	0.00	0.00	0.00	153.00	0.00	0.63		
Female : 1823	vi) Milk/milk products	6.67	4.97	139.00	104.00	1.25	2.17		
Av.HH Size	vii) Fruits	0.00	0.01	0.00	0.00	0.00	0.01		
: 5.02	viii) Meat/meat products	0.00	0.48	0.00	3.00	0.00	0.21		

Table 22.2 Contd.

Site	Foodstuff	Protein (gm)		Dietary Energy (Cal)		Expenditure (Rs.)		Income (Rs.)	
		1992	2001	1992		2001	1992	1992	2001
6. Pallipuram, Emakulam	Total	38.89	59.35	1495.00	1858.00	5.19	14.08	14.48	23.00
	i) Wheat & Rice	25.46	23.41	1312	1077.00	1.90	3.76		
	ii) Sugar	0.00	0.05	0.00	189.00	0.00	0.33		
	iii) Pulses	0.00	8.65	0.00	132.00	0.00	1.13		
HH : 14140	iv) Vegetables	3.40	1.93	80.00	45.00	1.20	1.14		
Pop. : 64054	v) Oil & Fats	0.00	0.00	0.00	191.00	0.00	0.74		
Male : 30746	vi) Milk/milk products	2.81	3.40	59.00	71.00	0.53	1.27		
Female : 33308	vii) Fruits	0.00	1.01	0.00	24.00	0.00	1.18		
Av.HH Size : 4.53	viii) Meat/meat products	7.22	20.92	44.00	129.00	1.56	4.52		

It will be premature to take this as an indication to the State that cereal intake is reducing countrywide because of this kind of shift in eating habits. But, similar shift in eating habits might be taking place at other places also and that may be a reason for lower off-take from the public distribution system. This inference will need further validation.

3.1.2 *Dietary Energy Intake*

The dietary energy intake has remained at the same level in three villages, viz, Singhu, Niglat, and Raipuria as showin in Table 22.3. It has improved in two places, viz, Madni and Pallipuram. It has substantially dropped in Peepalwas. This varied between 2191 cal/capita/day to 2623 cal/capita/day except for Pallipuram that registered an intake of 1858 cal/capita/day. The intake level is satisfactory as per the national level except for Pallipuram. The positive sign about Pallipuram is that the village has shown an upward shift from 1495 cal/capita/day to 1858 cal/capita/day.

Despite the satisfactory levels of average energy intake it has been noticed that pockets of malnutrition do occur, all across the income level, though mainly in groups that are below poverty line. The sample has recorded 35 per cent families below energy consumption level of 1800 cal/capita/day .

3.1.3 *Dietary Energy Intake at Household Level*

A comparison on the basis of the caloric intake has been conducted at five different levels. The average intake for those

Table 22.3 : Consumption of Dietary, Energy, Domestic Energy, Expenditure on Energy and Income

Site	Protein (gm)		Dietary Energy				Cooking Energy				Total Expenditure (Rs.)		Total Income (Rs.)	
			Quantity (Cal)		Expenditure (Rs.)		Quantity (Cal)		Expenditure (Rs.)					
	1992	2001	1992	2001	1992	2001	1992	2001	1992	2001	1992	2001	1992	2001
1. Singhu, Delhi	67.02	69.07	2343	2289	7.03	10.11	598	580	1.24	1.28	8.27	11.39	12.02	25.21
2. Niglat, Nainital	74.44	66.12	2191	2192	8.32	7.56	523	805	1.10	1.10	9.42	8.66	10.66	20.81
3. Peepalwas, Udaipur	86.09	48.51	2470	2127	3.34	3.97	581	452	1.22	0.60	4.56	4.57	3.50	5.68
4. Madni, Sikar	81.00	80.61	2388	2553	5.35	10.67	373	431	0.79	1.50	6.14	12.17	10.14	19.23
5. Raipuriya, Dhar	55.88	61.12	2613	2623	4.34	9.26	418	432	0.58	0.86	4.92	10.12	5.54	10.73
6. Pallipuram, Ernakulam	38.89	59.35	1495	1858	5.19	14.08	470	609	0.94	1.29	6.13	15.37	14.48	23.00

Table 22.4 : Relationship Between Income and Food Consumption Pattern

Income	Households Income Group							Households Income Group						
	<500	500-1000	1001-1500	2501-2500	2501-3500	3501-5000	>5000	<500	500-1000	1001-1500	2501-2500	2501-3500	3501-5000	>5000
Income per Capita (Rs)	4.58	7.49	9.08	12.92	18.48	22.79	39.88	4.58	7.49	9.08	12.92	18.48	22.79	39.88
Food Items	Food Consumption gm/capita/day							Dietary energy cal/capita/day						
1. Cereals & Cereals Product	433	468	484	525	515	483	516	1481	1602	1656	1795	1761	1652	1765
i) Wheat	303	310	341	362	342	334	371	1033	1056	1164	1233	1166	1140	1265
ii) Rice	130	158	142	163	173	148	145	448	545	492	562	595	511	499
2. Sugar	22	30	39	36	47	50	60	66	118	156	142	188	200	237
3. Pulses	20	26	27	26	32	28	31	70	90	96	90	113	99	106
4. Vegetables	160	212	142	145	160	156	180	64	85	57	58	64	62	72
5. Fruits	0	17	30	32	32	44	52	0	7	12	13	13	18	21
6. Meat/Meat Product	0	25	21	24	27	30	28	0	28	24	26	30	33	32
7. Oil & Fat	0	9	18	27	36	43	45	0	1	2	4	5	6	6
8. Milk/ Milk Products	43	288	307	293	406	407	381	29	194	206	197	273	274	256
								1730	2125	2209	2324	2447	2343	2495

below income of Rs. 500 per household/month indicate a figure of 1730 cal. However, it is interesting to note that there are about 30 per cent households below 1730 cal/capita/day in the sample. There are only 37 per cent households with an average dietary energy consumptions of over 2200 cal/capita/day.

3.1.4 Protein Intake

Protein intake has remained at the same level in Singhu and Madni villages; improved in Raipuria and Pallipuram villages; and reduced in Niglat and Peepalwas. Except for Peepalwas the protein level has remained over the recommended minimum level.

3.1.5 *Expenditure on Food*

Expenditure on food has increased at all the places, especially as the number of bought out items increased mainly in the drought-affected area of Peepalwas, Madni and Raipuria. The expenditure has almost doubled as shown in Table 22.3. In case of Peepalwas the increase is marginal and the corresponding lowering of energy intake has been witnessed. Expenditure has increased three times in Pallipuram bringing about the needed upward shift in energy intake. Only in case of Niglat the expenditure has come down mainly because of higher local production. Singhu has shown upward change because of higher consumption of vegetables, fruits and milk.

3.1.6 *Income*

Income has uniformly doubled at all the sites. It was still very low in Peepalwas. These average values of income increase may not give a true picture at micro level and there are pockets of poverty and associated malnutrition at a number of places.

3.1.7 *Status of Weight and Height*

Average weight and height have shown improvement or maintained the same level. But, there is no decrease-indicating trend towards stunted growth.

3.1.8 *Male to Female Ratio*

Male to female ratio in different villages has been observed to be 1.0 to 0.8 – 0.9. It is a matter of concern.

3.2 Relationship between Income and Food Consumption Pattern

Please refer to Table 22.4.

3.2.1 *Income and Dietary Energy Intake*

Data collected from different villages indicate that on an average the *dietary energy intake improves with income*. Also, *the diet becomes more balanced* shifting away from only cereal based to one rich in vegetables, fruits and milk and milk products. This is not to say that the cereals are given up. The level of cereal consumption remains almost same in all income levels at about 425 cal/capita/day indicating that cereals remain the staple diet for the predominantly vegetarian population. With higher income brackets other suitable foodstuff rich in vitamins, proteins and other micro nutrients are also added to the diet.

The increase in dietary energy or additional material does not bear any direct proportion to the income. It does show a remarkable improvement with increase in income.

A look at the dietary energy intake shows a much wider variation between groups by income. It varies from an average figure of 1730 cal/capita/day for the lowest income bracket to 2495 cal/capita/day for the highest income bracket. These average figures can be misleading. Some families in higher income groups have also registered lower dietary energy intake. The lowest income category is also the nutritionally vulnerable for reason of lack of purchasing power, which does not allow them access to food otherwise available. Only the government subsidy can help them.

3.2.2. *Nutrition level of children in age group 1-5 years*

Please refer to Table 22.5.

Table 22.5 : Nutritional Level of Children in Age Group 1-5 years

Site	Parti-culars	Severe Under-nutrition	Moderate Under-nutrition	Slight Under-nutrition	Normal Growth	Over weight	Total
Singhu	No.	20	21	36	41	43	161
	%	12.42	13.94	22.36	25.47	26.71	
Niglat	No.	3	4	17	38	33	95
	%	3.16	4.21	17.89	40.00	34.74	
Peepalwas	No.	100	60	39	44	8	251
	%	39.84	23.90	15.54	17.53	3.19	
Madni	No.	26	75	31	35	32	199
	%	13.07	37.69	15.58	17.59	16.08	
Raipuriya	No.	34	25	16	5	0	80
	%	42.50	31.25	20.00	6.25	0.00	
Pallipuram	No.	3	3	14	35	9	64
	%	4.69	4.69	21.88	54.69	14.06	
Total	No.	186	188	153	198	125	850
	%	21.88	22.12	18.00	23.29	14.71	

The nutrition level of children in the age group 1-5 years was assessed on the basis of the standard used by hospitals in Delhi to determine growth level of children by comparing age and weight. On this basis, it has been observed that about 22 per cent of the sample group suffered from severe undernutrition, 22 percent under moderate nutrition and 18 percent under nutrition. Only 23 per cent reflected normal growth and about 15 percent had the tendency of overweight.

Conclusion

It is interesting to note that the poverty indicator gives large populations as threatened by malnutrition or undernutrition but the ground reality is different. As the poor do their production, which is not reflected in their income. Their traditional knowledge also help them to eat locally available foods and minor forest produce, not recorded otherwise. However, there are households above poverty whose average dietary intake is low as those below poverty line.

The trend differs from 1992 in two ways :

i. Overall cereal consumption level has come down.
ii. Consumption patterns across all sections have become more balanced.

As has been asserted in the present Report containing six Case Studies, the spectrum of malnutrition and poverty is still haunting the country in spite of various steps taken with all sincerity for fulfilling the commitments that delved on us at the International Conference on Nutrition, 1992 and the World Food Summit, 1996. It is in this context the Indian Association for the Advancement of Science undertook to take up concrete case studies of six villages located in six different agro-climatic locations with wide divergence of conditions. The results have indeed been quite revealing and it is our hope that the information gathered will be of use to those who are entrusted with or have taken on themselves the task of poverty alleviation and combating against malnutrition.

23

Poverty and Food Security

K P A Menon
President
Indian Association for the Advancement of Science

For meeting the needs of the growing population and ensuring better nutrition to the poorer sections, the planners had envisaged a production level of 230 million tones by the close of the 20th century. It was their expectation that the realization of this, not too ambitious, target will enable the country to attain self-sufficiency in the field of food production with some provision for bad monsoon years and marginal surpluses for occasional exports. While assessing the situation at the turn of the century, claims are being made by some that progress in food grains production has been quite satisfactory since there was even a marginal surplus in respect of the main food grains and the Food Corporation of India was holding huge buffer stocks which, they were finding difficult to dispose of. Ironically, all this has been achieved without the country having attained a stable production level of even 200 million tonnes. Dose it mean that the National Commission on Agriculture had gone wrong in their calculations and come to wrong inferences ? Nothing could be farther from truth than such an assumption as any realistic assessment of the scenario would reveal.

If a country like China with a smaller area under cultivation of food grain crops and consistently producing double the quantity of grains as compared to India is, still, not feeling complacent about the future we have hardly any ground for rejoicing over our achievement. The calorie intake recommended by nutrition experts of our country can not, by any stretch of imagination be considered as immodest or over ambitious. Even with unsaleable surpluses in public and private godowns there are, not infrequent, reports of starvation deaths invariably being qualified as effects of malnutrition. In a Welfare State there can be hardly any distinction between the two since the government is under an obligation to provide adequate means of livelihood to every citizen. Surpluses are bound to be there if people have no access to food due to inadequate purchasing power. It was with such a realization, antipoverty programmes with special emphasis on employment generation were initiated.

"Irrigation to every field – Employment to every one" These were the two guiding principles on which a programme was initiated in one of the Eastern U.P districts during the days of Integrated Rural Development. It was indeed a bold challenge against the phantom of poverty. Rightly has it been mentioned that India is a rich country with poor people. If the rich resources are effectively used, poverty will become a memory of the past. For a land to become productive, three more resources are to be added. We are well endowed in respect of two out of the three no doubt i.e air and sunlight. If the fourth one in the form of water is also available in good measure and at the appropriate time, most of the regions of the country are capable of producing two or three crops without, in anyway, overstraining the land. In many cases even an intercrop has been found to be a possibility in addition to the three regular crops. So far as this essential resource is concerned our country is not ill endowed with it either. India's has one of the most potential of irrigation resources in the world and the country also records a high degree of precipitation in a good percentage of the land area. The great tragedy is that this rich resource is not being effectively and efficiently utilized in many cases. A logical sequence indeed that the rich country has got a good percentage of the poverty stricken people of the world !

Irrigation turns out to be a double edged weapon in the fight against poverty. While increasing the productivity of the land, it simultaneously generates employment opportunities. Where the crop intensity rises to 250 – 300 % the number of man days of employment also increases proportionately and increase in production could be more than proportionate. In the past, irrigation schemes were being executed on a large scale in more responsive and less risky areas. From the point of view of overall economic development the approach was not without its own logic at a particular stage of development. During the Third Five Year Plan period, when the country was facing a food crisis, certain emergency measures had to be planned for achieving quick results and saving the country from an alarming situation of severe famines. The Intensive Agricultural District Programme, popularly known as the Package Programme, was launched in 1960-61 where the districts were selected for intensive development on the basis of three criteria namely, availability of maximum irrigation facilities with minimum of natural hazards like floods and drought and easy access to agricultural credit. The programme did make a good deal of progress in the early stage and when a critical assessment was made of the progress achieved in the I.A.D.P. by an evaluation committee it appeared that the ground had been prepared for the total agricultural modernization of the country as a whole. At the same time, there was a feeling that such programmes had also the effect of widening the gulf between the rich and the poor on one hand and the well endowed areas and the handicapped areas on the other. With this realization came the programmes meant specially for the poor and for the ill-endowed areas including those like the Small Farmers and Marginal Farmers Development Agency Programme, the Drought Prone Areas and Desert Development Programmes etc. culminating ultimately in the Intensive Rural Development Programme (I.R.D.P).

Though this approach stands accepted at all levels for the last three decades and more, we cannot claim that the rain fed areas have received adequate attention. This is one of the factors contributing to the high percentage of persons living below the poverty line. There has to be a composite approach towards development if worthwhile results should be forthcoming. India can claim to be one of the countries giving special attention to Non-conventional or Renewable Energy resources. These can go very well with other programmes like Desert and Drought Prone Areas Development. Irrigation to each field and employment for every able bodied person has to become a reality if persons living below the poverty line are to have enough of purchasing power.

Modernization of agriculture by itself will not be a panacea for the eradication of poverty. The new strategy of agriculture based on high yielding verities might be area neutral but benefits accruing from any crop production programme will be proportionate to the area used provided the small farmers were are able to get their own fair share of the required inputs. Since the vast majority of farmers in the country are having small and uneconomic holdings, it was necessary to find a new capital base for the weaker sections. Programmes of animal husbandry where a good cross-bred heifer becomes a new capital base, composite fish culture, piggery and poultry development etc properly integrated with the tertiary sector should all be conceived in an integrated fashion. Where this has been attempted with emphasis on local level planning with the full involvement of the beneficiaries, the results have been most encouraging. The farmer should be made to take greater initiative in having a production programme where he gets an adequate share of the benefits of development. The existing scenario is that he is becoming what could be described as a double door mat. For his crop production he depends on inputs over which he has, in most cases, no control and is invariably exploited nor has he any control over the disposal of his products. After the harvest he is compelled to part with his products on some one else's terms in the absence of holding power or access to storage facilities on reasonable terms. For a good part of his daily needs he has to depend upon what comes from outside, thereby putting him to a second phase of exploitation.

The fast pace of urbanization that is becoming the order of the day is comparable in a way to the what had happened in England in the 18th century with the ushering in of the Industrial Revolution which subsequently spread to other Western Countries also. Urban habitations are becoming a veritable hell and rural areas are not being relieved of the bane of poverty either. It is true that this is a natural consequence of Industrialisation along with urbanisation with the interplay of the push and pull factors. A good percentage of the rural population is being pushed out of the villages due to inadequate employment opportunities and are being pulled into the urban conglomerations where they are finding new employment opportunities, some times developing the needed skills, but on some else's terms. We try to comfort ourselves by saying that the developed countries of the West had also gone through the same process and some kind of order ultimately came out of the chaos. Will it not be a more logical approach to benefit from others' experiences without going through the same mistakes, one might ponder over.

Large industries located in the urban areas are finding it an expensive proposition to build up new facilities needed for their ambitious programmes of expansion and modernization in many cases. It will only be a logical step to decentralize the production process by shifting some of the production units to the rural areas or entering into agreements with the rural producers. Necessary skills could be imparted to them and we know from past experience that Indian villagers are quick to learn. As far as possible production should be organized where the raw materials are available in bulk. This will also turn out to be more economic by cutting on the cost of transportation and storage for long periods. In this process the primary producer gets the advantage of value addition and the relation becomes symbiotic instead of being parasitic or exploitative.

Under these circumstances, it appears a new approach is called for in the fight against poverty which should be guiding principle for brining in food security on the basis of the following principles -

1. Acceptance of the value added concept by the primary producer with emphasis on local production with local resources—the old Indian concept which was the strength of our economy and which made the small Indian producers compete successfully even when the Industrial Revolution had changed the scenario of production in the West.
2. Farmers will attain strength through well orgranised Co-operatives and Farmers' Associations.

3. Rural Godowns should be organised through Co-operatives and Local Bodies at various levels. This will give better bargaining power to the farmers.
4. There should be a Decentralization of Industries without haphazard and unplanned growth in the urban areas.
5. Rural and urban development should be supplementary and complimentary on the basis of a Rural Urban Continuum, not one to the exclusion of the other or one trying to exploit the other.

ANNEXURES

ANNEXURE - I

Global Food Security Situation

(Abstracts from FAO's Report : The State of Food Insecurity in the World 2001)

The global attention on food security revolves around the pledges and commitments at the World Food Summit in 1996. As a quantifiable target was set for 2015 to reduce the number of hungry from 800 million to 400 million an assessment against this figure is tried and various projections emerge. The quantifiable target of reducing the number of hungry and malnutritioned to half remains the target which could bring prosperity to the world. Various political, national and geographical conflicts and natural and manmade hazards have drawn the political attention and financial resources in sectors other than food and agriculture. Lack of political and financial allocations is reflected in terms of widening gap between the targets and achievements. An analysis of the events since 1996 convey: progress has been made in reducing the absolute number of hungry people in the world; but, this is not happening fast enough to achieve the 1996 World Food Summit target.

What should be of major concern is : Is the number of poor coming down or not?

When such a target was set at the Rome Summit no body had the faintest of the idea about political will of the countries; infrastructure capabilities of the countries to undertake such a mammoth task and the financial resources required for achieving this target. This figure was projected because we wanted to reduce the number of hungry to half by 2015. The figure of 20 million each year was projected if the target was to be achieved that was a mathematical calculation.

Over the past decade the total number of chronically undernourished in the developing world has fallen by approximately 40 million (39 million to be precise), but the average rate of decline has continued to be slow, reaching only 6 million a year (compared with the 8 million reported in 1999). Consequently, the annual reduction required to reach the target by 2015 has grown from 20 million to 22 million people per year and hence the gap – between reductions realized and reductions needed – has widened. Continued at the current rate, it would take more than 60 years to reach the target.

FAO's latest estimates indicate that, in 1997-99, there were 815 million undernourished people in the world: 777 million in the developing countries, 27 million in transition countries and 11 million in industrialized countries. For the developing countries, the latest figure represents a decrease of 39 million since 1990-92 (the benchmark period used at the World Food Summit), for which the revised figure is 816 million undernourished. This means that the average annual decrease now stands at about 6 million people.

Clearly, there has been a slow down in the reduction of undernourished in the world. As a consequence, to achieve the World Food Summit goal of halving the number of undernourished in developing countries by 2015, the average annual decrease required is no longer 20 million but 22 million – well above the current level of performance.

The overall decline in the number of undernourished in the developing regions hides contrasting trends in different countries: only 32 of the 99 developing countries studied recorded a decrease in their numbers of undernourished between 1990-92 and 1997-99. The total reduction achieved by this group amounted to 116 million people. This compares with a total increase of 77 million recorded for the countries in which the number of undernourished rose. Because the first group includes several large countries, such as China, Indonesia and Thailand in Asia; and Nigeria in Africa, the total reduction achieved outweighed the total increase in the second, numerically larger group of countries. The net reduction reported is 39 million.

Thus, the number of undernourished has increased considerably in the majority of developing countries. (This analysis excludes Ethiopia and Eritrea, which were not separate countries in the early 1990s. It also excludes the nine developing countries in which less than 2.5 percent of the population was undernourished in 1990-92.)

When the number of undernourished is considered as a proportion of a country's total population, instead of in absolute terms, the picture is somewhat different. The proportion actually fell in the majority (58) of developing countries. However, this finding should not be interpreted too optimistically, since in 18 of these countries the fall coincided with a rise in absolute numbers. The decrease in the proportion of undernourished in these countries has not been sufficient to offset the effect of population growth. Continuing rapid rises in the number of mouths to feed imply further difficulties in meeting the World Food Summit target.

Asia Pacific Situation

Asia Pacific Region has a direct relevance for our country. This region still accounts for 64 percent of the 718 million hungry people in the developing world. They face a deficit in basic daily dietary energy ranging from 100 to 400 kcal. Food insecurity in Asia Pacific developing economies is essential a poverty problem, reflecting in large part a failure of food entitlements due to low returns to assets owned by the poor. Thus the bulk of the food insecure is also largely the rural poor. The prevalence of undernourishment co-relates well with poverty incidence. With 522 million or 44 per cent of the world's poor in 1998, South Asia correspondingly has the largest incidence of undernourishment (494 million or more than 39 percent of the world's hungry people). National incomes (measured by per capita GNP) are lowest in countries, where undernourishment is pervasive. In this regard, it is thus of great concern that countries with over 20 percent undernourishment showed only negligible improvement of per capita income during the last decades.

The percentage of undernourished people in Asian developing countries had fallen from 21 percent in 1990-92 to 17 percent in 1996-98. To reach the WFS targets it is necessary that the region reduces its hungry at a rate of 14 million per year.

Dr. R.B.Singh, Assistant Director General, FAO has summed up the concern as : 'The sad part of the reality is that this (undernourishment) is happening even in parts of the world where there is plenty of food to meet everyone's needs. The paradox of the existence of mountains of grains and millions of hungry is a shame to the humanity'.

Individual Country Performance

The overall progress achieved in decreasing the number of undernourished in the developing world between 1990-92 and 1997-99 hides sharply contrasting trends in individual countries. Some countries have made outstanding progress, while some have moved forward slowly or stood-still. Still others, however, have suffered reverses, in most cases moderate but occasionally severe.

Countries that perform well do so by following one or more routes. They may have devoted more resources to increasing agricultural production. Alternatively, they may have imported large amounts of food, either purchased in international commodity markets or received as food aid. Countries afflicted by long standing civil wars or recent short-term shocks may achieve better than anticipated performances by the later route. In addition, a good performance may reflect a recovery from a previous period of poor performance – for example, a sharp reduction in the proportion of undernourished as agriculture recovers after the end of a Civil War. The reverse is also true in the case of negative performances.

All other things being equal, changes in a country's number of undernourished will be proportional to size of its population – large the population, large the increase or decrease that may be expected. But, population also plays a conforming role in the statistics on undernourishment. While a rise in the proportion of undernourished implies a rise in their absolute number, a decline in the proportion does not necessarily imply a fall in number. A high population growth rate, for example may result in absolute numbers increasing. Thus, change in the proportion of undernourished provide a measure of performance, that is independent of the influence of population growth.

Analyses on this basis indicate that 12 countries may be singled out as "best performers" ,i.e., they reduced their proportion of undernourished by more than one percentage point per year from 1990-92 to 1997-99. These countries are: Peru, Chad, Ghana, Kuwait, Mozambique, Malawi, Angola, Sudan, Togo, Thailand, Vietnam and China. At the opposite extreme, there are ten countries that may be classified as "worst performers", since there proportion goes down by more than one percentage point per year.

It is interesting to note that the best and worst performing countries are found in all developing regions, including sub-Saharan Africa, where the proportion of undernourished in the total population is highest. In fact, seven of the best performers and four of the worst performers are in Sub-Saharan Africa.

The effect of a substantial population size is illustrated by India, where the percentage of undernourished is estimated to have declined from 25 to 23 per cent but the number of undernourished goes down by 11 million, owing to rapid population growth.

Among the 98 countries analysed, the two extremes of performance are represented by China, a country that achieved stunning aggregate economic growth in 1990s and the socio-economic transformation rivaling that of South East Asia in the 1970s and 1980s; and the conflict stricken Democratic Republic of Congo, a potentially very rich country, which has seen its proportion of undernourished grow from 35 percent in 1990-92 to 64 per cent in 1997-99. It should be noted that, despite China's good performance, the country is still home to the world's second largest number of undernourished people after India.

Variables Affecting Food Security

Two clusters of variables have been identified as being very significantly related to changes in the prevalence of undernourishment :

i) Variables that reflect " as measured by the frequency of food emergencies, loss of civil rights and decline in life expectancy"

ii) Variables that reflect growth in agriculture productivity.

In other words there is a strong inverse relationship between the occurrence of shocks (whether caused by natural or by human induced disasters) and progress in reducing the number of undernourished; and there is a strong co-relation between increased agricultural productivity and reductions in the number of undernourished.

A recent study by the International Food Policy Research Institute (IFPRI), examines the relationship between a variety of factors and reductions in the number of underweight children in 63 developing countries between 1970-1975. The study indicates that the statistical explanation of lowered numbers of underweight children centers on four following factors :

i) Level of women's education (43%)
ii) National per capita food availability (26%)
iii) Health and environmental factors (19%)
iv) Woman's status in society (12%)

FAO's analysis shows that food production and access to food are important, but they are not the only factors at work.

Towards More Equal Access to Food

Over the past three decades, world food production has grown faster than population. Between 1969-71 and 1997-99, the amount of food available per capita per day rose from 2410 to 2800 kcal in the world as a whole, and from 2110 and 2680 kcal in the developing countries. The remarkable growth in food availability achieved in the developing countries more than halved the proportion of undernourished in the total population from 37 percent in 1969-71 to 17 percent in 1997-99. This decrease was not sufficient, however, to halve the absolute number of undernourished in the developing world, estimated to be 956 million in 1969-71 and still as high as 777 million in 1997-99.

Clearly, world food production must continue to grow if the World Food Summit target of halving the number of undernourished by the year 2015 is to be met. In theory, a smaller increase in production would suffice if its growth were accompanied by more equitable access to food. This could be achieved through redistribution – of food itself, of the means of producing it or of the purchasing power needed to buy it – to those currently on the lower rungs of the food access ladder.

The assessment of changes in the inequality of access to food among and within countries – has been undertaken by FAO by using the Gini co-efficient, commonly adopted in distributional analysis. The Gini co-efficient theoretically ranges from 'zero', implying an equal distribution among the units under consideration to 'one' implying absolute inequality- in other words, concentration in a single unit. The more co-efficient depart from zero, the more unequal are the distribution. From the bunching effect, it is concluded that the growth in world food availability since 1969-71 has been accompanied by a re-distribution in favour of countries that previously had low per capita food availability.

Prevalence of Undernourishment vis-à-vis Poverty

FAO's measure of the prevalence of undernourishment is based on the distribution of household food consumption and availability, whereas, in the measure used by the World Bank estimate, the prevalence of extreme poverty is based on the distribution of household expenditure on consumer goods. There is a positive and *close relationship* between *'food consumption'* and *'expenditure on consumables'* in low-income households.

The *estimates* for 'extreme poverty' are *higher* than those for 'undernourishment'. The exception is the near

East and North Africa, where the prevalence of extreme poverty is estimated to be only 2% compared with 7.7% for undernourishment. This anomaly reflects the weaknesses in both of the organizations' approaches when they are applied for low-level prevalence.

In FAO's estimates, food consumption is expressed in terms of dietary energy and people in households consuming less than a certain minimum energy requirement are termed undernourished. The minimum daily requirement, which takes into account the calories needed to maintain body weight while performing light activity varies from country to country, but is approximately 1900 kcal/capita depending on age, sex and average height.

In the World Bank's estimates, expenditure on food and non-food consumables is expressed in terms of the international dollar, adjusted for purchasing power parity (PPP). People living in households with a per capita expenditure of less than PPP $1.08 per day are considered to be living in extreme poverty. The PPP $ 1.08 poverty line is obtained as the median of the ten lowest national poverty lines of the 33 calculated by the World Bank. National Poverty lines take into account the value of the basic food basket, which also involves estimates of energy requirements. These refer to the average requirements, which are approximately 2200 kcal/capita/day.

Therefore, the international poverty line used by the World Bank defining extreme poverty relies on a higher food consumption level than that used in the FAO definition of undernourishment. This explains the general tendency for the World Bank's estimates of extreme poverty to be higher than FAO's estimates of undernourished. It also reinforces the already widely shared belief that the undernourished are found largely among the poorest of the extreme poor. Hence combating undernourishment implies combating the most extreme conditions of poverty.

Unequal Access Among Households

Intra-country inequality of access to food is due mainly to difference in income or purchasing power among households. The best and most direct way of assessing this kind of inequality is to look at data on food consumption for households in different income classes. Comparable data on income distribution were examined for 23 countries in Latin America, Africa and Asia, covering the period 1970-1993. Based on this study, the following observations may be made:

i) Intra-country income inequality is much greater than inter-country inequality in food distribution.
ii) Across countries, the period-to-period changes in the given co-efficient are rather small, with no indication of either an increasing or a decreasing trend across all. In countries that have experienced rapid growth, all income classes tend to move up together, with little change in the distributional pattern.

The share of food in household expenditure declines with rising income. In addition, there are upper and lower limits to food consumption (expressed in kcal), whereas this is not true in the case of incomes. This means that actual changes in access to food, as opposed to income will tend to be small than those that can be detected from the analysis.

It can therefore, be detected over time, real changes in the equality of intra-household food consumption have tended to be very small, if at all perceptible. This is why countries need to organize special programmes to help raise the level of disposable income of people in the lower income classes, which has the highest rates of undernutrition.

ANNEXURE - II

NGOs/CSOs Statement in the Asian Regional Consultation on the World Food Summit - Five Years Later Bangkok, Thailand, 28-29 August 2001

End Hunger!

Fight for the Right to Live!

We, the representatives of more than 80 NGOs/Civil Society Organizations (CSOs) from 14 Asian countries are outraged that despite abundance of food to feed the world, more than 800 million, with two-thirds found in Asia, still go hungry everyday.

The programs and practices aimed at reducing hunger and malnutrition by the Bretton Woods Institutions, international financial groups and inter-governmental agencies have failed miserably and instead aggravated food insecurity.

The crucial promise of the 1996 World Food Summit to halve poverty and hunger by the year 2015 has been declared impossible to achieve by the same institutions that adopted it. Albeit an important one, this "crucial" promise is still insufficient and unacceptable to the 'other half' i.e., the rest of the millions who go hungry everyday. According to FAO, only 8 million undernourished people were made healthier in the 1990s --- far below the 20 million annual average necessary to meet the target of the 1996 World Food Summit.

Food has been declared a basic human right by many international agreements such as the Universal Declaration of Human Rights, the Preamble of the FAO Constitution, the International Covenant of Economic, Social and Cultural Rights, among others. Yet, the right to food is continually denied. Worse, it is now considered more as an item for trade than for sustenance.

After five years, we demand that national governments and international institutions accept the responsibilities and consequences of their failed "experiments" and make this acceptance known to the poor.

The grassroots communities, including the peasant farmers, landless agricultural laborers, small fisherfolk, rural women, indigenous peoples and forest dwellers[1] have a right of access to productive resources, such as land, water, forests, seeds, genetic resources and indigenous knowledge. They should be given the freedom to determine their own means to meet their food needs. Moreover, they have the primary right to benefit foremost from the transformation of their resources done with their prior and informed consent.

It is a paradox that peasants who produce food to feed the world are the ones suffering most from hunger and malnutrition. Subsistence and sustainable agricultural systems, which for centuries have been the basis of their livelihood, are being obliterated by the concentration of land ownership in a few hands and its corporatization, as well as the encroachment of agribusiness on smallholder farms. These activities dilute the culture and way of life of peasants with the ultimate aim of profit for the few.

The globalization process, perpetuated by the G8 countries and institutionalized by the World Trade Organization (WTO), international financial institutions, like the International Monetary Fund (IMF) and multilateral development banks, particularly the World Bank and the Asian Development Bank, has benefited merely a few transnational corporations. They have gained a monopoly of our food, genetic resources and agriculture and imposed the dumping of subsidized, unhealthy food and agricultural products and inputs, including chemical pesticides and fertilizers into our countries. This has created massive indebtedness, increased landlessness and displacement leading to rural out-migration, eroded our food sovereignty, worsened land and environmental degradation including the destruction of biodiversity, the biopiracy of indigenous knowledge, pesticide poisonings and unabated land conversions for non-agricultural purposes, mega-dams, mega projects and maldevelopment. It has further marginalized peasants particularly women and children.

---

[1] The term "Peasants" henceforth refers to peasant farmers, fisherfolks, landless agricultural laborers, rural women, indigenous peoples, forest dwellers and subsistence farmers.

The WB/IMF model of market-oriented land reform subverts national governments to implement genuine agrarian reform by imposing debt bondage. It does not aim to distribute land to the landless but rather increases the concentration of land with the landed elite. The Asian Development Bank, through its privatization program, is even attempting to transfer peasants' rights and access to water as a public a resource to private corporations and large-scale producers.

The rights of indigenous peoples are likewise on the verge of extinction with the uncertain recognition of their contributions to food security. There is a critical need to distinguish the contribution of indigenous peoples, local communities and farmers' rights especially on their own seeds under the forthcoming International Undertaking of Plant Genetic Resources

The peasants must be empowered to ensure the achievement of our goal of food for all. Food security can only be achieved if the world's cultivating peasants themselves own the agricultural lands and have access to resources required for healthy and safe food production and sustainable livelihood with gender equity.

In response to the Summit commitments, peasant movements and their partner NGOs/CSOs have also been working on their own initiatives towards ensuring food security. These include:

- Policy advocacy and lobbying to sensitize and strengthen peasant movements, although there is still a need to strengthen these initiatives further.
- Sustainable development programs to raise levels of self-sufficiency and self-reliance through increasing domestic production by establishing local-level seed and grain banks, conservation of biodiversity, formulation of village plans by the villagers, land, water and forest management, low-external input, sustainable agriculture, and utilization of local resources and local and indigenous knowledge systems.
- Forging the political will to uphold the Right to Food through people's participation, supporting efforts towards democratization, gender equity and improving agricultural services, especially in the provision of support services and

proper developmental management of food and emergency aid.

RECOMMENDATIONS

We recommend that our governments:

- Adopt an international code of conduct on the human right to adequate food to govern the activities of different actors including the state parties and international institutions to end malnutrition and hunger.
- Food aid should not be used as a political weapon. Governments should be accountable to guarantee the right to food of vulnerable populations including displaced persons, victims of disasters and internal conflicts, as well as refugees.
- Review the implementation of land reform programs including violations thereof and formulate and implement genuine agrarian reform founded on progressive land legislation, which ensures equitable access to resources, sustainable agriculture and gender equity.
- Ensure policies and programs that enable communities to own and manage productive resources and disallow mega development projects, which displace populations and peoples, destroy the environment, livelihoods, and indigenous cultures.
- Formulate effective strategies to combat the threats to food security and prevent the shift of the control of agriculture from the producers to the market forces.
- Reject the policies and practices of Bretton Woods Institutions, especially the conditionalities attached to debt relief, credits and other financial assistance.
- Rescind the WTO Agreement on Agriculture, Trade Related Agreements on Intellectual Properties (TRIPS), Sanitary Phyto-sanitary Measures (SPS), and General Agreement on Tariffs and Trade (GATT) and oppose the revival of MAI.
- Oppose the WTO General Agreement on Trade in Services (GATS) and the revived Multilateral Framework of Investments.

- "Deglobalize" and focus on strengthening domestic economy and optimal use of local resources for local communities.
- Remove burden of usurious debt affecting peasants particularly loans linked to the promotion of chemical-based agriculture.
- Create a public body or forum to review government expenditures and restructuring in favor of peasants and rural economies.

We recommend that the FAO and intergovernmental organizations :

- Adopt a World Convention on Food Sovereignty and Trade whose principles include the right of peasants and people to ensure their food and agricultural policies, food self sufficiency, control and access to land and resources, gender equity, fair prices and fair trade as well as sustainable agriculture.
- Support measures that restore food sovereignty to peasants where the people themselves can have control over the productive resources and make decisions on matters regarding their food security and discourage the establishment of corporate farms and big commercial fishing corporations.
- Recognize and operationalize farmers' rights in the International Undertaking of Plant Genetic Resources and install mechanisms to ensure that farmers primarily benefit from their traditional knowledge and contributions and resources.
- Assess the environmental, social and economic impacts of Genetically Modified Organisms (GMOs) on Food Security with the full and informed participation of NGOs/CSOs and prior and democratic consent of people in Southern countries and meanwhile call for a moratorium on all field-testing, commercialization and trade of GMOs in food and agriculture.

As NGOs and CSOs, we commit to :

- Make the right to food and food security as central to national and regional agenda without forgetting that this is a principal issue of peasants.
- Forge stronger alliance against anti-poor/peasant policies and put pressure against these entities including Transnational Corporations, World Bank, IMF, ADB and the WTO.
- Accelerate the process and implementation of genuine agrarian reform and other forms of resource rights entitlements for peasants to have control over their way of life and for the nation's sovereignty on its capacity to produce its own food
- Adopt a rights-based instead of the welfare approach to development work where entitlements for peasants are demanded on the basis of their rights and accountability of governments and other institutions are required because it is their duty to protect and uphold the rights of peasants.
- Continue the work of empowerment of the grassroots by raising their consciousness of their ability to secure food for themselves and their community and to preserve the community-based alternative livelihood systems that save them during times of emergencies. In addition, create awareness and understanding on the impacts of the globalization processes.
- Identify, document and publicize self-reliant, self sufficient, sustainable production and consumption practices, programs and initiatives.
- Work towards ensuring food security and promote partnerships and linkages between urban and rural poor.
- Conscienticize the general public about everyone's role in perpetuating an unjust and unequal social economic system through our consumption practices.

Our Calls today are :

- Assert that all people have the right to safe and healthy food.

- Implement Land to the Tillers.[2]
- Adopt and celebrate a World Peasants' Day.
- Oppose biopatenting and biopiracy.
- Demand End World Hunger. Take WTO out of Agriculture.

NGOs/CSOs Represented in the Consultation

REGIONAL FOCAL POINTS Asian NGO Coalition for Agrarian Reform and Rural Development (ANGOC), Institute for Motivating Self-Employment (IMSE), Pesticide Action Network-Asia-Pacific (PAN-AP) **BANGLADESH** Shikkha Shastha Unnayan Karzakram (SHISUK), Policy Research for Development Alternative (UBINIG), Unity for Programmed Action in Coastal Lands (UPACOL), **CAMBODIA** Cambodian NGO Alliance for Cooperation (CNAC), HEKS Cambodia, **CHINA** China Association for NGO Cooperation (CANGO), **INDIA** Asian Institute for Rural Development (AIRD), Association of Voluntary Agencies in Rural Development (AVARD), Centre for Agrarian Research and Education (CARTE), Church's Auxiliary for Social Action (CASA), Forum of Voluntary Organizations West Bengal, Gandhi Peace Foundation (GPF), Indian Association for the Advancement of Science (IAAS), National Alliance of People's Movement (NAPM), South Asia Rural Reconstruction Association (SARRA), Vikas Adhyan Kendra (VAK), Voluntary Action Network India (VANI), **INDONESIA** Lembaga Alam Tropika Indonesia (LATIN), Kongres Wanita Indonesia (KOWANI), PAN-Indonesia, Sekreatariat Petani Sumatera Utara (SPSU), Serikat Petani Jawa Tengah (SPJT), Yayasan Bina Swadaya, **JAPAN** Ja-Zenchu, **SOUTH KOREA** National Agricultural Cooperative Federation, **MALAYSIA** Consumers International Regional Office for Asia and the Pacific (CIROAP), South East Asian Council for Food Security and Fair Trade (SEACON), Education and Research Association for Consumers (ERA Consumer), **NEPAL** Action Aid Nepal, All Nepal Peasants'

---

[2] Land to the Tillers also include the right of peasant women to own land.

Association (ANPA), Community Welfare and Development Society (CWDS), National Cooperative Federation of Nepal (NCFN), NGO Federation of Nepal (NFN), Rural Reconstruction Network (RRN), **PAKISTAN** Peasant Development Programme, Rural Development Foundation of Pakistan (RDF), South Asia Partnership Pakistan (SAP-PK), **PHILIPPINES** Alternate Forum for Research in Mindanao (AFRIM), Asian Partnership for the Development of Human Resources in Rural Areas (AsiaDHRRA), Center Agrarian Reform and Rural Development (CARRD), Pambansang Kilusan ng mga Samahang Magsasaka (PAKISAMA), Philippine Association for Intercultural Development (PAFID), Philippine Partnership for the Development of Human Resources in Rural Areas, Philippine Rural Reconstruction Movement (PRRM), Project Development Institute (PDI), Southeast Asia Regional Institute for Community Education (SEARICE), Farmer – Scientist Partnership for Development, Inc. (MASIPAG), Kilusang Magbubukid ng Pilipinas (KMP), South East Asia Rural Social Leadership Institute (SEARSOLIN), Southeast Asian Ministers of Education Organization- Regional Center for Graduate Study and Research in Agriculture (SEAMEO-SEARCA), University of the Philippines- Department of Soil Science, **SRI LANKA** All Lanka Peasants Front (ALPF), Lanka Jathika Sarvodaya Shramadana Sangamaya (SARVODAYA), Movement for National Land and Agricultural Reform (MONLAR), National NGO Council of Sri Lanka (NNGOC), **THAILAND** Action Aid Asia, Alternative Agriculture Network, Asian Resource Foundation, Assembly of the Poor, CARE Regional Management Office- Asia, Asia Partnership for Human Development (APHD), Focus on the Global South (FOCUS), Institute for a Sustainable Agriculture Community, Northeast Alternative Network, Southern Alternative Agriculture Network, Sustainable Agriculture Foundation, Rural Reconstruction Alumni and Friends Association (RRAFA), **VIETNAM** Action Aid Vietnam, Rural Development Services Center (RDSC)

This statement from the Asian Regional Consultation of NGOs/CSOs on the World Food Summit-Five Years Later is the collective call of more than 80 NGOs from 14 countries namely, Bangladesh, Cambodia, China, India, Indonesia, Japan, Korea, Malaysia, Nepal, Pakistan, Philippines, Sri Lanka, Thailand, and Vietnam. The consultation was organized by the Asian NGO Coalition for Agrarian Reform and Rural Development (ANGOC) a regional NGO network, Pesticide Action Network in Asia-Pacific (PAN-AP) of Malaysia and the Institute for Motivating Self-Employment (IMSE) of India with the Food and Agriculture Oranization Regional Office for Asia-Pacific (FAO-RAP) last 28-29 August 2001 in Bangkok, Thailand.

Index